# Pathways through education for young people in care

# Pathways through education for young people in care

Ideas from research and practice

edited by Sonia Jackson

BAAF
ADOPTION
& FOSTERING

Published by British Association
for Adoption & Fostering
(BAAF)
Saffron House
3rd Floor, 6–10 Kirby Street
London EC1N 8TS
www.baaf.org.uk

Charity registration 275689 (England and Wales)
and SC039337 (Scotland)

British Library Cataloguing in Publication Data
A catalogue record for this book is available
from the British Library

ISBN 978 1 907585 72 2

Editorial project management by Miranda Davies,
BAAF Publications
Designed by Helen Joubert Associates
Typeset by Avon DataSet Ltd, Bidford on Avon
Printed in Great Britain by TJ International
Trade distribution by Turnaround Publisher Services,
Unit 3, Olympia Trading Estate, Coburg Road,
London N22 6TZ

BAAF is the leading UK-wide membership
organisation for all those concerned with
adoption, fostering and child care issues.

# Contents

# Acknowledgements

I must first of all thank Shaila Shah and BAAF for commissioning me to edit this second anthology of writings about the education of children and young people in care. In the years since BAAF produced my previous collection, *Nobody Ever Told Us School Mattered* (2001), the centrality of school and education in the lives of children looked after away from home has become much more widely recognised and many important publications have appeared. I am grateful to all the authors who gave permission for their journal papers to be reprinted here. Special thanks to those who agreed to revise and update their articles or to contribute new chapters.

I have learned a great deal from working with colleagues at the Thomas Coram Research Unit in the London Institute of Education, having previously been based in social work departments. I would like to thank them for many stimulating discussions and seminars. It has been a privilege to work closely with Claire Cameron over several years, especially on the *YiPPEE* project, which has given me the opportunity to meet and collaborate with academics and practitioners in different European countries. Seeing how things are done in places with other traditions and cultural perspectives is very valuable in making us question policies and practices that we normally take for granted. I greatly appreciated the chance to work with Ingrid Höjer from Sweden on a special issue of the *European Journal of Social Work* devoted to the education of children and young people in state care.

Other people who have helped to inform the thinking behind this book are Peter McParlin, Robert Flynn, Mike Stein, Judy Sebba and colleagues at Oxford University's Rees Centre, Peter Pecora, David Berridge, Roger Bullock, Nick Axford, James Wetz, Gerri McAndrew of Buttle UK, and the Who Cares? Trust which does so much valuable work on behalf of children and young people in care. Above all, I want to thank the very many people of all ages, who have shared their experiences of care with me over the years and whose stories continue to provide the incentive to keep trying to change things for the better.

I owe a great debt to my wonderful BAAF editor, Miranda Davies. She has taken a keen interest in the project and kept it on the rails throughout its sometimes erratic journey towards publication. I am also most grateful for her helpful suggestions on content and comments on draft chapters. Thanks to her support, compiling and editing this book has been a most interesting and enjoyable experience.

This book has been kindly supported by funding from the de Brye Charitable Trust.

# The Editor

**Sonia Jackson** is an Emeritus Professor at London University Institute of Education and Swansea University, a Patron of the Who Cares? Trust and a former Trustee of the National Children's Bureau. She read History and Natural Sciences at Newnham College, Cambridge and worked as a clinical child psychologist, education adviser and primary school teacher before obtaining her qualification in social work from the LSE. This interdisciplinary background made her aware of how seriously the education of children in care was neglected.

Sonia first drew attention to the issue in the 1980s and has since written or contributed to over 80 publications on child care and looked after children. These include a previous BAAF anthology, *Nobody Ever Told Us School Mattered* (2001), *What Works in Creating Stability for Looked After Children?* (2001), *Better Education Better Futures: Research, practice and the views of young people in care* (2001), *The Costs and Benefits of Educating Children in Care* (2002), *Going to University from Care* (2005) and *People Under Three* (1994/2004), as well as book chapters, reports for the government and European Commission and numerous journal articles, of which two are reprinted in this book. She edited a special issue on education for *Adoption & Fostering* (31:1, 2007) and most recently co-edited a special issue of *The European Journal of Social Work* on 'The education of children and young people in state care' (16:1, 2013).

Sonia has directed many major research projects on early years care and education and the health and education of looked after children and young people, notably *By Degrees*, the only UK research on going to university from care, and *YiPPEE*, a cross-national study of education for young people with a care background in five European countries. She was Chair of Children in Wales at the time of the successful campaign for the appointment of the first Commissioner for Children in the UK. She is an academician of the Academy of Social Sciences and was awarded an OBE in 2003 for services to children.

In addition to her research and writing, Sonia is a keen amateur musician and plays the cello and viola da gamba in several orchestras and ensembles. Her interest in children is not purely theoretical as she has helped to bring up six children and has 16 grandchildren, ranging in age from 0 to 21.

# Introduction

*Sonia Jackson*

## Background

It is 12 years since BAAF last published an anthology on the education of children and young people in care. The earlier book (Jackson, 2001a) was called *Nobody Ever Told Us School Mattered*. Happily that is no longer true, at least in the UK, but there is still a very long way to go before young people in care can hope to enjoy the same educational opportunities as those living with their own families. It always annoys me when I read in government documents or research reports that children in care tend to do "less well" than others. The truth is that the vast majority of those who spend a significant part of their childhood in care still do *much* less well than their classmates. They are unlikely to complete their basic secondary education successfully. According to government statistics, only 13 per cent of children looked after by local authorities in England achieve the "expected" standard of five GCSE passes at Grade A*–C including Maths and English, compared with 59 per cent of those not in care, and they are very much less likely to stay in full-time education beyond 16 or to go on to further or higher education (Jackson and Cameron, 2012)

Examination passes are only an indicator, not the purpose of education, but the enormous gap in academic attainment and participation between young people in care and others probably mirrors shortfalls in less easily measured aspects of their learning such as emotional well-being, health, self-care, and social and practical skills. Lack of qualifications and low levels of social competence put these young men and women at a massive disadvantage in competing for scarce jobs. Lacking family support or extensive social networks, they run a high risk of experiencing long-term unemployment and poverty in adulthood, which in turn puts them in danger of a whole range of other negative outcomes (Jackson, 2007).

## Overcoming adversity

It has been argued that this is not the fault of the care system. In the social class from which most children in care are drawn few children do well at school (Berridge, 1997). Moreover, children in the UK only come into care after the best efforts to keep them in their own families have proved unavailing. This usually means that they will previously have suffered from severe neglect and mistreatment. The high incidence of PTSD (post-traumatic stress disorder) in the care population was first pointed out by Kate Cairns over 10 years ago (Cairns, 1999) and has been repeatedly confirmed by subsequent research (see Chapter 11). Peter Pecora, Research Director of the Casey Foundation in Seattle, told the audience in a lecture at Oxford University that the level of PTSD among children entering their foster care programme was similar to that in veterans returning from service in Afghanistan (Pecora, 2013).

It is sometimes overlooked that the experience of entering care is in itself intensely traumatic for many children (Reimer, 2010). It is surely the duty of the state, when it takes on the role of parent, to make the most strenuous efforts to promote young people's mental health and help them to overcome the related emotional and behavioural difficulties that often cause them to be denied their right to education. Yet studies of children in foster and residential care and personal accounts have shown that services for those with mental health difficulties related to abusive experiences and chaotic family lives are generally inadequate and do not reach many who badly need them (Ashcroft, 2013).

The literature review by Penelope Welbourne and Caroline Leeson (Chapter 2) illustrates the strong tendency of researchers to focus on the "biographical disadvantage" of children in care rather than on what might be done to overcome it. Official policy statements pay lip service to the aim of enabling looked after children to "realise their potential". The truth is that we have no idea what their potential might be: too often it is defined by their care status rather than their personal qualities, as Collette Bentley (Chapter 3) reminds us. If we want evidence of this we need only look at the wide differences in the educational achievement of looked after children between local authorities with similar social characteristics.

## But things are getting better

At the time when BAAF commissioned the previous anthology it was hard to find any research papers or journal articles on the education of children in care. Since then three major journals have devoted complete issues to the subject – *Adoption & Fostering* (2007), the US journal *Children and Youth Services Review* (2012) and the *European Journal of Social Work* (2013). Two large-scale research projects have focused on a previously unexplored area, the post-compulsory and higher education of young people in and leaving care – *By Degrees* (Going to University from Care) and *YiPPEE* (Young People in Public Care: Pathways to Education in Europe) – and have had considerable influence on policy both in the UK and other countries (Budge, 2010; AcSS, 2013). Papers drawing on findings from both of those studies are included in this collection (Chapters 12 and 13).

There have also been important advances at the legislative and policy levels. The Labour Government (1997–2010) gave great importance to education right from the start and children in care were not forgotten. Frank Dobson, then Secretary of State for Social

Services, in launching the 1998 *Quality Protects* programme, described educational achievement as 'the single most significant measure of the effectiveness of local authority parenting'. The Children (Leaving Care) Act 2000, implemented the following year, put leaving care services on a statutory footing and made continuing in education beyond the official school-leaving age a practical possibility. The 2004 Children Act joined up care and education in a single local authority department under a Director of Children's Services and laid an explicit duty on authorities to promote the educational attainment of looked after children and young people. The government Green Paper, *Care Matters: Transforming the lives of children and young people in care* (DfES, 2006a), gave unprecedented space and emphasis to education and was followed by a White Paper, *Care Matters: Time for change* (DfES, 2007), which was full of innovative ideas and became the foundation for the 2008 Children Act and a number of pilot action research projects.

Probably the most successful of these was the idea of appointing a senior educationist to be the strategic leader of education services for looked after children in an area as if they were all attending the same school. The Virtual School Head (VSH) pilot was positively evaluated by a team from Bristol University (Berridge *et al*, 2009) and most local authorities took up the idea. The virtual heads formed themselves into a strong, mutually supportive network with an annual conference (see Chapter 10). The All-Party Parliamentary inquiry into the educational attainment of looked after children, *Education Matters in Care*, recommended that the appointment of a VSH should be a statutory requirement for every local authority and this has been included in the Children and Families Bill, before Parliament at the time of writing (APPG, 2012). It is remarkable that this is one of only five such mandatory officers whom every local authority is obliged to appoint. If the other 89 recommendations of this excellent report were implemented, there would be some hope of real progress towards narrowing the gap in achievement between children in care and the general population and, as the conclusion of the report puts it, 'help to create the stability, durability, focus and understanding necessary for looked after children to thrive by way of their education rather than merely survive the ordeal' (APPG, 2012, p 75).

The education of looked after children has a constant tendency to fall off the social care agenda, especially at times when the care population is rising and the need to provide roofs over heads becomes the most urgent priority. However, the fact that Edward Timpson, who chaired the cross-party inquiry, was subsequently appointed Minister for Children may keep it in the foreground and provide some protection against the effect of cuts to local authority budgets.

## The structure of this collection

This book is organised into four sections. The first part sets the policy and research context: Chapter 1, 'Reconnecting care and education' charts the progress that has been made in focusing attention on the educational experience of looked after children since the passing of the Children Act 1989. This Act provides the legislative basis for children's services in England (with similar measures in the other three UK countries) and the Guidance on education in care which followed two years later is still remarkably relevant. Welbourne and Leeson's research review (Chapter 2) analyses findings from 106 studies and concludes that care has the potential to enable some children to recover from earlier adverse experiences, but only if intensive educational help is coupled with skilled intervention to assess and treat mental health difficulties. Those who come into care early tend to do better, provided that they are not subjected to repeated unsuccessful attempts to return them to their birth families. Going back to an abusive family predicts the worst educational outcomes; even children who appear to be on track to do well are always vulnerable to "derailment", an observation that will resonate with most social workers.

## Raising expectations

There is a consistent finding that the attainment of children in care tends to decline relative to their age cohort even when their placements are comparatively stable (see Chapter 5). This is perhaps not surprising if we think about the content of secondary education as compared with earlier school years. As children get older, the educational level of their carers becomes increasingly important. It is an issue that is very seldom discussed, but it is thrown into sharp relief by the autobiographical account of a remarkable success story in Chapter 3. Collette Bentley was all set to follow the sad trajectory of too many young people in care when she had the great good fortune to be placed, in an emergency, with a highly educated couple who were determined for her to fulfil her educational potential. Almost as soon as she arrived at her new foster home, her carers took her shopping for a school uniform, a French dictionary and a hole punch and drove her the 40 minutes across the city to school. They spent 'endless hours' at the kitchen table patching up the gaps in her knowledge of algebra, chanted French irregular verbs on car journeys and let absolutely nothing stand in the way of her attending school and succeeding academically. Along with this they provided what she describes as 'an unparalleled sense of stability and nurturing tenderness and love' (p 51).

Collette might have spent her adolescence hanging out by the canal with her truanting friends from the children's home, smoking and drinking, or worse still ended up in a young offender institution. But thanks to her foster carers and her own determination, she returned to school, went on to get a first-class degree in languages and finally achieved her ambition to qualify as a doctor.

The other chapters in Part 2 focus on practical measures to raise attainment, most of which have been systematically evaluated and shown to achieve some success. Chapter 5 reports on one of the first attempts to track the educational achievement of individual children in care. Angela O'Sullivan and Rob Westerman found clear evidence of decline between earlier and later assessments of the same child – children who functioned close to the expected level at Key Stages 1 and 2 falling progressively behind their peers in secondary school. The authors are strongly critical of the quality of local authority data and inattention to school performance by social workers, for instance failing to record results of important tests. They found a clear association between falling levels of attainment and the number of school and placement moves, and made recommendations for improving practice. The *Way Ahead* project continues, and O'Sullivan with other colleagues has written a postscript on its development over the five years since the original article was published.

## Fostering a love of reading

The next three chapters are all about helping foster carers to offer better support for education. One of my own research studies, *Successful in Care* (Jackson and Martin, 1998) found that learning to read early and fluently was a key factor in doing well at school and in life after care. A love of books is a lifelong asset. So many of the young people I have interviewed have told me that their enjoyment of reading was what enabled them to survive their care experience. Reading gives you access to worlds other than the one you currently live in. You can escape into books, read about other countries, other times and other places, discover different ways of life. You can find out how to knit, make models, grow vegetables or just curl up in a corner and delight in the story, away from the pressures of everyday life.

The Letterbox Club is a highly imaginative scheme that bypasses the professionals and delivers packages of carefully chosen books and educational games directly to children in care placements. As Rose Griffiths writes in her introduction (Chapter 4), 'most of us enjoy getting something through the post' (as long as it's not a bill) and the Letterbox project uses children's excitement at receiving a parcel to encourage them to enjoy reading and playing number games at home. "Enjoy" is the key word here. Children have to want to learn: the missing element in so much writing about education is motivation.

The other chapters in this section reinforce the message of the earlier research review: foster children come from such severely disadvantaged backgrounds and have usually suffered so much disruption in their schooling before they come into care that they need intensive help to catch up with their peers. General support is not enough. The findings from the paired reading project reported by Cara Osborne and colleagues (Chapter 9) were very encouraging. On average the children's reading age improved by 12 months after an intervention lasting only 16 weeks, with children previously identified as "poor" readers making the biggest gains. Demands on foster carers were minimal: they only had to undertake to read with the child three times a week for 20 minutes, although, sadly, even that was too much for some of the potential participants. This underlines the urgent need to recruit foster carers who value education and people who love books. There also needs to be much more emphasis in their training on reading aloud to children in a way that engages their interest and makes them want to read for themselves.

## The school's responsibility

Most writing about the education of looked after children comes from the social care rather than the education perspective. Schools, and our inflexible and target-driven education process, which pays little attention to the differing circumstances of individual children, must take more responsibility for the under-achievement of children and young people in care. The In Care, In School project described by Richard Parker and Mike Gorman (Chapter 10) is an innovative collaboration between a university education department and a local authority virtual school designed to help teachers and students understand the situation of children in care and respond to them in a more helpful and sensitive way. The project is rooted in the young people's direct experience and was developed in very close co-operation with the local Care Council.

One of the things it is very important for teachers to understand is how children's learning might be affected by a traumatic family life before care and by the process of coming into care itself (Reimer, 2010). Tedeschi and Calhoun (1995) say that children who are victims of PTSD need 'safety, stabilisation, therapy, social attachments and *the possibility of joy*'. Schools need to be aware of these needs quite as much as social workers and carers, and can play a key role by providing safety and stability which are too often missing from other parts of the children's lives (Höjer and Johansson, 2013). They can also advocate for young people to receive therapy instead of throwing them out for difficult behaviour. A high proportion of children in care suffer from bullying, both verbal and physical, and often are further punished when they respond to provocation (Brodie, 2001).

The balance of current opinion is strongly in favour of including children with learning difficulties and disabilities, including social and behavioural problems, in main-stream school, but there are some children for whom the standard school environment is not well suited. As Maria Poyser argues in Chapter 12, from her experience of being in care, her doctoral research and from teaching in special schools and pupil referral units, that is not an excuse for giving up on their education. Learning can go on alongside therapy and educational achievement is therapeutic in itself.

## Managing transitions

The final part of the book focuses on the education of young people making the transition to adulthood. Chapter 13 reports findings from a comparative study of young people from a care background in five European countries (Jackson and Höjer, 2013). At a time of high youth unemployment throughout Europe, educational qualifications are essential. The vast majority of school students now continue into upper-secondary education but for those in care the way is much harder. In every country they suffer delay and disruption in their schooling, and even those with proven academic ability are steered into low-level vocational training aimed at providing economic independence as early as possible. In all countries there seem to be more barriers than facilitators to educational achievement. Care leavers need better informed advice, higher aspirations and much more generous financial support (see also ButtleTrust, 2013).

Chapter 15 from Ala Sirriyeh and Jim Wade discusses the educational pathways of young refugees and unaccompanied asylum seekers, who make up an increasing proportion of the care population. Despite their multiple disadvantages, they tend to do better in education than UK-born children. Might exploring the reasons for this surprising finding provide clues relevant to all young people moving forward from care?

Despite the many obstacles to continuing or returning to education beyond school, some people manage to do it, and that includes some who might be considered failures of the care system, such as young parents. Claire Cameron (Chapter 16) found that having a baby could be a powerful incentive for young women who had dropped out of school to go back to study with greater application and success. In the final chapter, the themes of resilience and motivation are taken up by Jenny Driscoll in a small-scale qualitative study which found a high level of support among her interviewees for the raising of the school leaving age (implemented 2013 and 2014). Chapters 13 and 16 both highlight the crucial role of foster carers in encouraging and supporting young people they look after to continue and do well in further and higher education.

## Concluding thoughts

A book like this cannot hope to be comprehensive and several important subjects have been left out. One of these is residential care, or rather, group living. Evidence from the *YiPPEE* study suggests it could have a positive contribution to make as it does in countries where children's homes are staffed by highly qualified social pedagogues or social educators. Why must we think of them only as a last resort for children unsuited by their behaviour to family life? In an earlier publication I suggested that some children's homes might be designated as places for young people to live while they pursued their educational ambitions in a protective environment, but the proposal fell on stony ground.

At the same time as working on this book I have been preparing a third edition of a previous publication, *People Under Three* (Goldschmied and Jackson, 2004), and it struck me how little is written about education for young children in care. Almost a quarter of children in the care population are less than five years old. It is the largest age group apart from teenagers (DfE, 2011a). Yet the very extensive literature on early childhood care and education barely mentions out-of-home care. The two fields exist side by side without ever connecting, just as used to be true for school and care (Jackson, 1987). But we are now fully aware that education begins at birth, if not before, certainly not at three or five years old. Differences in developmental progress are already substantial by the age of two.

Despite these omissions, and no doubt others, I hope this collection will be useful to the many teachers, social workers, policy makers and children's services managers who understand the urgent necessity to improve the school experience and educational opportunities of children and young people in care if they are to enjoy their childhood and make a successful transition to adult life.

# PART 1

## OVERVIEW

# 1 Reconnecting care and education: from the Children Act 1989 to *Care Matters*

*Sonia Jackson*

*The Children Act 1989 ended a period of four decades during which the education of children and young people in care was almost entirely neglected. However, it was another 20 years before education took its rightful place at the centre of provision for the care of children away from home. This chapter, reprinted from the* Journal of Children's Services *(5:3, 2010), explores some of the reasons why the education of children in state care was neglected for so long and considers how obstacles to their achievement might be overcome.*

## Introduction

It is now generally recognised that education is the key to social integration and that, conversely, lacking educational qualifications carries a high risk of long-term unemployment and social exclusion. In most advanced western economies unskilled jobs are disappearing fast and those that remain are insecure and low paid. There was a steep rise in youth unemployment in all European Union countries between 2008 and 2009. The experience of previous recessions is that unemployment hits young people first and they are the last to get back to work when things improve (Jackson and Cameron, 2009).

Longitudinal research has shown that, of all the identifiable groups in society, young people who have been in state care are the most likely to experience poor outcomes in adult life, including early parenthood, health problems, depression and criminality (Jackson, 2007). All these misfortunes are strongly associated with unemployment and dependence on welfare benefits. When jobs are scarce, care leavers, with at best basic education, little family back-up and poor social networks, find it hardest to get work. An estimated 70 per cent of new jobs created over the next 10 years will require graduate-level skills. Figures for 2007–8 show that only 14 per cent of 16-year-olds looked after by local authorities achieved the basic expected level at Key Stage 4 of five GCSE passes graded A*–C, compared with 64.8 per cent of all children (DCSF, 2010a) and only nine per cent continue into any kind of higher education. The Labour Government (1997–2010) made strenuous efforts to increase the proportion of 19-year-olds in education, training or employment but the 2009 figures show that 20 per cent of them are NEET (not in education, employment or training), and this is likely to be an underestimate because not all young people who have been in care maintain contact with their local authority (Hauari *et al*, 2010).

During the 19th and early part of the 20th century, there was a clear perception that "education" was important in equipping children for their future lives, even though the conception of what children needed to learn in Poor Law institutions or the large homes run by voluntary child care organisations was extremely limited by modern standards. The Curtis Report, which provided the basis for the 1948 Children Act, complained that there seemed to be only two destinations envisaged for those leaving care: domestic service for girls and the army for boys (Curtis, 1946). A remarkable report by a Victorian lady, Mrs Nassau Senior ("the first woman in Whitehall") on the education of workhouse girls found that, because of their inadequate training and poor socialisation, many were virtually unemployable. Even those who did find employment quickly lost their jobs and were returned to the workhouse, or alternatively resorted to prostitution. Mrs Senior and her helpers followed up 182 of these girls and discovered that many were already dead by the age of 20 (Oldfield, 2008).

Jeanie Senior's ideas about education were far ahead of her time and went much beyond literacy and domestic training. She advocated covering the grim walls of the workhouse with 'paintings and scrolls and illuminations and texts and bits of poetry, all in bright colours'. Children should dance and play games, have books to read and have lessons in health, hygiene and physiology: 'anything that would raise new ideas and thoughts in the minds of the children would be of service to them' (Oldfield, 2008, p 207). Corporal punishment should be banned. Such suggestions aroused angry opposition from the other inspectors (all men) who, in accordance with the less eligibility principle, mostly believed that life in the workhouse, even for children, should be made as unpleasant as possible.

Some of the voluntary child care organisations put considerable emphasis on education. A study of National Children's Homes (NCH) using records going back to the end of the 19th century found a high level of concern to equip care leavers for future employment and a commitment to supporting any who showed educational promise, for instance by paying for them to attend grammar schools (Jackson, 1988).

## Losing sight of education

By the 1950s this perspective had been almost completely lost. The key decision in 1948 was to give central responsibility for children's services to the Home Office, and later the Department of Health (DH), instead of the Department for Education. Roy Parker (1990) suggests that this resulted from the heavy demands on the civil servants of implementing the Education Act 1944, which deterred them from bidding for control of children's departments set up under the Children Act 1948. Whatever the reason, children in care became almost exclusively the concern of social workers for the next half-century.

During the 1960s and 1970s psychoanalytic theory still provided the basis of much social work thinking. Theories of attachment came to dominate child welfare policy in

Britain and the United States to a much greater extent than in non-English speaking countries. This led to a preoccupation with placement issues and a lack of attention to children's daily lives, including school (Jackson, 1987, 1994; Parker *et al*, 1991).

Some enlightened thinkers, such as Mia Kellmer-Pringle, the founder of the National Children's Bureau, advocated much greater attention to education for children in care because of its intrinsic value (Pringle, 1965), but in relation to future employment, education may have seemed less important because in the 1960s there were plenty of unskilled jobs in manufacturing requiring no educational qualifications. Secondary modern schools, to which 80 per cent of children were allocated, generally did not enter them for national examinations. Children in care were identified with other working-class children, who nearly all left school at 15, the first legal opportunity, but could usually expect to find some kind of work. Britain was still a very class-based society and the intense concern for their children's education characteristic of middle-class parents even then was only shared by a small minority of working-class families (Jackson and Marsden, 1962; Jackson, 2010a). Part of the explanation for the apparent indifference of social workers to educational matters, discussed later, may lie in their failure to adjust to the entirely different employment environment of the late 20th century.

## Education in the Children Act 1989

The Children Act 1989 can be seen as a first step towards ending the neglect of education within the care system, but it still does not give the matter much prominence. Almost the only reference in the Act itself is the duty (1.3(b)) to meet the physical, emotional and educational needs of looked after children. Schedule 2 to Regulation 5 on six-monthly reviews of care plans, headed 'Considerations to which Responsible Authorities are to have Regard', includes 'the child's educational needs, progress and development'. In 'Matters for consideration in the Review', arrangements made for the child's education come well down the list at number 10, whereas 'whether the plan makes necessary provision for the child's religious persuasion, racial origin and cultural and linguistic background' is number 4. Among those who might be invited to attend a review, the child's school teacher is listed right at the bottom, even though the teacher is the person who sees, or should see, the child every day.

Probably the most important change in relation to education brought about by the Act was the repeal of the Education Act 1981, Schedule 3(9), under which non-attendance at school was one of the grounds for compulsory reception into care. Coming into care rarely improved children's attendance but cut them off from their families and often started them on a steep downward path, especially if they were placed in children's homes (Berridge, 1985). Education supervision orders under Part III, section 12, were designed to introduce a less punitive approach to problems of truancy and school phobia, in line with the overall philosophy of the Act to move away from coercion and work in partnership with parents.

The principles underpinning the Act are set out in the official publication, *The Care of Children: Principles and practice in Regulations and Guidance* (DH, 1990). It states that:

> The various departments of a local authority (e.g. health, housing, education and social services) should co-operate to provide an integrated service and range of resources **even when such co-operation is not specifically required by law**. (Principle number 28 – emphasis added)

The only other mention of education is in the acknowledgement that 'change of home, caregiver, social worker or school almost always carries some risk to a child's development and welfare' (p 17). Although the principle of co-operation may have been accepted, in practice it was widely disregarded (Firth and Fletcher, 2001). In particular, placement moves were often arranged without reference to school timetables or consultation with schools or education departments, resulting in many children spending long periods out of school and losing any sense of continuity in their education. Alternatively, children might be torpedoed into a completely strange school environment with no attempt at liaison with the previous school and no information given to the new one.

## Assessing outcomes

The Guidance which accompanied the implementation of the Act two years later goes into more detail about what "having regard" to education might mean, although only Volume 6 on *Children with Disabilities* devotes a whole chapter to 'Working with education services' (DH, 1991a). The other relevant volumes, *Volume 3, Family Placements*, and *Volume 4, Residential Care*, give it less than two pages each (DH, 1991b; 1991c). However, these sections do take account of some of the research carried out during the 1980s, in particular the deliberations of the Department of Health Working Party on outcomes in child care, chaired by Professor Roy Parker. The Working Party's report, published at the same time as the Guidance, proposed a system of assessing outcomes of care based on what "ordinary" parents might want for their children (Parker *et al*, 1991). It commented that up to that point almost everything that could be called "outcomes research" centred on a single measure – the breakdown or continuance of placements, ignoring the question of how far the placement actually contributed to the child's well-being. The report argued strongly for an interdisciplinary approach, pointing out that:

> the fact that social work is the profession with responsibility for child care has tended to produce a distorted picture of outcome, with the focus being on what concerns social workers rather than on the overall development of the child. (Parker *et al*, 1991, p 81)

The Working Party proposed that the concept of "outcome" should be broken down into seven dimensions, of which education was the second. It comments on the evidence from the wider educational literature on the close association between parental interest and children's achievement and, conversely, on the low priority given to educational matters by social workers:

> Such attitudes permeate the care system, symbolised by the fact that the responsible government department requires no statistics on the school-leaving qualifications of children who may have spent their whole lives 'in care' and that local authorities do not systematically collect this information. (Parker et al, 1991, p 89)

## Better opportunities

The Guidance on the education of children in foster care (DH, 1991b, Chapter 2, paras 2.33–2.39) begins with the important statement that:

> Children who are looked after or accommodated have the same rights as all children to education, including further and higher education and to other opportunities for development.

However, it was another 10 years before this could become a reality, when the Children (Leaving Care) Act 2000 made it a statutory duty for local authorities to provide the practical means and financial support for looked after children to continue their education beyond the age of compulsory schooling.

Other points made in the Guidance have been reinforced by later research – for example, the risk that the ability of looked after children may be underestimated both by themselves and others, and that they need extra help to compensate for early deprivation and disrupted schooling due to changes of placement (para 2.33). It urges authorities to take a long-term view, providing educational opportunities and support and promoting educational achievement. The authority should offer support to carers; social services departments and education authorities should collaborate; and children should be encouraged and given opportunities to develop and pursue leisure interests and any special gifts they may have. Unfortunately, the educational perspective is conspicuously absent from the rest of the volume. For instance, the section (para 3.54) on the training and support of foster carers makes no reference to school or education. The substantial chapter on foster placements includes only a brief statement that visits during the first weeks are important to check that arrangements made for schooling and contact are "working smoothly" (DH, 1991b, Chapter 4). The low educational level of foster carers is a longstanding obstacle to raising attainment which has never been effectively tackled or even acknowledged. I have argued elsewhere that minimum standards of education should be set for carers and that specific educational support should be offered to fostered children whose carers are not able to provide it.

The Guidance on residential care (DH, 1991c) acknowledges that young people accommodated in children's homes can be especially disadvantaged educationally and advises that they should be given every opportunity to take full advantage of educational opportunities. It urges care staff to recognise and applaud a young person's achievements and provide support and encouragement when he [sic] encounters disappointments. They should be alert to the possibility that the child may be bullied or discriminated against at school, work closely with teachers, attend school social events and parent evenings and report back to the young person. There should be appropriate quiet conditions for homework and access to reference books. Sadly, there is evidence that, 10 years later, for many children in residential care, perhaps the majority, none of those things were happening (Rees, 2001). The continuing very poor educational outcomes from residential care appear to be at least partly attributable to the low level of education and qualifications of care staff, compared with their counterparts in other parts of Europe (Petrie and Simon, 2006).

The statement in the earlier volume quoted above about further and higher education is repeated even more emphatically:

> It is sometimes too readily accepted that further education is not appropriate for young people in homes. This belief needs to be countered forcefully. Young people who have the ability should be encouraged most strongly to continue their education beyond compulsory school age. Staff in homes need to emphasise the value of education . . . Every encouragement should be given to young people to undertake higher education when they have demonstrated ability to benefit from it. (1.112)

This admirable exhortation was not very realistic considering that most residential units only accommodated children up to age 16 and even before that were thinking of moving them on to independent living. Training in independence skills took precedence over any possibility of continuing in education.

The only study to date of university students who have been in care as children found that one individual out of a sample of over 150 had gone into higher education directly from a children's home, and even he could say nothing positive about his residential experience (Jackson et al, 2003). About a third of the study sample were living independently, usually in council flats, at the time of applying to university, and some of them showed great determination and resilience in coping with the demands of independent living while continuing to study, although all had found it very hard. Among this group, many had come to the UK as unaccompanied asylum seekers and their backgrounds were not typical of other children in care (Jackson et al, 2005). The young people who did best were those who had stable foster placements, at least from about the age of 14 onwards (Jackson and Ajayi, 2007), with foster carers who valued education and continued to support them practically and emotionally through their higher education.

## How effective was the Children Act 1989 in improving educational opportunities?

Before 1989, the DH already had a strong track record of commissioning and supporting research, much of which contributed to the thinking behind the Act. No research specifically on education was commissioned but for six years (1989–1995) the Department supported the further development of the Looking After Children (LAC) system proposed in the report of the Working Party on Outcomes (Parker *et al*, 1991). The prototype Assessment and Action Record (AAR) (pp 141–192) became the basis for a comprehensive set of materials with age-related schedules covering the seven chosen dimensions of outcome: health, education, identity, family and social relationships, social presentation, emotional and behavioural development and self-care skills. Although the focus of the work increasingly shifted from research to the goal of improving practice, studying the implementation of the system included examination of completed AARs for 204 children looked after in five local authorities and 379 children living at home in the community (Ward, 1995).

Criticisms of the Records expressed by departmental advisory groups and social workers in relation to the education section are very revealing. Some people argued that the AARs promoted middle-class values that were irrelevant to looked after children. Objections were raised to straightforward questions that might have been considered basic to welfare, such as how well a child was doing at school. Many critics seemed to assume that all children in care have learning difficulties (the actual figure is about three per cent) and therefore it would be "insensitive" to say anything about attainment. Most controversy concerned questions about access to books and libraries, whether children were learning to play musical instruments and if 10 to 15-year-olds had a quiet place to do homework. Such criticisms came exclusively from professionals and social workers, not from any respondents in the community group, which included all social classes (Ward, 1995).

The underlying assumption was clearly that it is somehow inappropriate, and indeed unfair, to encourage looked after children to aspire to academic success. Reading is not for the lower orders. As for musical instruments, the research found that nearly half of children from all social classes were learning to play, including a third of looked after children aged three to nine. However, the attitudes expressed in these objections certainly contributed to the lack of attention given to the education of children in care before and for many years after the implementation of the Children Act 1989. They can be traced back to the less eligibility principle of the Poor Law and assumptions about the level of education appropriate for working-class children (Jackson, 2010a). There is also a substantial education literature on the self-fulfilling relationship between teacher expectations and pupil performance – the "Pygmalion effect" (Good, 1987). Children and young people frequently complain that they are not expected to achieve at school

17

simply because they are in care (Jackson, 1987, 2000; Martin and Jackson, 2002).

The education section of the five to nine AAR was modified in response to feedback from advisory groups and professionals (Ward, 1995, Appendix 2). The key change is in the final section in which the aim 'the child's educational attainments are average or above' is replaced by 'the child's educational attainments match his/her ability'. In other words, an objective statement about level of attainment is replaced by a subjective judgement. But, in the absence of a standardised test, this feeds into the underestimation of looked after children's potential identified in the Guidance to the Children Act 1989 (2.33).

## Losing sight of education

Examination of completed AARs both in the pilot study and at the implementation stage showed that the education section was the least well completed and was sometimes left entirely blank, especially when the child was either excluded from school or had no school place due to a change of placement – precisely the circumstances in which action would seem to be most necessary. A high proportion of those in children's homes were not attending school; in some homes a culture of non-attendance seemed to have taken root and staff appeared powerless to influence it. This finding was repeated in several subsequent studies of residential care (e.g. Sinclair and Gibbs, 1996; Berridge and Brodie, 1998).

The Social Services Inspectorate (SSI) carried out a detailed inspection of 33 children's homes in 11 local authorities in 1992–2003 to see how well the standards set by the 1989 Act were being met. Their report was highly critical of many aspects of the care provided, especially the lack of attention to education (SSI and DH, 1993). The general picture was described as "depressing": school exclusion was a significant problem in all homes, 'most children's case files lacked educational histories and there was very little evidence of educational planning as part of overall care planning' (p 44). Social services and education departments were failing to work together in the way envisaged by the 1989 Act, and children were suffering as a result. Essentially this report provided further evidence of the serious weaknesses already identified in the Utting Report, *Children in the Public Care* (Utting, 1991).

Despite the good intentions of the Act and the LAC system, the 1990s were the period when children in care probably experienced the worst educational disadvantage by comparison with those living with their own families. It was a time of rapid change with constant reorganisation of services within local authorities, dissatisfaction among social workers about increasing bureaucracy and chronic instability within the care system (Jackson and Preston-Shoot, 1996; Jackson and Thomas, 1999).

A survey of 2,000 children carried out by the Who Cares? Trust found that almost a third had moved placement more than six times and nine per cent of children under 11 had moved more than 10 times (Shaw, 1998). It was not uncommon for children to experience over 50 placements in the course of their care career. Many of these moves would have involved changes of school, especially damaging during the two-year run-up to GCSE but disruptive at any time. The trauma and anxiety caused by this constant movement made it very difficult for children to concentrate on school work and impossible for them to make plans for the future, knowing that their lives might be turned upside down again at any time, often without consulting their views or wishes (Jackson, 2000). The high proportion of looked after children not even entered for GCSE is partly due to the loss of coursework during placement moves and the failure of social workers to understand the vital importance of ensuring that this does not happen (O'Sullivan and Westerman, 2007, reprinted in this volume).

In addition, the educational legislation during this period was in complete conflict with the Children Act 1989 and had the effect of locking large numbers of children out of school and denying them access to education, sometimes for as long as a year at a time (Blyth and Milner, 1996). The Education Reform Act 1988 and the Education Act 1993 decisively shifted power away from the local education authority (LEA) in favour of individual head teachers. If it was hard previously for LEAs to accept the idea that they had special obligations towards children in public care, it became still more difficult once head teachers could make their own decisions about the allocation of school places (Benson, 1996). Fletcher-Campbell (1997) found that children were refused places because of fears, often unfounded, that they would be a disruptive influence in the classroom and interfere with the work of better motivated students. For the minority who did have real problems, the answer was to throw them out with little concern for the effect on their educational opportunities or future lives (Firth and Horrocks, 1996; Brodie, 2001). At best they would be allocated to pupil referral units (see Chapter 10), where they might get more sympathetic treatment but would be 'categorised out of normal education' and have no chance of acquiring useful qualifications (Tomlinson, 1982).

In the fiercely competitive climate engendered by the "reforms", looked after children were seen as a liability, unlikely to contribute to league tables of GCSE and A-level scores. In addition, social workers often moved children's placements in the middle of the academic year when places in desirable schools were all taken up, so looked after children tended to find themselves in schools where no one else wanted to go. The requirement in the Education Act 2005 to give preference to looked after children even when the school was officially full thus represented a very important advance.

## A better education for children in care

Towards the end of the 1990s, evidence was accumulating of the severe educational disadvantage associated with being in care. Some local authorities had already taken the initiative to set up educational support services for looked after children, spanning the divide between education and social services, on the model first established by the

Manchester Teaching Service for the Social Services (Walker, 2002). A study by the National Foundation for Educational Research (NFER) found that these services were greatly valued and did an excellent job of advocating for looked after children and supporting them and their carers (Fletcher–Campbell, 1997). Unfortunately, not being part of core services, they were chronically underfunded, patchily distributed and always vulnerable to cuts, which may still be the case. The NFER study, like many others before and since, found that the lack of priority given to education by social workers and their inadequate understanding of the education system continued to be a major problem (Jackson and Sachdev, 2001).

A contributory factor may also be that many entrants to the social work profession come by unconventional routes, such as access courses, and may have a negative view of schools because of their own experience (Millham *et al*, 1980). This may be less true since social work became a graduate profession with more emphasis than in the past on continuing professional development. However, the report of the Social Work Task Force (2009) commented on the poor educational level of many social workers, which prevents them from engaging effectively with other professionals and, in particular, limits their capacity to act as advocates for looked after children (Berridge *et al*, 2009).

The Who Cares? Trust, a voluntary organisation which advocates for looked after children, played an active role during the 1990s in raising awareness and produced several publications informing children of their educational rights, as well as guides for school governors and elected members of local authorities (Who Cares? Trust, 1994; Fletcher 1996, 1998). This was followed up by the *Equal Chances* project, funded by Gulbenkian UK, an ambitious attempt to create an integrated care and education service for looked after children in two local authority areas (Firth and Fletcher, 2001). Although it did not achieve the aim of bringing the performance of looked after children up to the same level as those not in care, it can be seen in retrospect as having pioneered many ideas that have now become part of mainstream thinking, such as the inclusion of young people in the planning and implementation of children's services, helping them to communicate their views to managers and policy-makers and measures to combat bullying and discrimination.

A similar project, *Taking Care of Education*, was carried out by the National Children's Bureau in three different local authorities (Harker *et al*, 2004a). It produced valuable evidence and some significant improvement in educational support for looked after children, but, as with *Equal Chances*, it was much more difficult to prove that the changes put in place, such as better study facilities, training for foster carers, anti-bullying strategies, access to out-of-school activities and celebration events, actually had any impact on measurable performance. Both projects ran into similar problems created by the division between social care and education services and the difficulty in getting them to work together at grassroots level, even when that was the clearly declared policy of senior managers (Harker *et al*, 2004b).

## Making education a priority

The Labour Government elected in 1997 immediately declared the intention of raising educational standards and improving opportunities for all children, and the following year that aspiration was extended specifically to looked after children in the form of the *Quality Protects* initiative (DH, 1998). Frank Dobson, then Secretary of State for Health, wrote to every local authority elected member in England and Wales emphasising that the most important thing they could do for children in their care was to give them a good education. A total of £885 million of new money was allocated to local authorities to improve the care of looked after children. Disappointingly, later research found that a very small proportion of these funds was used for educational purposes, in line with previous findings that social work concerns always tend to predominate over educational aims (Berridge *et al*, 2008). *Quality Protects*, like the Children Act Guidance, explicitly linked educational attainment and future life chances, on which the British Cohort Studies provide conclusive evidence (Feinstein and Brassett–Grundy, 2005). It also challenged the low expectations that had dogged the LAC project. The government went on to commission an enquiry into the education of children in care by the Social Exclusion Unit (SEU, 2003). Importantly, the Department of Health also began to require social services departments from 1999 to produce figures on the educational attainment of looked after children at key stages and to compare them with the average attainment of children not in care. This, at last, provided objective evidence at a national level of the very low achievement of looked after children (DfES and DH, 2002). Research by the *YiPPEE* project[1] in five EU countries has shown that collecting statistical evidence is the essential first stage in raising awareness of this as a significant policy issue (Hauari *et al*, 2010; Jackson and Höjer, 2013).

The government did not wait for the SEU to report before taking action. Two further landmarks were the first ever Joint Guidance on the education of children in care, issued by the DfES and the DH in 2000, with some of the items having statutory force, and the Children (Leaving Care) Act 2000, implemented in 2001 (DfES and DH, 2000).

The new legislation addressed many of the serious problems experienced by young people in transition from care to independence that had been identified by leaving care researchers since the 1980s (Stein, 1997; Broad, 1998). It resulted in the setting up of leaving care teams in most local authorities. Most importantly, for the purpose of this paper, it gave legislative force to the aspiration in the Children Act 1989 Guidance for young people in care to continue their education beyond compulsory school age. Local

---

1  *YiPPEE* is the acronym of a project funded under the European Union Framework 7 Programme on Youth and Social Inclusion, Young People in Public Care: Pathways to Education in Europe. The five countries which form the *YiPPEE* partnership are England, Sweden, Denmark, Spain and Hungary. The final report can be accessed on the website: http:/tcru.ioe.ac.uk/yippee. See also Chapter 14.

authorities were now obliged to provide financial support and vacation accommodation to young people who wanted to go to college or university, whereas before this had been done on an ad hoc basis so that prospective students were deterred from applying to university because they did not know how they would be able to support themselves. The study of young people with a care background at university referred to earlier found that those who started their courses before the Act was implemented were four times more likely to leave prematurely than those who could claim local authority support as a legal entitlement (Jackson *et al*, 2005).

The SEU Report, *A Better Education for Children in Care*, was published at the same time as the Green Paper, *Every Child Matters* (DfES, 2003a), which set out five desirable outcomes for all children, two of which, 'enjoy and achieve' and 'achieve economic well-being', are clearly related to education. As pointed out earlier, it is now very difficult to achieve economic well-being without having at least basic school-leaving qualifications.

In his Foreword to the SEU report, which he had personally commissioned, Tony Blair, then Prime Minister, wrote:

> . . . the Government is committed to giving children in care all the same life chances any parent would give their child, and none is more important than a good education which is crucial to a brighter future. (p iii)

The Report, though watered down through successive drafts, made it clear how far that aim was from being achieved. It set a revised Public Service Agreement (PSA) target, 'substantially narrowing the gap between the educational attainment and participation of children in care and that of their peers by 2006', followed by more specific targets. They are still far from being achieved in 2010, and due to the success in raising standards generally the gap in attainment has actually widened. Perhaps most significantly, secondary analysis of official statistics produced for the *YiPPEE* project reveals huge variations in the performance of different local authorities that cannot be explained by the characteristics of the area or of the children looked after. For example, one of the last government's top priorities was to increase the number of 19-year-old care leavers who are in education, employment or training. The range in 2007–2008 was from 29 per cent in the worst performing authority to 96 per cent in the best. The percentage of children in care achieving five A*–C level GCSE passes varied from none to 46 per cent. Although these figures can fluctuate greatly from one year to another due to small numbers, within-authority trends over three or four years are remarkably consistent (Hauari *et al*, 2010).

## Obstacles to closing the gap

The underlying problems were identified by the SEU from its review of research over the previous 20 years and surveys of local authorities: vacancy rates and turnover in the social care workforce and lack of training on educational needs of children in care; lack of commitment at senior level; poor strategic planning and use of resources; 'a widespread absence of joint working between frontline workers and local authority officers in different departments'; and negative attitudes and low expectations. At an individual level, the SEU listed five key reasons for low achievement: instability – changes of care and school placements; time out of school both when living at home and in care; lack of help to catch up after falling behind due to gaps in schooling; 'carers not expected or equipped' to provide sufficient support and encouragement for learning; and lack of attention to physical and mental health and difficulty in accessing mental health services.

The SEU Report, together with a study by the Institute of Education which showed the enormous costs incurred by the failure to educate children in care (Jackson and Simon, 2006), produced decisive government action. The Children Act 2004, in an amendment to section 22(3)(a) of the 1989 Act, which came into force in July 2005, placed a new duty on local authorities to promote the educational achievement of looked after children. The Statutory Guidance issued by the DfES (2005) stated:

> Local authorities as [their] 'corporate parents' should demonstrate the strongest commitment to helping every child they look after, wherever the child is placed, to achieve the highest educational standards he or she possibly can. This includes supporting their aspirations to achieve in further and higher education.

Education rose decisively to the top of the agenda for looked after children with the *Care Matters* Green and White Papers (DfES, 2006a; DCSF, 2007), which underpinned the Children and Young Persons Act 2008. They carry forward the principles of the 1989 Act and the LAC system in their emphasis on the local authority's duty to support the education of looked after children as a good (and well-informed) parent would. There was admirable honesty in admitting past failures and acknowledging, as seldom before, that the fault lies with the system and not with the children. For the first time, education was at the centre of the vision for improving outcomes for children in care, and this was education in its broadest sense, including the earliest years and leisure and cultural activities. Perhaps the most encouraging change was the recognition that all aspects of care and education are inter-related, so that in addition to Chapter 5, entitled 'A first class education', learning in and out of school was discussed at numerous points throughout the Green Paper.

The *Care Matters* papers put forward a range of innovative ideas, many of which were commissioned by the government as evaluated pilot projects (see below). Some were directly related to education and others, such as the right to remain in foster care beyond

18, had an important indirect impact. The responsibility of the school to support the education of children in public care (DfES, 2003a) was reiterated and the role of designated teacher was made statutory.

## Post-compulsory education

It is a shocking fact that the UK has the lowest proportion of 17- to 19-year olds in education of any western industrialised country. The school-leaving age was fixed at 16 as long ago as 1973 and at the time of writing it is unclear if the Labour Government's commitment to raise it to 18 by 2013 will be honoured.[2] For looked after children, there is still a strong, and damaging, assumption that education ends in Year 11, with GCSE (or GNVQ) as the highest qualification to which they can aspire. There is currently no government target for A-levels or higher education. Only the most recent figures distinguish between employment and education after 16.

Expectations of education after Year 11 are still far too limited by the assumption that young people in care, regardless of ability, are more suited to vocational than academic routes. Nevertheless, increasing numbers of care leavers are able to access higher education and the *Care Matters* papers laid a strong emphasis on increasing participation (DfES, 2006a, pp 90–1). In 1999, the feasibility study for the *By Degrees* research cited above reported a young man being told by his social worker: 'You can't go to university – you're in care' (Jackson and Roberts, 2000). Now local authorities compete to get more care leavers into university than their neighbours. Social workers are still not well informed about educational matters, but at least they know that they should be.

## Can *Care Matters* change opportunities and outcomes?

Some of the *Care Matters* pilot initiatives have now been formally evaluated with mixed results. For example, broadly speaking, the virtual school head (VSH) evaluation was a success (Berridge *et al*, 2009). In most of the 11 pilot authorities the VSH adopted a clear strategic remit, addressing some of the structural weaknesses identified by research, raising the profile of looked after children within the authority, challenging low expectations and aspirations, developing protocols with other authorities to ensure that children placed out of area are not overlooked and mounting training programmes for designated teachers, social workers and foster carers. One of the most important aspects of the role was

---

2  Instead of raising the *school* leaving age the Coalition Government decreed that all pupils must stay 'in some form of education or training' until the end of the academic year in which they turn 17 in 2013, and 18 in 2014. This need not mean full-time education in school or college; it includes apprenticeships and full-time (20 hours or more) employment combined with part-time education or training, i.e. a very much reduced requirement for continuing *education*. It remains to be seen how this will affect the educational opportunities of young people in care.

facilitating the still new and incomplete integration of care and education within children's services and helping the two arms of the service to communicate more effectively.

The VSH, usually a former secondary school head or deputy, with high status within the education system, was able to act as an effective advocate for looked after children, particularly in relation to deflecting threatened exclusions and securing places for them in the most suitable schools. This had a clearly beneficial effect in most of the 11 pilot authorities, with some showing remarkable improvement in Year 11 examination results. Another task of the VSH in four of the pilot authorities was to oversee the private tutoring scheme funded by HSBC Bank, and this proved extremely helpful and popular with children, carers and social workers.

The Boarding School Pathfinder (placing "vulnerable" children in ordinary boarding schools rather than in residential or foster placement) was also judged to be successful by the Department and rolled out across the country, but seems unlikely to be suitable for more than a small minority of children on the margins of care (Maxwell *et al*, 2009). The Budget-holding Lead Professional scheme, designed to give social workers freedom to be adventurous and creative in finding ways to improve the care experience for children, including in relation to education, seems to have been a more or less complete failure: perhaps it required too great a shift in the culture of social care (Walker *et al*, 2010). Other initiatives have yet to report and there is a question mark over how far the present government will be willing to promote or sustain ideas proposed by its predecessor, especially in a time of increasing financial stringency.

## Conclusion

The educational experience and outcomes of children looked after by local authorities are intimately bound up with other aspects of their lives and care. We are beginning to understand better how class, gender, ethnicity and less tangible factors like learning identity interact to influence educational achievement (Ball, 2005). Although there have been many developments and considerable improvements in practice since 2003, most of the underlying problems identified by the Social Exclusion Unit (SEU, 2003, pp 3–5) continue to blight the educational chances of looked after children. As a result, progress has been disappointingly slow, but if we look back to 1989 we can see that it has happened. Back then it was unusual for looked after children even to be entered for examinations and very few obtained any but the lowest grades. The 2009 figures show that 14 per cent of the looked after cohort obtained five or more GCSEs at grades A*–C, still far below the general population for whom the latest official figure is 64.8 per cent but over twice as many as in 2001 (DCSF, 2010a).

There are fundamental problems within the care system which make it far more difficult for a looked after child to achieve educational success than a child growing up in his or her own family, but there is some encouraging evidence that a clear focus on educational attainment for looked after children can have measurable effects. Being happy and doing well at school and, especially, continuing into further and higher education, can enable young people to escape the problems experienced by their birth families and enjoy a better quality of adult life. In retrospect, the Children Act 1989 can be seen as the first small step along that road.

## 2    The education of children in care: a research review

*Penelope Welbourne and Caroline Leeson*

*This chapter explores three key aspects of the education of children in care: the composition of that population of children and the extent to which they differ from the general population of children due to difficulties most of them have experienced prior to as well as after entering care; issues relating to the identification of causal relationships and the extent of under-achievement by children in care; and any evidence that care may provide more positive opportunities than is often supposed. It is presented in the form of an extensive literature review of existing published research into social policy and practice of caring for looked after children. The significant factors that contribute to better achievement for children in care are placement stability and support at school, but for some children therapeutic help and specialist assessments are necessary to improve outcomes. Different analyses produce different results and the scrutiny of children's trajectories indicates better outcomes than one-off comparisons with children not in care.*

*The review is reprinted from the* Journal of Children's Services *(7:2, 2012) with kind permission from Emerald.*

## Introduction

*The gap between the educational achievement of looked after children compared with children not in care has long been identified as a cause of concern: recent practice guidance describes this as 'not doing as well at school as their peers'.* (NICE, 2010, p 57)

While researchers have highlighted 'the devastating impact of being in care on young children's attainment' (Connelly and Chakrabarti, 2008, p 348), a careful analysis of the evidence available relating to the attainment of looked after children suggests a more complex picture. Achievement by looked after children may be greater than has been suggested (Heath *et al*, 1994; Harker *et al*, 2004a; Forrester, 2008; Gaskell, 2010), and where they have poorer outcomes, the reasons for this appear to include a range of individual and contextual influences that need to be understood and addressed if children in care are to have similar opportunities for educational success as their peers, and therefore, similar lifelong opportunity (Berridge *et al*, 2008).

## Policy context

It is has been known for 25 years that children in care achieve, on average, lower GSCE results than the average child (Stein and Carey, 1986; Jackson, 1987). Only 13 per cent of children in care obtain five GCSEs at Grade A*–C compared with 59 per cent of all children in the same age group; 37 per cent achieve no GCSEs compared with two per cent of all children (DCSF, 2008b).Other countries have noted similar problems (Weyts, 2004; Egelund and Hestbæk, 2007; Fernandez, 2008; McClung and Gayle, 2010). This is routinely described as under-achievement, implying that the expected level of attainment should be higher, but the comparison group against which their attainment might reasonably be measured is seldom specified (Berridge, 2007). The disparity in attainment has been used as evidence of failure of local authority "corporate parenting" (Fletcher-Campbell, 1997; Archer, 1999; Forrester, 2008).

There is better policy support for the education of children in care now than at any previous time. *Care Matters* made educational achievement of looked after children a priority for local authorities (DCSF, 2008a). Local authorities have a duty to promote their educational achievement; all children in care should have a personal education plan, and specialist designated teachers have been created to promote their attainment (Children Act 2004; Hayden, 2005; DfES, 2007; DCSF, 2008a, c; 2009c; Children and Young Persons Act 2008). Virtual school heads have a co-ordinating and facilitating role with additional resources of £500 available for each child in care (DCSF, 2008c; 2009d).

The Department for Education (DfE) in England is monitoring progress for all children looked after continuously for 12 months or more. They are expected to progress two curriculum levels in English and maths between each Key Stage from the age of seven, and one level at Key Stage 1. This will be monitored using information from the National Pupil Database (DfE, 2011b). Targets have been set:

- 20 per cent to achieve five A*–C GCSE grades;
- 55 per cent to reach level 4 at Key Stage 2 in mathematics;
- 60 per cent to reach level 4 at Key Stage 2 in English (DCSF, 2008a).

This tracking offers the possibility of building a more comprehensive picture of the impact of care on the education of children in care, although only for children who stay in care at least a year (DCSF, 2009b).

## Research context

Berridge (2007) prefers the term "low achievement" to "under-achievement" for children in care, since the academic potential of the children concerned is not easily established. Such information is often unavailable or very difficult to measure at the point when a child enters care. The unexamined belief that the care system is largely to blame for children's educational difficulties is an obstacle to improving matters (Stein, 2008a;

Hannon *et al*, 2010). There is little hard evidence about how decisions about educational provision have been made in the past (Davey and Pithouse, 2008) and difficulty identifying 'what affects what' (Hare and Bullock, 2006, p 26), so planning how to improve matters presents a policy challenge. As Brodie and Norris (2009, p 1) comment:

> There is a serious lack of evidence about the complex learning and behavioural needs of many looked after young people and the ways in which they do or do not benefit from recent policy and other initiatives.

In this chapter, we use the terms "children in care" and "young people in care" to refer both to those who are in care by reason of a court order, and those who are in care by agreement with their parents or carers.

Gaps in existing knowledge are all too apparent, including knowledge about why children in some areas do better than others. National cohort data often appear incomplete (Jacklin *et al*, 2006). Retrospective studies are particularly vulnerable to poor data gathering and recording because older records have less reliable data in many areas (O'Sullivan and Westerman, 2007). Attainment to the "baseline" standard (5 A*–C GCSEs) varies widely between local authority areas from 0 to 39 per cent of young people in care, and variation in the proportion of care leavers in education, employment or training is even more varied, between 0 and 100 per cent (DCSF, 2008a, p 35). Some variation in attainment to the "baseline" standard may reflect contextual local variables, some may reflect recording practices, but the extent of variation suggests that there may be something to learn by exploring the differences in outcome between areas (Wade *et al*, 2010).

Absence of key data is an obstacle to interpretation of the data we do have. Data about the low attainment of children in care (such as GSCE passes) do not on their own establish causal links between level of achievement and being in care. We have evidence about differential average outcomes; it is the complex causality behind this that we wish to explore here. To know how care affects education, we need to look at the trajectories of children's educational achievement throughout their time in care, as well as levels of attainment, and ideally we need to know what happens to them after they leave care too.

Many – perhaps most – children in care come from families in which they have been children in need, according to the definition in section 17 of the Children Act 1989. The Welsh Assembly Government's Child in Need Audit for 2011 links data about children in need to information about educational attainment (Ceredigion County Council, 2010). One aim of this is to support formulation of 'sound policies that will tackle the underlying causes of poor outcomes for looked after children' (Welsh Assembly Government, 2010, p 23). The audit shows that the attainment of children in need living at home is actually lower than that of children in care (Welsh Assembly Government, 2011), challenging established beliefs and suggesting that coming into care is more likely to be helpful than impair educational progress. This positive effect was found to be the case for children in every Key Stage. As with children in care (discussed in detail below), children in need at home achieved better at younger ages, and as they got older they fell further behind the average level of attainment. The widest difference was between boys in care and not in care in Key Stage 2: thereafter the gap narrows as both groups' attainment relative to the average declines; 18 per cent of children in need at home attained five GCSE A*–C passes compared with 21 per cent of children in care. This similar pattern for both groups of falling further behind their peers with increasing age suggests that all children in need, wherever they are living, need tailored educational support, not only those in care. The educational problems of both groups may reflect lifelong interaction between economic disadvantage, parental difficulties and children's responses to those problems. It also suggests that even if being in care is not the primary cause of the problem, significant difficulties often continue to affect achievement after children enter the care system.

## Research questions

We consider three key questions:

1. Who do we mean by "children in care" in terms of age of entry, time spent in care, and other aspects of their profile?
2. What is the effect of:
   - trauma;
   - some common familial risk factors on children's educational attainment, whether or not they are in care?
3. What known factors support resilience in the recovery or maintenance of educational potential in the context of child/family difficulties?

## Methods

As a first approximation to answering these questions, we carried out a non-systematic literature review, chosen as an initial way of exploring and scoping gaps in existing research.

We searched through the research literature available via web-based searches for academic papers with keywords including "education", "looked after children", "attainment" and "care". We then searched for additional material relating to early brain development and educational attainment related to early experience of abuse and neglect and parental difficulties, including depression and poverty. We do not claim that this was an exhaustive search, nor have we reported all the research we discovered, selecting that which had the most direct relevance to our research questions.

## Exploring the characteristics of the looked after child population

It is important to consider the profile of children in care as a group in order to understand research describing their achievements and difficulties. They are not a homogenous group: they enter at different points in their childhood, for different reasons, and leave after different intervals (Forrester, 2008; Walker-Gleaves and Walker, 2008). In England and Wales, at least 80 per cent have experienced abuse, neglect, family stress or family dysfunction before entering the care system. Time in care is often a relatively small part of their life and accounts for a small proportion of their educational experience (DCSF, 2009a; Hannon *et al*, 2010). Despite their family history, many soon return home: half do so within a year and a quarter leave within eight weeks (Mooney *et al*, 2009; Hannon *et al*, 2010). On the other hand, re-entry is common. About two-thirds of care leavers return (Wade *et al*, 2010). Nearly half of all entrants to care are aged 10 and over, with several years at school behind them before coming into care. Many children in care have significant experience of living with their own families, and many move between home and care a number of times during their education. Difficulties with education may begin before or during time in care. For the purposes of addressing those difficulties, it would seem very important to know why the problems began and what perpetuates them. This is likely to be complex, with the working of the care and education systems among a number of causal factors.

The age and timing of entry to the care system suggest some reasons why children in care may do so much worse educationally than their non-care peers. Sinclair *et al* (2007) (summarised in Mooney *et al*, 2009) describe the age and composition of the care population in England in the following way. Young entrants (43%) aged under 11 at entry became looked after primarily due to abuse and neglect. Adolescent graduates (26%), who had lived within the care system for some time, first entered the care system for similar reasons to young entrants, but now being older, tended to have more difficulties at home, at school and with behaviour than younger entrants. For abused adolescents (9%) first admitted to care over the age of 11, usually for reasons of abuse or neglect, on average their behaviour was significantly more challenging than that of the adolescent graduates and they were also doing much worse at school. Adolescent entrants (14%) also first admitted over the age of 11, but usually because relationships at home had broken down. Their families had fewer problems than those of the previous groups, but the young people showed challenging behaviour and were often doing badly at school. Children seeking asylum (5%), who were almost always over the age of 11, tended to do comparatively well at school and displayed less challenging behaviour than any other group. Disabled children (3%) (16% had a disability but this was not always their primary "need code") had comparatively high levels of challenging behaviour, were on average older than other groups and had been looked after for longer. The exact nature of the difficulties and challenges children usually experience often leave a legacy of educational and

31

behavioural attitudes, apparent from the time they become "looked after".

Fernandez (2008) carried out a prospective, longitudinal study of younger children in long-term foster care in Australia with a "quasi-control" group of children not in care. At entry to care, over half the children in care had specific school difficulties including attitude, behaviour or motivational problems and poor academic attainment. They had high levels of psychological need affecting mood, behaviour and relational capacity, and significant problems with attention, social interaction, anxiety and aggression. One in five was behind their age-appropriate grade, and over a third were in the clinical range for one or more emotional and behavioural problems. Carers reported a pressing need for additional help with skills such as reading.

Children in care more often have educational issues that are predictors of poorer-than-average outcomes, such as school exclusion and truancy (Jackson and Sachdev, 2001; Connelly and Chakrabarti, 2008). They are eight times more likely to be excluded from school (Ofsted, 2008) and in 2007–2008, 13 per cent missed at least 25 days of school (DCSF, 2008b). Conduct disorder is more frequent in older children in care and is predictive of poor academic performance, especially when associated with attention difficulties (Cassen et al, 2008). Conduct and behavioural difficulties appear linked with educational problems for many children in care.

A fifth (20%) of children in care have a special educational need (Jacklin et al, 2006; O'Sullivan and Westerman, 2007; Davey and Pithouse, 2008) and nearly a third have statements of special educational needs (DCSF, 2008b). Although they may span the full range of academic ability (Jackson and Martin, 1998), they include a high proportion of children with specific educational difficulties. The current consultation on special educational provision is highly relevant for both groups of children, and for them much rests on getting the review process right (DfE, 2011b).

Not all evidence supports the idea that being in care is detrimental to attainment. A retrospective longitudinal study of a large cohort of children born in the 1950s found only mild adverse effects of being in care at any time during childhood:

> . . . men but not women who had a history of care were less likely to achieve higher academic qualifications [2 A-levels or degree level education]. However, [. . .] those with a history of care were not more likely to leave school with no qualifications, and a higher risk for school exclusion was only found among women, suggesting that school failure in this group reflects childhood socio-economic disadvantage as well as the effects of local authority care. (Viner and Taylor, 2005, p 897)

Most avoided significant disadvantage: they were not over-represented in the lowest income quartile. They were more likely to have high scores on the Rutter Malaise Inventory and to have had mental health problems, but not at the level reported in studies of adolescents currently in care (Richardson and Lelliott, 2003; McAuley and Young,

2006). Factors other than being in care appear to be important in explaining the difficulties care leavers experience:

> ... *the disadvantage associated with public care is substantially less than is reported by studies of those who leave care at 16 to 17 years and by cross-sectional studies during adolescence that fail to account adequately for other causes of disadvantage [...] the great majority do not experience significant long-term health or social adversity.* (Viner and Taylor, 2005, p 898)

There is evidence that being in care at age 16 to18 is associated with high risk of poor mental health (Blower *et al*, 2004; Ford *et al*, 2007), homelessness, unemployment and early pregnancy (Sergeant, 2006). One possible explanation for the difference between Viner and Taylor's conclusions and other studies is that theirs captured information about children who stayed in care for shorter periods or left earlier as well as long stayers/ late entrants. Studies of older children in care include many young people who had longer damaging pre-care experiences (Stein, 2008a). It may be harder to achieve felt security for older entrants (Cashmore and Paxman, 2006), and relational difficulties may be harder to resolve (Akister *et al*, 2010). The consequences for education may include the emotional and behavioural problems highlighted above.

## Adversity, trauma and child development

In this section, we consider some contextual factors that potentially impact on educational attainment by children in care.

Four out of five children in care have experienced abuse, neglect or chaotic, frightening, family life: many have vivid memories of it (Winter, 2008). Comfort (2007, p 29) argues that the belief that a stable placement will solve problems with education '... is a misconception. Both looked after and adopted children bring with them histories that continue to interfere with their progress even in a settled placement.'

All forms of abuse potentially undermine development across a broad spectrum. Emotional abuse and neglect are traumatic, often chronic, and link to difficulties with cognitive development, including problem-solving and emotional coping skills (Newman, 2004). Many children in care have psychiatric symptoms or psychological difficulties that may affect their ability to learn (Jackson and McParlin, 2006). Their educational needs may not be related to ability so much as enduring mental health difficulties and emotional needs (Cairns, 2002).

Many children in the general population also experience traumatic events, especially those from more deprived areas (O'Connor and Russell, 2004). Exposure to trauma is linked to lower educational attainment. The risk of lower attainment is highest for children with low levels of attainment pre-trauma: being successful is a protective factor.

Low attainment is a risk factor for post-trauma difficulties of different kinds, not just educational attainment. The more traumatic events experienced and the more varied the types of trauma, the more probable it is that a child will display post-traumatic symptoms.

These may include behavioural disturbance, hyperactivity and inattention in school (O'Connor and Russell, 2004). The relevance for children in care is clear: many enter care after traumatic experiences, coming from socio-economically stressed families, and coming into care is itself often traumatic (Beckett and McKeigue, 2009).

The same emotional and intellectual attributes that children need to cope with the demands of being in care and education may have been impaired by prior experiences. Physical and psychological adaptive responses that may have helped children cope in the past have the ability to impair positive adaptation when children are placed in more supportive environments (Iwaniec *et al*, 2006). Being at risk of coming into care may indicate vulnerability to educational underperformance, among other things, possibly compounded by the event of coming into care (see Chapter 12).

A recent research review (CWIG, 2009) explores the effect of maltreatment on brain development. Early neglect and under-stimulation may lead to withering of neuronal pathways underpinning language development, cognitive-behavioural and socio-emotional development (Scannapieco, 2008). Persistent fear and hyperarousal may lead to over-production of cortisol, with lasting effects on brain development (Glaser, 2003; CWIG, 2009). Impaired ability to tolerate stress and regulate emotion presents challenges for children in classroom situations. They may suffer chronic activation of fear responses, causing over-reaction to triggers that other children find non-threatening: '... often labelled as learning disabled, the reality is that their brains have developed so that they are constantly alert and unable to achieve the calm necessary for learning' (CWIG, 2009, p 9). The dissociative stress response of "zoning out" has possible implications for memory and retention. For adolescents, a long history of abuse may have implications for cortical development, creating difficulties with tasks that require higher-level thinking and feeling (CWIG, 2009). The effect of neglect and abuse on attachment patterns may lead to lasting difficulties in maintaining meaningful relationships (Perry, 2001; 2002). The relevance of this research for those seeking to support children and young people in care is that without an understanding of both physical and psychological sequelae of early trauma, it is likely that interventions aimed at helping them will either fail to have the expected benefits or, in the worst cases, exacerbate difficulties they are experiencing. Conversely, such understandings may underpin future approaches that tailor educational support to fit in with other types of support needed if such children are to thrive.

## Risk factors in children's family and immediate environment: poverty, employment and qualifications

In this section, we consider environmental and familial risk factors that may affect children coming into care disproportionately. Many children in care come from families experiencing chronic poverty (Bebbington and Miles, 1989). Vulnerability to "derailment" of educational progress is not specific to children in care; it is shared by most economically deprived children. The question of persistence of difficulty is the mirror of resilience. Persistence of poor results is highest among children from poorer families, and good performance at primary and early-stage secondary school is less likely to be maintained by children from poorer families (Feinstein and Bynner, 2004). Nearly 30 per cent of children from households without a member in full-time work or with parents in manual work achieve five A*–C GCEs (Berridge, 2007). Just over a quarter (26%) of white British boys eligible for free school meals do not obtain five or more GCSEs (Poverty, 2010) (children from other ethnic groups receiving free school meals mostly exceed the performance of the poorest white children) but even this lowest-attaining group attains five GCSEs at a higher frequency than children in care.

An attainment gap appears early on between the children of the poorest and their better-off counterparts, with children of the poorest parents developmentally up to a year behind those of better-off parents by age three (Feinstein and Bynner, 2004). Developmental delay and significant cognitive impairment are more common among children whose parents are persistently poor (Petterson and Albers, 2010), and the experience of poverty at any time during childhood significantly increases the risk of growing up to be poor and without qualifications as an adult (Hobcraft and Kiernan, 2001).

Poverty, depression and parenting ability interact to affect child development, which may selectively disadvantage children entering the care system. Sheppard (1997) found that one parent in three involved in child protection procedures was depressed. Depression among poor mothers is almost twice as prevalent as among non-poor mothers, with single-parent status increasing vulnerability (Brown and Moran, 1997). Maternal depression is a risk factor for educational attainment (Hay et al, 2001) as well as social adjustment (Hay et al, 2010). Children of mothers who were depressed three months post partum showed significant deficits in intellectual functioning at age 11, including attention problems and difficulties with mathematical reasoning, and were more likely than other children to have special educational needs (Hay et al, 2001). Children of depressed mothers are four times more likely to suffer from psychiatric disorder: half the children of mothers suffering from depression in a socio-economically deprived area had a psychiatric illness at age 11 and children of mothers who met DSM-IV criteria for psychiatric disorders showed significantly higher rates of teacher-rated behavioural and emotional problems (Pawlby et al, 2008, p 244). Petterson and Albers

(2001) found maternal depression significantly associated with children's lower scores on a range of developmental dimensions including cognitive and motor development. Many children in care may be educationally disadvantaged by the impact of their family's socio-economic circumstances on maternal mental health and parenting capacity as well as the invidious effects of poverty itself.

## Age and educational progress in care

Heath *et al* (1994) found that children in care were progressing educationally at the same rate as other children, but because of their initial academic disadvantage they did not catch up. This left them behind their peers, despite working just as hard. They made the same absolute progress, but not relative gains: they could not catch up (Heath *et al*, 1994, pp 257 and 258). Children in care do not fail to progress, but they have difficulty making up prior deficits, which leaves them unrewarded by the work they do (Harker *et al*, 2004a; Forrester, 2008; Gaskell, 2010).

Younger children entering care are more likely to do so because of parental difficulties, while children aged over 12 are more likely to do so because of problems with their own behaviour (which does not exclude parental conduct as a contributory factor). The latter group does least well educationally (McClung and Gayle, 2010). Older children have less time available to make an educational recovery and potentially more ground to make up, so compared with younger children, greater relative gains are needed. Some may have had more prolonged exposure to abuse, neglect and parental problems. Behavioural difficulties and attitudes to education have also had longer to become entrenched. Communication difficulties may also be a factor in some educational and behavioural difficulties observed in children in care: untreated, they can lead to a range of negative psychosocial effects, which may directly or indirectly impact on education (McCool, 2011).

Age and low academic attainment appear linked for children in care, as for children in need. The problem of under-achievement increases with age. A relatively modest gap in reading and writing attainment at age seven to eight between children in care and other children is wider by age 12. Lower attainment in mathematics is evident in older children but not younger ones (Connelly and Chakrabarti, 2008). At secondary school, the gap continues to increase from Key Stage 3 to 4 (Ofsted, 2008, p 4). It appears to be harder for older children in care to do well in school than younger ones.

Studies using GCSE results and other outcomes for 16+ care leavers focus on a subset of the care population, which may not be representative. Children who stay in care longest appear to be those with the least satisfactory resolution to their family's difficulties, the most severe histories of abuse and exposure to chaotic parenting, who may have difficulties of their own and are more likely than those who return home to have disabilities (Wade *et al*, 2010). Pre-care experience and ongoing family difficulties may contribute to continuing low attainment. Expectations that a stable placement (if one is found) and targeted educational support will be enough to "turn things around" appear unrealistic. Specialist assessment across a range of psychological, communication and educational areas seems indicated for older entrants to care as much as younger ones.

While a stable foster placement may not on its own solve children's emotional and educational problems, instability (frequent placement moves) is associated with poor academic performance (Aldgate *et al*, 1992; Berridge *et al*, 2008). Children with the most changes of education placement at Key Stages 2 and 3 were least likely to be entered for any GCSEs (Fletcher-Campbell and Archer, 2003), and just six per cent of children who moved more than 10 times in care achieved any GCSEs at all (O'Sullivan and Westerman, 2007). Frequent moves are also associated with familial risk factors, such as a family history of violence and abuse (Osborn *et al*, 2008). Patterns of causality seem complex and interlinked: prior abuse may affect capacity to attain stability in the care system as well as academic attainment, with instability being a primary cause of academic difficulty (Jackson and Thomas, 2001).

Foster care appears to be a more positive environment for achieving academically than either residential care or care with parents (McClung and Gayle, 2010), although there is little detailed research on the relationship between foster care and educational achievement (Berridge *et al*, 2008). It should be noted that children in residential care tend to be older, with correspondingly complex histories that will have significantly affected their educational achievement. There may be specific complex interactions affecting the education of children in residential care: a nexus of interacting risk factors, including a history of abuse and trauma, emotional difficulties, instability and educational difficulties. Research into distinctive approaches to supporting educational achievement offered by residential special schools for children with behavioural, emotional and social difficulties may offer some valuable insights into working with looked after children (Berridge *et al*, 2008).

## Factors supporting resilience and recovery of educational potential

General resilience factors for young people in care include: stability of placement; being able to make alliances with others and use help; a positive sense of self-efficacy and self-esteem; being able to plan and be in control; and having someone to help them understand why they are in care and address their feelings of rejection and resentment (Biehal *et al*, 1995; Stein, 2008a). Many of these factors are vulnerable as a result of the experiences that bring children into care. In order to make educational progress, these children will often need support to cope with the emotional after-effects of neglect and abuse as well as specific educational inputs.

## Anticipating "derailment"

Children's adaptive responses for short-term physical and emotional survival can become an impediment to engagement with learning in supportive environments when defensive adaptations to adversity underlie ingrained patterns of behaviour. Instead of re-channelling their energies and developing more positive attitudes and behaviour, children whose special educational needs are misunderstood may develop attitudes and behaviour that are incompatible with learning (Fletcher-Campbell and Archer, 2003). There is then a risk of misdiagnosing emotional problems as educational ones:

> Children who have defied and survived severely injured childhoods tenaciously hold on to the behaviours and attitudes that served them well in a former time, even when they are counterproductive in their current situation. (Cairns, 2002, p 00)

The disrupted attachment histories of many children in care may make them disinclined to ask for or accept help (Bebbington, 2005; Phillips, 2007). Their trust in adults as sources of support may be low, and some may opt for choices that are safely manageable and non-threatening, rather than participating in activities providing the challenge that adults think may benefit them (Phillips, 2007).

Being in care can mark children out as "different" from their peers. Many experience bullying and cite this as a factor in their struggles with educational achievement (Harker et al, 2004b). In one recent study nearly half the children reported having been bullied and, for more than half of them, the bullying did not stop after being reported to school staff (McClung and Gayle, 2010).

Although there is general improvement in children's overall well-being during their time in care (Forrester et al, 2009), in the case of educational achievement the effect reduces with age, with later entry predicting poorer results. Garnett (unpublished, cited in Evans, 2003) found that children who entered care at 10 or younger performed considerably better educationally than those entering care in their teens. The educational progress of children in Key Stage 2 was above expectations, with better than predicted outcomes for the child, but by Key Stage 4 there was no correlation between prior attainment and GSCE grades (Evans, 2003). Early success seems fragile, easily undermined or "derailed". Children in care who achieve at primary school are not markedly more likely to achieve in secondary school than children who have not (Gilligan, 2007). By contrast, early failure to achieve seems to persist and become embedded unless some significant change breaks the pattern (Davey and Pithouse, 2008).

## Support for success

There are examples of good recovery from educational disadvantage by children in care, often when support is available from a good foster carer or an inspirational teacher

(Jackson *et al*, 2005). In this section, we explore what is known about the relationship between quality of care and support and educational attainment.

The period while care proceedings are ongoing may be bewildering, so the first year in care may be particularly difficult (Beckett and McKeigue, 2009). Security, stability and a positive sense of self can be very difficult to achieve while care proceedings are in process. Good support and information about what is happening are critical, during pre-care investigative processes (Woolfson *et al*, 2010) and afterwards. Stability of social worker is important as well as stability of carer. The quality of the relationships between children in care, their teachers, social workers and carers are important to ensure their continuity and success (Celeste, 2011; Leeson, 2009).

Good literacy skills (which promote independence in learning), friendships outside care and out-of-school interests may be nurtured by consistent support from an engaged adult (Jackson and Martin, 1998). Aldgate *et al* (1992) found that reading attainment over a wide age range (8-14 years) improved in stable foster placements, but stability is not enough on its own: children do not achieve good results in every stable placement, and carers and children need quality support to promote progress.

Moving is not always negative: finding a placement that meets a child's needs may take some time. In about a third of cases moves are planned and happen for broadly positive reasons (Wade *et al*, 2010). Equally, moving between placements is not an insuperable obstacle to achievement: quality of final placement seems more important than number of moves (Jackson *et al*, 2005). However, the search for stability comes at a cost: attempts to provide permanence may feel to the child like a '. . . rollercoaster of raised expectations and potential serial losses', with a negative impact on the child's psychological well-being (Schofield *et al*, 2007, p 636). Expectations about educational attainment should be linked to holistic support that acknowledges the burden of children's past experience: '. . . extreme thoughts, fears and experiences that are far beyond the understanding of most of their classmates and teachers' (Comfort, 2006, p 30). Children who have not developed a sense of well-being and self-worth may not be able to sustain the effort required to maintain good educational progress under difficult conditions (McMurray *et al*, 2008).

Planning for educational success needs to include curriculum and learning style considerations and therapeutic support. Things that help children in care with their learning include: an individualised approach that is flexible and involves the young person in choosing the focus of their learning; developing long-lasting trusting relationships between staff and young people; and using activities that encourage the development of resilience (Connelly *et al*, 2008).

The majority of Jackson *et al*'s (2005) sample of "high achievers" had spent over five years in care, reflecting other findings that entering care before the age of 11 may be a better starting point for recovery of educational potential than later entry (Jackson and

Simon, 2006). Another important factor is a relationship with someone who shows care, concern or pride in the young person. Teachers and social workers can negatively influence achievement through having lower aspirations for children in care, but professionals and carers who have strong meaningful relationships with children are most likely to be able to convince them that their efforts are worthwhile (Harker *et al*, 2004b; Jackson *et al*, 2005; Phillips, 2007; Fernandez, 2008; Gaskell, 2010).

After two years in stable foster care, with additional input from a range of professionals, Fernandez's (2008) sample of children in care made gains exceeding those of the non-care children. They improved in all areas of adaptive functioning, were rated as happier than the non-care children, and were functioning near the 50th centile. The non-care children also showed significant gains, but of less breadth or magnitude (Fernandez, 2008). The impact of stability plus focused professional support with emotional and educational problems appears, unsurprisingly, to be an effective way of helping children to avoid educational under-achievement as well as behavioural and emotional difficulties.

The evidence indicates that for many children entering care before the age of 10, care provides an opportunity to make better-than-average educational gains and recover educational potential. Older children struggle to regain educational attainment, perhaps especially when they have experienced prolonged or severe adversity at home. Children can show notable resilience, with the right support, but this needs to be carefully planned around the child's educational and psychological needs. Care does appear to promote attainment compared with being in families with complex problems: children who remain in care after experiencing abuse, especially neglect or emotional abuse, tend to do better on a range of indicators of well-being, including educational adjustment, than those who go home (Wade *et al*, 2010). Returning to a formerly (possibly still) abusive home may damage education more than remaining in care, suggesting that care status is only one educational risk factor for some children, and is probably not the most significant. This is confirmed by findings relating to the relative achievement of children in care and children in need in Wales.

## Conclusions

There are well-evidenced grounds for concern about the educational attainment of children in care. However, the evidence that being in care damages educational outcomes for children in care is less strong, and there is some evidence that this view is incorrect (Berridge *et al*, 2008, p 179):

> Hence our conclusions that official statistics on the educational achievement of looked after pupils are misleading and misunderstood; most young people we interviewed felt that they had received good quality care; educational supports are generally good; most make some social, behavioural and educational progress . . .

The very poor outcomes of many school leavers in the care system seem to reflect their high level of vulnerability based on a wide range of known risk factors. This is not an argument for complacency about the educational needs of children in care. It is, rather, an argument that more careful assessments of the needs of children in care are required if their education is to be effectively promoted, and any discharge home should be carefully planned, with the risks for staying in care and leaving care with appropriate after-care support carefully weighed.

Current approaches to supporting the education of children in care include specific support in school, with an emphasis on placement stability. However, stable placements are unlikely to be enough to help most children overcome educational difficulties, even with additional support in school. Specialist therapeutic support may be required, especially for older children, along with knowledgeable support for carers and teachers. The critical protective factors of trust, felt security and a feeling of self-worth may take time to develop, especially for more severely and chronically ill-treated children.

Children in care as a group are clearly not failing to progress educationally, but research confirms that many of them need specialist help to enable them to make the necessary gains to catch up with their peers. Recognition of the gains they make as well as the deficit they have to make up is important for them and their self-esteem. There is a danger that educational deficits may seem overwhelming if the gap between the children's performance in school and that of the majority of their peers is slow to decrease. This highlights the importance of tracking children's trajectories of development, as well as their level of attainment.

The most important message from this review of research appears to be that the opportunities to provide educational support created by recent policy changes will only offer substantial benefit to children if coupled with therapeutic support where needed, including specialist assessment of needs in relation to education.

## Implications for practice

- Assessment of the educational needs of children in care should be integrated with holistic assessment of their emotional, psychological and behavioural needs.
- Stability of placement and continuity of social worker are important in helping children feel secure, but it should not be assumed that security and stability will be enough to support children in care, many of whom have experienced significant ill-treatment, to recover their academic potential.
- Evaluation of the progress made by children in care is as important as assessment of their actual level of attainment; the trajectory of attainment is a better indicator of the effectiveness of the care system in promoting children's educational outcomes than grades.

- While every effort is needed to address the educational difficulties experienced by many children in care, care should not be seen as a second-best option for children on the basis of an unconfirmed belief that children will do less well educationally if they come into care.

# PART 2

# RAISING ATTAINMENT

# 3   Great expectations: supporting "unrealistic" aspirations for children in care

*Collette Isabel Bentley*

*Six years ago Collette wrote a passionate plea, 'Don't we deserve a good education?', in a special issue of* Adoption & Fostering *(31:1, 2007). At the time she was about to graduate from Birmingham with a degree in Modern Languages but her long-held ambition to become a doctor looked unachievable. Here she continues the story and reflects from her own experience on the obstacles that stand in the way of educational achievement for looked after children.*

At six years old, my usual reply to any adult enquiring about my aspirations was: 'I want to be a doctor when I'm older.' Today, as a doctor, I hear these words almost daily from my paediatric patients. I usually acknowledge them with a word of advice and an encouraging smile. However, one little girl's words are firmly etched on my mind. In a bid to distract and calm the elfin 11-year-old whose heart I was auscultating I had asked her what she wanted to do when she grew up. 'I'd like to be a doctor,' she replied, her eyes fixed on my purple-rimmed stethoscope. I could have been forgiven for interpreting the shudder that reverberated through the instrument seconds later as a childhood murmur, but this girl's heart was perfectly healthy. The cause had been the foster mother's comment. Unaware of the journey that had brought me to wielding this stethoscope, she had glanced across at me, raised her eyebrows and remarked: 'Flamboyant ambitions for a foster kid, eh?' This invitation for me to share in her contempt for the little girl's dreams left a strong and disturbing impression on me. For that child, the subliminal message of scornful discouragement, poorly disguised behind a derisory comment, will have left an indelible mark. I know because I had once been that child, ridiculed and talked about in the third person.

I stood for a moment, paralysed by this unexpected and emotionally charged interaction. I briefly considered an impulsive retort but reminded of my obligation to professional conduct, opted for a diplomatic though personally frustrating rejoinder. 'Well, if you want to be a doctor, you have to be good at science and look REALLY stylish with a stethoscope,' I joked before draping mine around the little fashionista's nape. 'What a feeble response,' I scolded myself after they had gone. I felt I had failed as an advocate for children in care.

Later, debating the merits and pitfalls of medical professionals challenging toxic discourse when a child's emotional health is at stake, my consultant cautiously remarked how easy it was for "us" to be idealistic when we had been born with a "silver spoon in our mouths". I could not suppress an inward smile at his presumptions: independent education, a path to the medical profession smoothed by thorough academic instruction . . . I wish!

Perhaps that moment when a consultant considered me as one of his kind should have made me brim with pride. After all, as one of 65,000 children in care in the UK, I was five times more likely to have ended up with a criminal record than wearing a mortar board. Instead my life, which for so long had been characterised by a lack of parental ambition and had set me apart from most of my university peers, had culminated in this moment, where I was indistinguishable from the archetypical newly qualified doctor, with a privileged upbringing and an expensive private education behind me.

That would be success to shout about, wouldn't it? What a testament to the system, for a child to emerge from state care so inconspicuous that the usually indelible mark left by life in the "looked after" system was no longer visible! Yet, it is not pride I feel; moments like this leave me with a sense of pathos at the reality of my history. It is precisely at such times that my mind flashes back to a pivotal moment when I was 13 years old and juxtaposes the woman I am today with the woman I would have been had I continued in the care system.

The details of my story are by the by. Suffice to say that my early formative years were scarred by emotional, physical and intellectual abuse, followed by further deprivation and neglect in state foster care. Yet despite this traumatic journey, I was a child with a vivacity and zest for life as unquenchable as my own "flamboyant ambitions"; I often remarked how much I wanted to be a doctor. These hopes and dreams survived many an insult from my birth family, but died within the care system. On my 13th birthday, my aspirations were still intact, even if my self-esteem had been badly marred. Six months later, these ambitions had not only diminished, but life felt so treacherously bleak that I attempted suicide.

This chapter draws on my story to expose a pattern of low expectations common to the care system and explore how this contributes to what I perceive to be a dual disadvantage for "looked after" children. Although my analysis entails a considerable amount of criticism of the system, I have tried to resist the temptation to engage in emotional diatribe, or indeed, self-pity. Instead, by contrasting my early negative experiences in care with a rather unique foster placement in my teenage years (which led to my emotional and educational restoration) I hope to make a productive contribution to the ongoing debate on how to improve the care system.

## My early life

Between the ages of three and 10, I spent long periods of time shut in a dark, cold outhouse, graced by the occasional presence of my birth parents at the hands of whom I was humiliated, tortured and abused. In addition to actively ill-treating me, my birth family denied me access to books, television, social engagements and almost any form of stimulation. It was not just the pain and boredom that I suffered in the present but also the fear that, through a thwarted education, I would never be able to establish a functional and independent life in the future.

Reflecting on these early formative years and the abuse I suffered from my parents, I often marvel at my apparent resilience in the face of adversity. Somehow I retained my zest for life. Now, as a professional who often encounters patients from similar backgrounds, I have come to believe that children are fundamentally resourceful. In a bid to make sense of their surroundings and ensure survival, they develop an inherently dualistic world view in which all aspects of their environment are classified as black or white, good or evil. This allows children to contain the destructive elements of their life in a controlled manner and stop these from invading other functional parts, thus drawing a protective barrier around themselves. This explains why, having gone through years of demeaning condemnation, when the children in my class were asked to describe themselves, my answer, aged 10, was indistinguishable from those of my peers: 'I'm kind, funny and clever and I want to be a doctor.'

Abuse is clearly damaging. However, the trauma I suffered at the hands of my birth parents was not as destructive as one might imagine, for by effectively compartmentalising my life I achieved a sufficient degree of damage limitation. The clear message from my parents was that I was bad, dirty and worthless. But my self-perception was not simply a product of what they told me; it was a blend of the many diverse messages I received. In my mind, my parents were "bad". I perceived them to be disagreeable people, whom I did not aspire to be like and whose opinions were not important to me. Teachers, on the other hand, were mostly pleasant-natured characters whose values and beliefs I consequently trusted. As such, their opinions of me carried a greater weight than perhaps they did for my classmates who had nurturing parents. It mattered to me greatly what teachers thought of me. As a result, I was compliant, conscientious, easy to engage and had an unquenchable thirst for both relationships and information. I blossomed at school. It was my haven, a place of academic stimulation where I was expected to do well and, in line with the well-known educational theory of self-fulfilling prophecy, I invariably did.

School was a place where, through hard work and dedication, I could be like all the other children, score 10/10 in a maths test and be rewarded with praise in return. Very quickly the positive feedback loop was established and despite the chaos at home, I thrived academically. Thus, school built up my sense of worth, functioning as a psychological counterweight to my home life. However, there was a down side. Since school had become my only source of happiness and stimulation, I was over-reliant on a successful and fulfilling educational experience for my emotional well-being. When life in the care system disrupted my schooling, this last lifeline very quickly broke down, leaving me without hope and unable to contemplate a future.

The academic year before I went to secondary school was one of the most chaotic periods of my life. Having moved foster homes more often than I care to remember, changed schools with similar frequency and endured three stints back with my abusive birth parents, my emotional health was fragile. A sense of helplessness and disillusionment had begun to erode my optimistic and expectant outlook. School specifically and academic endeavour generally could only function as compensation for my otherwise dire circumstances as long as they formed a relatively firm, constant part of my life. Around that time, my head of year proudly reported at my foster care review that despite all the disruption to my education and home life, I was on track to represent my school at the regional heats of a Spelling Bee at the end of that academic year. If only I had stayed long enough! School saw the potential in me but was equally at the mercy of "the system".

Of course, the mission of the care system is clear and justified: first, safeguard the survival of our looked after children, before venturing into the loftier heights of Maslow's hierarchy of needs, where sound relationships, intellectual endeavours and academic achievement become the focus of our attention. Problematically, however, whether it is due to a lack of resources, will or ambition (or a combination of all three), most elements of the care system seem to be content with ensuring survival and show little desire to push or even gently nudge the child beyond the merely physiological-needs base of Maslow's pyramid. I vividly remember moving into a new foster placement at 11 and asking when I could go back to school. The answer: 'Don't worry about school right now; there are more important things to sort out first.'

On a separate occasion with a different family, on asking for help with homework one evening, I was told by a foster carer not to bother with French since she had never learned any and it hadn't done her any harm in life! This is somewhat ironic considering I later went on to university to read Modern Languages. For me, these episodes epitomise the insidious culture of low expectations within the care system.

Time after time, my education was subjugated to other seemingly more pressing needs. The demands of my birth parents to be reunited with me, foster carers' pleas to enrol me at a different school to save their commuting times, relentless and unnecessary foster placement changes, and a string of different social workers meant that, despite my best attempts, slowly but insidiously my patchwork life was mirrored in my patchwork education. Now, more than ever, I needed the care system, my corporate parent, to prioritise, protect and promote for me the one thing on which my self-esteem depended: my education. Instead, I was greeted with a chronic lack of interest in my learning, reflected in my foster carers' failure to attend parents' evenings, inadequate provision of educational materials, and absence of aspiration and expectations for my future.

In other instances, my chances of good, and more importantly, consistent education were hampered by absolute parental neglect. This is illustrated by another memory from my early teens. That chaotic year, when I was 12 years old, culminated with me moving into a children's home where, due to overcrowding, my bedroom comprised a fold-out sofa-bed in the games room. The consequent disorganisation meant that for my first few weeks, I attended school without a uniform or my PE kit. This had the double effect of setting me apart from the other pupils, hindering my attempts to make myself inconspicuous and incurring the inevitable chastisement from teachers, thus creating a bad impression and diminishing any expectations they might have had of me. As I became increasingly conspicuous at school, my self-esteem took another battering. I was mortified. I had worked hard to blend in and assume a conscientious and committed attitude. I had battled the disability of my early childhood yet now I found myself struggling with an added insult: I was battling against the system that should have been facilitating my restoration. My lovely middle-class peers began to question why I was constantly in trouble, why I didn't have the correct uniform, why I looked tired and withdrawn, why they couldn't come around for tea, or why I was taken to and from school in a taxi. Inevitably, I was less than forthcoming and slowly those relationships became strained.

I still remember asking around the children's home for a compass to complete my "angles" homework for maths, a challenging quest since only two of the nine residents attended school. All I found that evening was insults from the other children for being a "nerd" and some cannabis hidden down the back of a sofa, which I later traded for £5.63 and a bag of Maltesers! The next day, I couldn't face the embarrassment at school, so instead of submitting the failed maths homework and risking another blow to my self-esteem, I absconded with my £5.63 to the railways tracks behind school. Here I struck up a friendship with a fellow truant, who convinced me to share my Maltesers with him and purchase a packet of cigarettes, and subsequently introduced me to a wider group of truants to whom I began to turn for support and approval. This sometimes involved committing crimes during school hours, thus further contributing to my dénouement.

One afternoon we were caught lighting a fire on the railway lines and I was returned to the children's home by the police. Staff at the home later jokingly observed how the "nerd" had turned "rebel" and sarcastically remarked why I even bothered going to school in a taxi if I was merely going to end up lingering around the train tracks. So, I stopped going to school and instead stayed around the unit with the other kids. Very soon I started to feel low, dejected and worthless. Life had lost all purpose. In a desperate bid to turn things round, I took three buses to visit my birth parents and begged them to take me back.

Thus, failure to promote a looked after child's intellectual and educational progress can very easily lead to a situation where low expectations and chronic under-performance perpetuate one another in a vicious cycle of under-achievement, low self-worth and even delinquency. A fulfilling school life and academic experience, promoted by teachers and foster carers alike, has a central role in the lives of children in care. Education serves not only as a means to markedly improving a young person's employment prospects and chances of becoming a self-sufficient, dignified, and productive adult; it also has a more immediate function as an affirmative counterweight to the impermanence and inconsistency of home life. My education wasn't preserved and protected and this is what led to my downfall, not my abusive and loveless home life per se. My only opportunity to experience consistency, routine, predictability and a safe place from which to explore, learn and venture out into the world, was gone the moment the care system stopped expecting me to achieve in the way that other parents expect of their children.

## Restoration

Aged 13, I ended up homeless in a cell at the local police station. Police officers phoned the local vicar whose summer camp I had attended and I found myself lodging temporarily with him and his wife "until a suitable foster placement can be found". Weeks turned into months and eventually everyone realised that this was the suitable foster placement that we had been looking for; in fact, it was more than suitable. These people were young, dynamic, emotionally intuitive and educated. They were university graduates who shared my zest for living and whose bookshelves brimmed with classics like Chaucer and Newton. More important though, was their holistic approach to "dealing" with me as a person. Unlike the traditional foster care placements I had experienced before, they never set out to simply "look after me" and just take care of my physiological needs; in the spirit of Abraham Maslow's idea that 'all that a person can be, they must be', they set out to restore and develop me.

Of course the metaphorical baggage I brought with me that night from the police station was a challenge even to the most seasoned foster carer. I had been on the run from an emergency foster placement where I had spent the previous month living on yet another sofa-bed in the living room, had been permanently excluded from school and had recently attempted suicide. Clearly providing me with access to a proper education was not at the top of the agenda, least of all mine. I was happy simply to have some respite from my chaotic, peripatetic lifestyle. Nonetheless, two weeks after moving in, my new foster carers took me shopping for a school uniform, a French dictionary and a hole punch, and drove me the 40-minute car journey across the city to school, with the expectation that whatever was going on in my home life, I would not only go to school but also achieve my potential. They recognised my ability and understood the critical role that education would play in my restitution, so they let absolutely nothing stand in the way of my attending school or succeeding academically.

Life carried on being unpredictable in many ways, with court hearings that disrupted school, counselling sessions, ongoing conflicts with birth parents and surging insecurities, but through all this my "new parents" continued to prioritise my education. They spent endless hours at the kitchen table with my algebra book, patching up the gaps in my knowledge, bought numerous bottles of paint for art projects (only to later discover their new carpet speckled with blue dots), joined in my chanting of French vocabulary on the way to school in preparation for my tests and shared in my delight when I did well. It wasn't all plain sailing but as far as I can remember, my perception of my foster parents' philosophy and approach was that I was not given any latitude. There was not only an expectation that I would attend school, be courteous to teachers, learn my spellings and establish functional friendships; it was assumed that I would do all of this irrespective of what obstacles continued to come my way.

They somehow recognised that allowing me to remain in a place of special dispensation would only have perpetuated my state as a "victim" and stifled the process of normalisation. Lack of aspiration and expectation is itself doubly disabling. For someone like me, who was desperate to shake off the shackles of an identity that had been forced upon me ("the poor kid in care who has no hope"), it was liberating. Indeed, I would go as far as to say that it was the key to my salvation. The subliminal message was: 'You are normal, you are capable of being normal and we expect that from you.' I believe the most rewarding approach to caring for a child like me is one that offers a supportive hand, a leg-up, but ultimately expects the same as would be expected from any other child.

In this context I recall a poignant conversation my foster mum had with my history teacher to whom I had been very rude following a particularly emotionally charged court hearing. In keeping with the way that she had vehemently instilled in me the basic need for courtesy, whatever the storm, she argued: 'Yes, Mrs Smith, Collette has had a very difficult life, you're right, but this does not preclude her from basic human courtesy . . . [and] it does not prevent her from learning her French vocabulary.' With this approach, in conjunction with an unparalleled sense of stability and nurturing tenderness and love, relatively quickly one subliminal message replaced the other. That is when I flourished.

It would be misguided to suggest that a good education constitutes a panacea for all the woes of a looked after child, but I do maintain that what we expect of children educationally is often a marker of our broader expectations of them and for their future, and consequently colours our entire approach to how we raise them.

Although my new foster parents were highly educated, which helped in my particular case, this is not a prerequisite for providing a foster child with the support necessary to achieve recovery and fulfilment through education. Time and time again, my education was a vehicle through which my "parents" transmitted a crucial message: 'You are worthy of our time, love, care and expectations.' As a child who had been rejected and abused, humiliated and shamed, it was overwhelmingly invigorating to have an adult care enough to learn my French vocabulary with me. It left an indelible impression to have an adult buy me an appropriate PE kit so I wouldn't have to face humiliation at school, never mind spend their free time painting papier mâché art projects or standing in the rain on a Saturday morning to cheer for me to win the 100m-sprint at the inter-school competition.

This kind of support had an immediately positive effect on my general attitude towards life. My social worker at the time approached me several years later and recalled how my behaviour had seemingly been transformed overnight. In reality, of course, it took a lot longer. But gradually the gregarious, determined extrovert that I had once been came back and I eventually started to expect things of myself. Slowly my hopes and dreams were rekindled and eventually I went on to achieve first-class honours at university, get married and train as a doctor.

Had I not been lucky enough to escape the system at the age of 13 and benefit from steadfast love and consistency, enveloped in high expectations, I can guarantee that I would never have gone back to school. And I certainly would not be standing in clinic wielding a stethoscope and cheering for other little girls to defy the odds and go on and do the same.

# 4    The Letterbox Club: educational possibilities in a parcel

*Rose Griffiths*

*Most of us enjoy getting something through the post. The Letterbox Club is a project that uses children's excitement at getting a parcel to encourage them to enjoy reading and playing number games at home. The project also aims to support foster carers, adoptive parents and other family members who would like to help the children do well.*

*The intervention started on a small scale with just 20 children aged seven to 11 in 2003 in Leicester, and has developed into a national programme involving over 5,000 children and their families each year across the UK. This chapter outlines the early stages of the Letterbox Club's development, explains how it is organised now and discusses the benefits it provides.*

## Families and educational support

The low standards of educational attainment of looked after children have been well-documented elsewhere, as have many of the possible reasons for this (see Chapters 1 and 2). For any child to do well, attending a good school is an important element in their success. Alongside school, the support and encouragement the child has from the adults who care for them is invaluable – and for most children who come into care, that support has been missing in the past. A third crucial element in this interaction is the child's own positive engagement with learning; they need to feel willing to try something and be interested and optimistic about their learning. Promoting this feeling of 'positive disposition' (Kilpatrick *et al*, 2001) is particularly important when working with children who are convinced they cannot do well in school and who have perhaps spent most of their time and energy in finding ways of avoiding school work.

School, home and the child are linked in a complex manner and we need to think about all three when aiming to raise a child's level of educational achievement. But while it is generally agreed that parents, carers and schools should work in partnership (Muschamp *et al*, 2007), it is not always easy to put this into practice. Any parent who has tried to help their child with homework set by the school will know that tiredness, anxiety and sometimes an inappropriate level of homework can all be barriers to both adult and child. In some cases, foster carers' own disappointing educational experiences may mean that they feel uncertain about challenging or supporting what a school expects, or about asking for suggestions from the school as to how they can offer help. Teachers, foster carers and adoptive parents may also underestimate the importance and value of less formal, more manageable activity undertaken with a child, both in improving their educational outlook and in making them feel more settled and secure (Gilligan, 2000).

## Developing the Letterbox Club: small beginnings: 2003–2006

Our initial aim – to find a method of helping to raise the attainment of children in reading and mathematics – was constrained by issues of capacity that meant it was not realistic to involve schools directly, nor to devise a project that required high levels of staff time (such as individual tutoring) or travel or premises costs (such as training for foster carers). For the programme to be sustainable we needed something that was comparatively low cost.

The central idea was to provide books and mathematical activities for each child directly to the home, but at first it was not clear what would be the best way of doing this, so an action research design (Carr and Kemmis, 1986) was used to develop the project. In focus group discussions with foster carers (all with foster children in the age range 7 to 16), carers described how difficult it could be to persuade children to complete even small amounts of homework, a view echoed in the research of Solomon *et al* (2002). Even carers who had been successful in supporting homework activities said that if materials were sent to them, they would feel obliged to try to persuade the child to use them, and they did not want to be made to feel guilty if they were unsuccessful.

The obvious solution was to address the materials to the child. Personalised marketing has long been a successful way of operating in the commercial world because it can make the "customer" feel special. It seemed likely that children would feel positive about materials sent to them rather than their carers. Three further principles were established:

- The materials would be provided in installments, to avoid the child feeling over-whelmed, and to provide an element of novelty and excitement each time the child received a parcel.
- The child would be told they were a member of a club, the "Letterbox Club", to reduce any feeling they were being given compulsory homework.
- The parcels would be sent through the post, as this would make distribution simple, including for children who were placed outside their local authority area.

In successive years from 2003 to 2006, we experimented with different items in the parcels, different times of the year to send them, different kinds of packaging and different age groupings, working with cohorts of 20 or 30 children each year in each of two local authorities (one urban and one more rural), to find the combinations that seemed to work best from the point of view of the children and foster carers. Each child was assessed before and after they received the parcels, to check their progress in reading and number. The children and carers had questionnaires that asked them their views of the books, mathematics activities and stationery items they received, and a sample of children were interviewed to find out more about how they used the materials.

By 2007, the form of the intervention was very similar to the way the programme runs now. Rather than offering the Letterbox Club once to every looked after child aged seven to 11, it was organised to have half the children as members each year, with two different age groups. Each child could be a member twice, starting when they were aged seven or eight (with Letterbox Blue) and then again when they were nine or ten (Letterbox Red), if they were still in care.

The packaging of the materials was changed from a plain brown padded envelope to a brightly coloured blue or red one, with a Letterbox Club sticker and the local authority information on the back. This made the parcels look more attractive and also made them easy to identify, which was reassuring for foster carers where contact with birth families was restricted. It was important that children should be able to open their parcels themselves, rather than the foster carer having to check them first.

The timing of the parcels was altered from the original six months covering October to March, to include the school summer holiday, with children receiving parcels from May to October. The long holiday is a time when children's skills in reading and some aspects of mathematics can decline (Galton et al, 2003), so providing reading materials and number games could help prevent children falling behind. The new timing also meant that children would receive the parcels across a period when many would be experiencing a change of teacher, moving from one school year to the next. This is a stressful time for many looked after children who do not find it easy to cope with change (Cairns and Stanway, 2013), and it was evident that the additional support and attention from being a member of the Letterbox Club was useful.

At first, the books we chose (a mixture of fiction, poetry and non-fiction) were differentiated in two ways: by the child's age and by their attainment in reading. This was complicated and time-consuming to do and we realised that the most important element was that the books should be of interest to children of the particular age group. Children's responses to our questionnaires were used to draw up guidelines to help with the book selections each year (Dymoke and Griffiths, 2010).

The mathematics materials were provided at different levels depending on the child's recorded attainment when they got their first parcel, and this did seem to be helpful. The mixture of explanations discussed in the literature of low attainment in mathematics includes problems caused by children being given work that is not well matched to their current level of understanding, and children's fear, lack of motivation or disengagement from their work in mathematics (Allardice and Ginsburg, 1983). Games at a suitable level provided a less threatening prospect than worksheets and can, of course, be played over and over again to build understanding and fluency.

Stationery was initially provided just where it was needed to accompany the mathematics activity – for example, a pencil to fill in a worksheet or scissors to cut out a game. When an exercise book was included, the children's responses on the questionnaires were so enthusiastic that a larger range of writing and drawing materials was added to subsequent parcels.

In the first few parcels, we included a list of the contents. This was changed to a letter addressed to the child, telling them what we had sent them.

## Extending the initial pilot to a larger scale: 2007–2010

The results from the first four years of trialling were very encouraging: children enjoyed the parcels, there were improvements in children's attainment in reading and number, and foster carers reported that they were sharing books and playing games with children at home. The next step was to test the initiative on a larger scale. Booktrust, a well-known national charity that already ran book-gifting schemes for children, agreed to become the University of Leicester's partner in a national pilot for 2007 and 2008, funded with a major grant from the DCSF (Department for Children, Schools and Families: now the Department for Education), and with additional support from the publisher Pearson and from each participating local authority.

During those two years, we worked with 1,500 children and their families, in 52 local authorities spread across England. It gave us the opportunity to collect data on a larger scale, to check whether the intervention was effective and to explore some of the key features in more detail. Importantly, it also enabled us to set up an effective central organisation, so that the programme could continue as part of Booktrust if this research showed it was worthwhile.

Each local authority that took part was asked to collect data before, during and after the children received their Letterbox parcels, but changes in staff and children's placements meant it was sometimes difficult for them to complete this. We were therefore pleased to receive useful information from 34 local authorities in total.

Reading and number assessments were carried out before children received their first Letterbox Club parcel and again around four weeks after their last one – a period of around eight months overall. Reading was assessed using the section on reading accuracy from the Neale Analysis of Reading Ability (Neale, 1997), a standardised test suitable for this age range. For mathematical attainment, National Curriculum "levels" had proven an unsuitable measure in the earlier pilot, as they were designed to show progress over a period of two years. Instead, more detailed tasks were devised (Griffiths, 2009) to assess children's progress in counting, place value and mental arithmetic (matching the mathematical content of the number games in the Letterbox parcels) over a shorter period of time. The outcomes of these tests could be matched to National Curriculum levels, so that the child's first assessment would indicate which level of number games was most suitable for them.

Children were sent questionnaires after every two parcels, to collect their views of the books, games and stationery, using a three-part rating scale: 'Liked it', 'It was OK' or 'Didn't use it'. There was space for comment for both children and foster carers to complete if wished.

To find out whether children continued to use their Letterbox materials over a longer time period, we conducted interviews with a sample of children and their foster carers, six months after the children had received their last parcel. These explored the families' views about each aspect of the Letterbox Club in greater detail.

The results of the reading and mathematics assessments showed that a majority of children made good progress, and the positive evaluation of the programme for England in 2007 and 2008 encouraged Fostering Network in Northern Ireland and the Welsh Assembly Government to sponsor pilots for every eligible child aged seven to 11 in 2009 and 2010. In addition, the Siobhan Dowd Trust provided funding in 2010 for us to develop a new age range, Letterbox Green, targeted at children aged 11 to 13. All of the pilots followed a similar pattern of data collection, using assessments of reading and number, questionnaires and interviews. The findings are considered together in the next sections.

Most of the data discussed below have been reported before in the evaluation reports for each pilot (e.g. Griffiths *et al*, 2010) and are also presented in Griffiths (2012). I have considered four aspects in this chapter: the children's attainment in reading and number; the importance of focusing on the child; children's favourite materials; and interactions within each foster family.

## Improvements in reading and number

Reading and/or number assessments for children aged seven to 11 were collected for 852 children in England, 112 in Northern Ireland and 165 in Wales; the small pilot for children aged 11 to 13 collected results for 38 children.

Children's reading scores were recorded as standardised scores (adjusted for chronological age) with a mean score of 100 and a standard deviation of 15. Before they received their first Letterbox Club parcel, the proportion of children in each cohort who recorded low reading scores (i.e. below 90) was notably higher than the national figure of 23 per cent. For example, in 2008, 42 per cent of the Letterbox children returned standardised scores of less than 90. While some of the children were classed as very good readers (scoring above 110) there were fewer children in this category (14%) than the expected national figure of 23 per cent. These baseline results matched the national picture of low attainment for children in public care (DfE, 2010a).

All of the children were tested again for reading about four weeks after the delivery of their final parcel. Since the six months of receiving the Letterbox Club materials included about nine weeks of school holiday and a change of class teacher, when attainment may drop, it could be argued that simply maintaining average progress in reading proficiency (i.e. a zero gain in the standardised score) over this period would indicate some success. In fact, in the 2008 cohort children across both age groups made an average gain of 3.9 on their standardised scores. The table below shows results for the different age groups across four pilot years.

*Table 1*
**Average gain in children's standardised reading scores for each pilot**

| Year of pilot | Country | Number of children assessed | Average gain, ages 7 to 11 | Average gain, ages 11 to 13 |
|---|---|---|---|---|
| 2007 | England | 316 | 4.4 | – |
| 2008 | England | 449 | 3.9 | – |
| 2009 | Northern Ireland | 112 | 3.4 | – |
| 2009 | Wales | 165 | 4.0 | – |
| 2010 | UK | 38 | – | 3.0 |

While standardised scores are the most reliable scores to use when looking at children's progress, many people find it helpful to think of a child's situation using "reading ages". Jamie is an example of a child whose standardised score improved by three. He was 10 years 5 months old when he was first tested, with a standardised score of 92, and a "reading age" of 8 years 11 months. Eight months later, after Letterbox Club, he was 11 years 1 month old; his standardised reading score was 95, and his "reading age" was now 10 years 1 month. In other words, he had made about 14 months' progress in the eight months between his two tests.

It would not be reasonable to attribute all of the children's progress to the Letterbox Club, since the majority of them were, of course, attending school for most of this period, but many carers and children did feel that receiving the materials had provided important additional support and encouragement to learn. For example, the carer of an eight-year-old boy wrote:

> The parcels have played a big part in Hamza becoming more enthusiastic about reading. Even made him keen to bring home school books.

Improvements in number were more difficult to judge against national norms. The Letterbox mathematics results were converted into National Curriculum levels for each child, to give a score of level 1 or below, level 2, level 3, or level 4 or above (Qualifications and Curriculum Authority, 1999). For children progressing at an average rate, the usual expectation would be that about 33 per cent of children would move up from one level to the next in a period of about eight months (calculated from an expectation of one level every two years). In 2007 and 2008, 36 per cent of the Letterbox children made this improvement, which was encouraging, particularly in view of the slow progress many of the children had been making previously. Again, while the improvement cannot be attributed solely to the Letterbox Club, many carers and children felt it had had a positive impact. For example, eight-year-old Daniel said:

> Mr Quinn [my teacher] done a test on us today and I got 20 out of 20 on it. Because I answered all 20 of them right, because I've been playing the maths games and it's helped me with my adding up.

## The importance of materials addressed to the child

Again and again in the questionnaires and interviews, children commented on the importance of having materials sent to them with their name on them: many said that it made them feel important and that someone was interested in them. Kayleigh's foster mother said, 'It may not seem a lot, but when you've not had much attention in your life, it is.'

Children clearly felt they could make decisions themselves about what to do with the materials and were usually keen to share them:

> Jake felt rather special as he loved the postman delivering the parcel for himself each month. He enjoyed getting everyone together and playing with his games and reading his books.

The bright envelope was important to many: 'Brandon watches the post and can immediately identify "his" package.' Many children told us they kept each envelope, 'because it has my name on'.

Children who had been in the Letterbox Club before were still very enthusiastic when they were members again. One carer said that her foster daughter had had the Red parcels 18 months before and when her first Green parcel came she 'just ripped it straight open . . . [She was] excited and straight into it!' In the daughter's words:

> It's a great thing and it makes you feel a bit happier . . . To get the parcels, it'll take a lot of money to put together for people, but it makes people happy.

If a child moved home or left public care, they still received their parcels for their full six months' membership. The fact that the parcel is delivered to the child's home address was particularly important to children who had moved recently or often. One boy (age 9) in the earliest pilot had expressed this very poignantly: 'So somebody knows where I live?' A significant proportion of children in care will move placement in any year; during the pilots for seven to 11-year-olds, about 15 per cent of Letterbox Club members moved. In the older age group, 11- to 13-year-olds, around 30 per cent moved placement during their six months as members.

The foster mother of a girl (age 10), who had moved three times in a year, commented:

*The Letterbox Club was the continuity, something that stayed the same when she moved from A to B. She'd had so many ups and downs and I think something like that, that stays the same, is quite important to children and it was very important to Kelly.*

A carer with two foster daughters (age 11) confirmed this:

*They love just getting the parcels and that was important to them, especially when they hadn't been here very long, it was like 'somebody from the outside knows I'm here'.*

Some foster homes had comparatively few books suitable for the children they cared for, so the Letterbox Club parcels were a valuable resource. Even where foster families were already well provided, many carers commented that a critical element in gaining children's interest was that the Letterbox books were their own. For example, the carer of a nine-year-old boy said:

*We've got a cupboard absolutely full of books, but he never paid them any attention at all, so it was nice that these came just for him.*

The carer of a 10-year-old boy commented:

*I'm very surprised that Nathan has taken the book in his hand. He won't read library books and doesn't like doing his homework.*

But Nathan evidently saw the Letterbox Club books as being different. The foster carer of a seven-year-old boy, who had received the *Wizard of Oz* book, said: 'Evan says if he was to become the Wizard of Oz he would grant his own wishes and send himself books!'

Lewis (age 8) told us: 'It was good fun because I've never been in a club before.' The aspect of being a member of a club seemed to have encouraged many children to tell their teacher at school about the books and games they had received. Perhaps 'I'm a member of a club' provided a simpler, less problematic explanation than the more emotional 'I'm getting books and games because I'm in care.' Elements in the parcels that emphasised "being in a club" (all marked with a Letterbox Club logo) were consistently popular, including personalised sticky labels with 'This book belongs to . . .' and the child's name printed on them.

These feelings of belonging, of being noticed and having materials that you can use by yourself or share if you wish (i.e. ownership and control), all seem likely to contribute to building children's resilience, self-esteem and self-efficacy, and perhaps to reducing anxiety (Flynn *et al*, 2004). As one carer of a nine-year-old boy said:

> *I wish you could have seen his face light up when he came in from school and saw his parcel waiting for him to rip open – these parcels gave extreme and lasting pleasure.*

## Children's favourite books and games

The questionnaires which were returned by children and their foster carers were used each year to guide the choice of materials for the next year; overall, they noted a high level of satisfaction with the books, number games and stationery. The interviews confirmed that children continued to use many items for months after their last parcel and sometimes for years: Kezia (age 12) was interviewed six months after receiving her last Green parcel and said one of her favourite books was still *Hansel and Gretel*, which she had received two years before in a Letterbox Red parcel.

Children liked the element of surprise, not knowing what books they might get, and carers, too, commented that this broadened the range of books their children used. Aaliyah (age 9) said:

> *It was nice because I could read a lot of different books, not just the ones that I choosed, because I'd probably pick up the same book every time.*

Children's reasons for wanting to read a book included that they had seen something on television or a film, or they were working on a topic at school, or someone important to them had shown interest in the story or topic. Nine-year-old Kian was asked whether he had a favourite book, in an interview six months after his last parcel. He replied:

> *I still read the Oceans book. I'm tied between the Oceans book and the Killer Cat Diary. And I love the Oliver book. I seen it on the telly, the film. I like 'Consider yourself one of us'.*

One only has to think about a few lines of that song to realise why it might be especially relevant to a child in care.

Children enjoyed *Where's Wally?* for its social qualities – one carer of an eight-year-old girl wrote: 'We all had a go at *Where's Wally?* – even the teenagers wanted to have a go.' There were many reports of children reading to each other and asking others (both adults and children) to read to them. For example, Kyle (age 12) told us he read excerpts from the *Guinness Book of World Records* to his younger brother: 'I'd show him stuff that was a bit weird and stuff. Like the dog with the longest tongue.'

Children in Wales were sent a range of books in Welsh as well as in English. This was not very successful in the pilot year (2009), largely because the choice of books was evidently too difficult compared to the Welsh-language levels of the majority of children and, often, of their foster carers. The revised choices of books in more recent years have taken account of the need to support language learning. The parcels have included bilingual books, two versions of the same stories (one in English and one in Welsh), and dictionaries, lift-the-flap vocabulary books and snap cards. One useful addition for the future would be to be able to include audio material, too, as this would help children and carers improve their fluency in Welsh.

In all the parcels across the UK, at least one in each age range included a story on CD with its accompanying book. Many carers commented that they had not previously thought of using audio stories with their foster child, but said they were often used at bedtime or on car journeys. The carer of Damon (age 11) said: 'He's of an age where he wouldn't appreciate a bedtime story from me, but he listened to the CD at bedtime.'

Another, with a foster son aged eight, wrote: 'Best gift ever . . . He never seems to get enough of it.'

The English pilot had shown that fewer children used the CDs than used the corresponding books, and this often seemed to be because they did not have a CD player. Consequently, Fostering Network Northern Ireland provided a small personal machine for each Letterbox child, and this was clearly much appreciated. As a carer of a boy in Primary 4/5 remarked, 'The CD player was a great one.' Several foster carers were pleased that their children used the CD player for music, too: 'I've been able to get him to sing now . . . with the CD player.'

Earlier versions of the mathematics games had required children to colour in and make the games themselves, and each child had been given just one game in each parcel. As an improvement from 2011, each parcel has included two full-colour games, one at an easier and one a more challenging level of difficulty. However, even with the earlier versions of the games, many foster carers commented that they had enjoyed them. For example, the carer of an eight-year-old boy wrote: 'The games are really fun for us. His favourite game is the bingo'; and another said, 'The money games are especially useful.'

As well as playing the number games, many children used the equipment provided in other ways. For example, Kezia (age 12) said:

*I liked the money games, cause . . . I get stuck on anything with money. I used to pretend that the five-pound notes with tigers on, like, was real money. I took the fake money in [to school]. Pretending I was rich.*

## Interactions within the foster families

Almost all the foster carers who took part in the pilots were pleased that their foster child had been a member of the Letterbox Club; only five carers said they thought the parcels were not suitable (or, in one case, that the child did not deserve them). The majority of carers (over 80%) indicated that the parcels had helped them do more with the child. The high level of participation by foster carers in reading, discussion and playing games had also been noted by many children, and, as in many studies of looked after children's views on educational progress (e.g. Harker *et al*, 2003), children valued the interest shown in what they were doing.

As other authors have reported in relation to literacy (e.g. Gregory *et al*, 2004), the range of people in the home setting who are interested in helping a child do well can be very wide. For Letterbox Club, this included siblings, foster carers, grandparents, birth parents on contact visits and social workers. Non-fiction and poetry books and the number games were especially suitable for short but purposeful interactions with children, including those who found it difficult to concentrate for long. The foster carer of a girl aged 10 said, 'She loved doing the sticker book with her granddad; many an hour they spent in the kitchen together doing it.' Another carer wrote that 'the whole family got involved', and the carer of a boy (age 10) said, 'He enjoyed telling the jokes!' from *Jeremy Strong's Laugh-Your-Socks-Off Joke Book*.

Some carers expressed initial worries about their ability to help, or said that they valued reassurance and new ideas of how to assist their children. Support for parents (including foster carers) through any intervention needs to be both accessible and acceptable (Brodie, 2010). Ghate and Hazel (2002) note the importance of parents feeling they have control over aspects of their participation, and comment on the positive role of informal support in building capacity. Many foster carers said that they looked forward to the parcels arriving as much as the children. For example, the foster mother of Janie (age 8) wrote:

> *Everything in the parcels was excellent, but* The Diary of a Killer Cat *was superb and the CD is used in the car all the time – I love it, too!! Hope we can have more parcels one day.*

One aim of the project was to entice foster carers into joining in with their children and the design of the intervention was successful in this respect.

The variety of potential activities provided in each parcel was valued by foster carers as well as children. The focus on money, counting and learning number facts in the mathematics games was seen as relevant and useful, and many carers commented favourably on the fact that a zip-top bag to keep the games in was included in each parcel. They enjoyed every genre of book the children were sent; one foster father said, 'Poetry,

I'd never have thought of that, but it's great!' Non-fiction was similarly praised by foster carers: 'I've learned such a lot.' Classic books, where many foster carers would already know the story, were welcomed. For example, when Danny (age 10) received *The Silver Sword*, he said, 'My [foster] dad knows this story, he read it when he was at school.' Children were pleased at these connections with their foster carers' childhoods.

Many carers commented on the value of the materials in helping them make better attachments with their children. The carer of 10-year-old Marley wrote that she 'found it a great way to bond with my daughter', while the carer of Danny (age 9) said, 'He has had fun, and we have spent a lot of time together because of Letterbox Club.' As the carer of Jamie (age 11) commented:

> It's nice to have something to do with Jamie, where he doesn't feel I'm forcing my attentions on him. He finds it very hard to be close to anyone, but he's been keen to be read to and to play the games he's made. It's made me feel more comfortable with him.

Some books in the parcels had been chosen to provide opportunities to discuss difficult topics. For example, Michael Rosen's *Sad Book*, which describes how you feel when someone dies but also offers a positive view of the future, was included with some more light-hearted books in a Letterbox Red parcel. As Sacha (age 11) wrote, 'It was a very sad book and it was very good' and Finbar (also 11) said, 'It helped me with my feelings.' Jaqueline Wilson's book *The Worry Website* received similar praise because it gave children a chance to talk about problems they might have. *Tracy Beaker* was another thought-provoking choice; to quote eight-year-old Owen's foster carer: 'Owen says he hopes Tracy finds a real family like he has and he will be glad for Tracy.'

It is possible that providing educational support in a non-threatening and enjoyable way could contribute to improving the stability of foster care placements. Certainly, the parcels raised the profile of educational activity among children and adults in many of the participating families, and for some children it seemed to have begun a "virtuous circle" of improved engagement at school and improved feelings of well-being in the child, with consequent feelings of relief and positive engagement for the foster carer. As Kezia (age 12) said:

> When you come home [from school], you're not expected to read or write, are you? Cause it's sort of your spare time. But because I got the Letterbox Club, I did sometimes read or write at home, and it helped me at school because I was prepared to do it at school.

Her foster mother's pleasure at the improvement in Kezia's attitude to school was evident when she was interviewed.

## Conclusion

The form of this intervention is simple – to send attractive educational materials to children over a sustained period of time, leaving it up to them to decide how or whether to use them, and with whom. There seem to be four aspects in particular that lead to the Letterbox Club being successful in having an impact on educational achievement among many participating children:

- *Feeling special*: the parcels make children feel "noticed" and cared about.
- *Doing things for yourself*: children respond to having control and responsibility for the materials, and become more aware of ways in which they can direct their own learning.
- *Doing things together*: children ask the adults and children around them to join in and help with their activities.
- *Good materials*: the books, games and stationery items provided have been carefully chosen, guided by feedback from children and foster carers.

Since 2009, the Letterbox Club has been open to every local authority in the UK on a subscription basis for each child, for children in care and for post-adoption support. The benefits have, of course, varied from one child to another, and this intervention can only be one element of a repertoire of actions to improve educational outcomes. In some local areas it has acted as a catalyst for additional work to support families – for example, where local authorities have begun to explore ways of using their public library services more effectively to engage with foster families. For further information about the programme see www.letterboxclub.org.uk.

# 5    Closing the gap: investigating the barriers to educational achievement for looked after children

*Angela O'Sullivan and Rob Westerman with Peter McNamara and Antony Mains*

*The main part of this chapter, reprinted from the education special issue of* Adoption & Fostering *(31:1, 2007), reports on one of the first attempts to track individual looked after children through their school careers. It found that instability was a crucial factor in preventing many children in care from achieving the outcomes predicted by their earlier Key Stage assessments. In the postscript O'Sullivan, McNamara and Mains provide an update on progress over the last five years and the obstacles that still remain.*

## Background

The education of looked after children has acquired increasing importance among researchers and policy-makers over the last 15 years (Goddard, 2000). Early analysis of the National Child Development Study data showed that children who had spent time in local authority care were less successful educationally than the rest of the population (Essen *et al*, 1976). This finding had little impact but a later paper by Jackson (1987) ignited academic and political interest leading to increasing numbers of reports and studies (Heath *et al*, 1989; Fletcher-Campbell and Hall, 1990; Jackson, 1994; Borland *et al*, 1998; Coulling, 2000; Harker *et al*, 2003). Most recently this has included the Social Exclusion Unit Report, *A Better Education for Children in Care* (SEU, 2003), as well as the study of care leavers going to university (Jackson *et al*, 2005), and two reports severely critical of the poor educational opportunities provided for children in care: *Failed by the System* (Barnardo's, 2006) and *Handle with Care* (Sergeant, 2006).

Partly driven by this interest, there have also been significant changes on the policy front. The Guidance associated with the Children Act 1989 required local authorities to provide both opportunity and support for education and to include it in the care plan (Goddard, 2000). Circular 13/94 issued jointly by the then Department for Education (DfE) and the Department of Health (DH) stressed the need for greater co-operation between local education authorities, schools and social services (DfES/DH, 1994). However, these measures failed to have much impact, and in 1995 a joint inspection by the Social Services Inspectorate (SSI) and the Office for Standards in Education (Ofsted), finding that low standards were the norm particularly in secondary education (SSI/

Ofsted, 1995), set the scene for contemporary debates (Goddard, 2000).

The government's response was twofold: firstly, targets were set for local authorities, creating both a motivation for change and a body of previously non-existent statistical data; secondly, the Department for Education and Employment (DfEE) and DH (2000) issued joint guidance on the education of looked after children. Although perhaps more an attempt to codify and spread existing best practice rather than introducing radical change, at least this meant that all local authorities were working to the same guidelines. In particular, each school was to have a designated teacher responsible for supporting looked after children and each looked after child was to have a personal education plan (PEP). Care placements were not to be made (except in emergencies) without first securing an education placement. Section 52 of the Children Act 2004 strengthened this guidance by adding a new duty to promote the educational achievement of looked after children. A critical weakness, however, is that this duty does not extend to schools who are *merely* "expected" to take a proactive approach to co-operating with and supporting local authorities in discharging this duty [emphasis added]'. The duty was introduced too late to affect the children in this study.

An important innovation introduced by the present government is the idea of using statistics in a planned way to drive up standards (Simon and Owen, 2006). Local authorities are set two sets of targets by central government: one set relates to the educational attainments, school attendance and permanent exclusion rates of children of compulsory school age, who have been looked after for a year or more on 30 September each year; the other relates to educational attainments of those young people aged 16 or over who ceased to be looked after during the year ending 31 March. Authorities are also asked to report on whether those young people previously looked after, whose 19th birthday fell during the same year, are in education, employment or training.

The Leicestershire Aim Higher partnership is a leading national project, funded by the Higher Education Funding Council for England. It seeks to raise aspirations, achievement rates and participation in further and higher education for children in care. Known as "The *Way Ahead* Project", one of its aims was to track the achievement of specific cohorts of looked after children to identify potential causal links with poor achievement in order to inform government policy and front-line practice.

## Summary of current research

There is universal agreement among academics and policy makers that looked after children as a group do less well educationally than the rest of the population (DH/DfEE, 2000; Goddard 2000; Martin and Jackson, 2002; Evans 2003; Fletcher-Campbell and Archer 2003; SEU, 2003; Jackson *et al*, 2005). At 30 September 2005 there were 44,700 children who had been looked after continuously for at least a year by English local authorities (DfES, 2006b), mostly (68%) in foster placements. The majority (78%) were of school age and, since 2000, the collection of GCSE results and end of Key Stage results have provided comparative national data that reveal the significant gulf between the levels of achievement of children in care and the rest of the population. In 2005, 86 per cent of all children in the appropriate assessment age group achieved level 2 at Key Stage 1, 80 per cent achieved level 4 at Key Stage 2 and 73 per cent achieved level 5 at Key Stage 3. The comparable respective percentages for children in care were 58 per cent, 44 per cent and 27 per cent (DfES, 2006b). The higher the level of assessment, the bigger the gap becomes.

In 2005, 96 per cent of all school children obtained at least one GCSE or GNVQ, compared to only 60 per cent of looked after children. Even worse, 36 per cent of them did not even sit such an examination. The figure used in school league tables is the percentage obtaining at least five GCSEs (or equivalent), at grades A*–C. Only 11 per cent of looked after children achieved this in 2005 (which is a marginal increase on 9% in 2004), compared with 56 per cent of all children in 2005 and 54 per cent in 2004. Again, the higher the level of achievement the wider the gap (DfES, 2006a).

In this context, it is hardly surprising that by the age of 19, only 19 per cent of care leavers are in further education and only six per cent progress to higher education, compared with 38 per cent of all young people who progress to further or higher education (DfES, 2006a). For many "widening participation" students, even those who *do* have the support of a stable home life, the barriers can seem insurmountable. For the small number of care leavers who achieve the entry requirements for a university degree, the lack of support and guidance can mean their dream often remains just that (Jackson *et al*, 2005).

These problems are not new; an earlier study undertaken by researchers in Coventry of children who were in care for two consecutive Key Stage SATs found that the negative influence of being in care on their potential achievement was most noticeable in the shortfall between their Key Stage 4 results, compared with the predictions from their Key Stage 3 results (Evans, 2003; SEU, 2003). However, the study could not track children in care through their whole school career or care history because at the time there was no statutory requirement to collate such data for looked after children.

The DH declared in 2004 that the data quality of the yearly returns from local authorities was improving year on year. However, Jackson (2001a) noted that gaps remained in local authority baseline data and Fletcher-Campbell and Archer (2003), in their cohort study of children looked after in the summer of 2001, described the information on the children's educational careers as 'frail'. They commented that the existing data were incomplete, contradictory and not regarded by many social workers as relevant to their work.

Instability in both home and school placements is almost universally cited as contributing to poor educational outcomes for looked after children (Jackson, 1998; Francis, 2000; Jackson and Thomas, 2001; Evans, 2003), and the students least likely to be entered for any GCSE exams are those who experience the most changes of placement (Fletcher-Campbell and Archer, 2003). Moving schools is in itself disruptive to a child's education but as a significant number of youngsters enter care in their early teens, moves are very likely to disrupt GCSEs. Coursework may be lost or they may transfer to an establishment that does not provide the same curriculum. Losing touch with friends and with supportive teachers who know them also reduces the young people's chances of success. Again, these findings are not new (e.g. Stein, 1997), but the research reported in this chapter suggests that change is happening much more slowly than one might have hoped.

## Methodology

In this study three cohorts of looked after children from two neighbouring local authorities were tracked back from their GCSE/GNVQ results through Key Stages 3, 2 and 1. Their achievements were analysed in the light of their gender, ethnicity, special educational needs and the number and type of their care placements and schools. The timing of their placement and school moves was also analysed and the GCSE pass rates achieved by other children at the schools have been considered. This novel approach has enabled the researchers to study the same children throughout their educational career, regardless of when they entered the care system.

### Data collection

Data recording and access problems that have hindered previous researchers were still reflected in the collection of data for this study, in particular the problem of information being held in a variety of places. The starting point for the research was the past three-yearly return made by the local authority on the educational attainment of looked after children of compulsory school age, who had been in care for a year or more on 30 September. Year 11 students from each of these cohorts were chosen as research subjects because they had already received their GCSE results.

Unfortunately, this return does not include a full list of care placements, school placements or historical end of Key Stage test results. Data on care placement, gender and ethnicity were sourced from the social services electronic database and were generally of good quality once permission to access the information had been negotiated. Historical end of Key Stage test results, levels of special educational need and school placements were sourced from the education department's separate electronic database but here there were significant gaps.

The historical nature of the end of Key Stage test results also proved problematic. A child sitting his or her GCSEs in 2005 would have sat their end of Key Stage tests in 2003, 2000 and 1997. They might or might not have been looked after at the time of sitting these tests and, in any event, local authorities did not have to return these data for looked after children prior to 2001. The education department collects test results for all children but does not separate those who were looked after, nor does it hold results for children who sat the tests in another authority's school.

Some of the gaps were filled by checking the social services database and asking the education authorities data co-ordinator to look them up, but again, the information was often so old that it wasn't recorded. The five A*–C GCSE pass rates for the schools where children sat their exams were available from the DfES website. The combined data were collated, in one authority by the team supporting the education of looked after children and in the other by their management information team. The data were coded for anonymity and passed to the *Way Ahead* researcher.

Even where data did exist the information was often presented ambiguously. If a student was recorded as "Did not sit" GCSE examinations, it is not clear if this means that the student was not entered or failed to attend. It was also often hard to tell whether the reason why end of Key Stage tests were missing was because the data had not been recorded or because the child had not sat the test. In addition, local authorities are not required to record when a placement move also results in a school move, how long a child is without a school place or what qualifications they achieve post 16. Clearly, standard recording systems and codes are required across education and social services departments.

Even before the data were analysed then, two findings became clear. Information on looked after children's current educational situation is generally of good quality if not always easily accessible. However, historical information of the sort needed to assess their progress over time and understand the "life story" of their education is still largely missing from local authorities' records.

The low academic achievement of looked after children compared to the rest of the population is now well documented but for recommendations to be effective, they must be based, as Lord Dearing stated, on 'evidential research' (*Hansard*, 9 February 2005). The authors' intentions are to provide such evidential research data but the problems encountered during the collation process have limited a full analysis of the data to date. The "missing" data are still being tracked and when the data collection is complete, a number of correlations will be investigated that may reveal less obvious trends and causal links.

## Preliminary findings

One hundred and eighty-seven children were included in this study and their gender balance and ethnic origins are comparable with national statistics for looked after children. In general, more males than females are in care at any one time and this was also true of the group studied (55% males; 45% females). The majority of children in the group were of white British ethnic origin. Although 17 per cent were recorded as being of other ethnicities, the variety of sub-groups within this number was so large that a separate investigation of each group's results would not be statistically viable. The ethnicity data have therefore not been analysed but it would seem that there is a clear opportunity here for a wider study in this area, using the same tracking methodology with the significantly larger groups that would be needed.

Nationally, there has been a steady increase in the number of looked after children achieving at least one GCSE, up from 49 per cent in 2000 to 60 per cent in 2005. However, variations between authorities are large and the overall figure remains a long way off, both the government's target of 90 per cent for 2006 and the 96 per cent achieved by the population as a whole in 2005. Progress has also been seen, although at a slower rate, in increasing the proportion of looked after children who passed at least five GCSEs at grades A*–C. This has risen from seven per cent in 2000 to 11 per cent in 2005 (DfES, 2006b). The two authorities in this research study have also seen significant improvements in their LAC achievement in this time period. Data on looked after children's achievements in post 16 education did not exist.

The Special Educational Needs (SEN) and placement postcode data are still at the collation stage for one authority and have not therefore been analysed yet. Preliminary data show that the number of children with statements of special educational need is comparable with national statistics for looked after children (27%), very much higher than the three per cent of all children with SEN statements (DfES, 2006a). The SEN data in this study will be compared against the number of placements to see if stability is less likely for children with statements. Special educational needs have been cited as correlating with lower educational attainment (DfES, 2006a) and may have an impact on both entry to the care system and to increased instability within it. However, statements are in themselves only a broad-brush measure of special educational need; looked after children are particularly vulnerable to falling through the gaps in the assessment system.

A brief overview of the postcode data collated so far has revealed a clustering of foster placements in areas which are frequently the catchment areas for the poorer performing schools. The local authorities involved in the study, aware of this problem, have prioritised looked after children for school places in the better achieving schools. They have invested substantial time in supporting social workers and carers to choose the best school for each child – pre-empting the warmly welcomed recommendations of the government Green Paper, *Care Matters* (DfES, 2006a).

The data collection problems outlined above highlight the difficulty that care workers, school teachers and education advisers actually have in seeing the whole picture for a child in care. It is hard to envisage how an effective PEP can be developed when so many pieces of the jigsaw are missing. At the outset of this research project, the aim was to identify students from early SATs results who had the potential to achieve well at Key Stage 4. The intention was to track them through their school and placement moves and identify the impact not only of the number of placement and school moves, but also the timing of these and, if applicable, the impact of entering care on their educational progress. This analysis will still be possible, but there are still a number of missing elements to be found.

Nevertheless, we are able to report on the emerging trends and they do provide the beginnings of the "evidential research" we have been seeking. Placement moves are inevitably disruptive to children and in this study, of those who were moved more than 10 times during their time in care, 60 per cent did not sit any GCSE examinations and 34 per cent sat their examinations but achieved no A*–C grades. In fact, of all the children who were moved more than 10 times, only six per cent achieved any GCSE passes at grade A*–C and none achieved five passes at grade A*–C.

There are some obvious reasons why instability has such a detrimental impact on achievement. Moving house is one of the most stressful events that adults experience, paralleled with traumatic events like bereavement and divorce. For looked after children placement moves are often not planned and follow the breakdown of their relationship with their carer. The added stress of this, coupled with feelings of guilt and/or rejection make such a move far more stressful than that of an adult moving home. Many of these children have been through other traumatic experiences, which then lead to a life punctuated with insecurity.

Another influence on a child in care is the movement of other children in and out of their placement. This remains a largely unexplored area but offers a further topic for future research. Such instability can have an effect not only on the number of GCSEs passed but also on the grades achieved. The local authorities included in this study are aware of instability as a barrier to educational achievement and the authors are pleased to report that in both authorities the average number of placements per child in their care is steadily declining. This reflects positive actions that have been initiated to meet government targets.

The number of placement moves needs to be considered along with an analysis of the *timing* of those moves and this is the direction that the further analysis of this study will take. Ten placement moves may occur in the form of one every year of a child's school life, or all 10 in the year before they sit their GCSEs. Clearly, moves at crucial times, such as before assessment points, are likely to influence measured achievement markedly, but we hope to be able to identify the other likely pivot points in a child's life in care when moves may be more damaging. These may be different for girls and boys.

The data presented in *Care Matters* (DfES, 2006a) clearly show the negative correlation between the number of placement moves in Years 10 and 11 and achievement; we hope to be able to expand on these findings.

Moving placement may also mean a move of school, although as local authorities are not required to report on this, any conclusions must be drawn from correlating the dates of such moves. As GCSEs are two-year courses, moving school in Years 10 or 11 can potentially mean that children are unable to complete their studies in some subjects as they may not be on the new school's curriculum. Likewise, there could be problems with coursework completion and modules may be taught in a different order at the new establishment. All these factors add to the likelihood of the student not being entered for the examination. In this study, approximately 50 children moved schools in Year 10 or 11; half of them did not sit any GCSE examinations and those who did might well have achieved better grades if they had not been moved at this crucial time. When all the retrospective data are tracked and collated it will be possible to predict, from their Key Stage SATs results, how much these moves and other synergistic factors have prevented them from achieving their potential.

When interpreting these data we must not lose sight of the fact that some school moves can be advantageous to the child, especially if they move to a better achieving school. This is something the government has recognised with key *Care Matters* recommendations to encourage local authorities to actively place children in care in the better performing schools and providing the authorities with 'the power to direct schools to admit children in care even when the school is fully subscribed' (DfES, 2006a, p 58). Further analysis of the correlation between looked after children's GCSE attainment and the overall achievement of the school where they sat their GCSE exams should provide additional supporting evidence.

## Conclusions

This research study was intended to identify the barriers to educational achievement for looked after children. The data obtained from the two authorities have been combined to obtain statistically viable numbers; but it must be recognised that the authorities are in themselves very different and have different constraints upon them. Nevertheless, both authorities involved in the research are to be commended for the way in which they have co-operated, shared information and worked to bridge the information gap between social services and the education authorities.

The data collection for this research has highlighted the difficulties that remain in accessing information on looked after children's educational careers. Some of the barriers to information gathering are created by the way local authorities are required to report on looked after children's educational outcomes and, as such, are likely to be a national problem. Our experience also leads us to expect that each local authority area may have its own local practices which may or may not be helpful to research of this kind. However, if the barriers were broken down, the information would be readily available to allow projects like this one to compare regional variations. It would also ensure that children in care, who are relocated to different regions, will be supported by professionals who have access to their educational and care history.

From a practical point of view it would seem safe to say that what is hard for researchers to locate will be equally, if not more so, for social workers, carers and teachers.

If the methods of tracking and analysing the educational "life history" of looked after children are to be embedded in national practice, the authors would like to make the following preliminary recommendations:

## For government

- Require local authorities to report on the number of placement moves that are made without first securing a school place.
- Require local authorities to report on the number of looked after children who are without a school place for more than 20 days.
- Set more meaningful targets for care leavers' educational attainment post 16. These should include the number achieving further educational qualifications and the number going on to university rather than simply the current number in education, training or employment.

## For local authorities

- Social workers, designated teachers and education authorities should have access to a shared and updated database.
- Where this is not possible in the short term, education and social services departments that have separate databases should have in place arrangements to allow social workers to access education data, both current and historical, relating to looked after children on their caseload.
- Local authorities should put in place written agreements as to who stores what education data and the coding system to be used.

## For social workers and foster carers

- Knowing the child's previous end of Key Stage test results and how to interpret them is an essential part of the personal education planning process.
- Potential achievement must be monitored against actual end of Key Stage test results and extra support requested for children who seem not to be achieving their full potential.
- Choosing the right school for each child is crucial. Looked after children are more likely to achieve in a school where achievement is the norm rather than the exception. Social workers and carers should know what the GCSE pass rates of their local schools are. Choosing a school is a major decision and should be part of the care plan.
- Placement and school moves should be minimised, particularly in school Years 10 and 11.
- Children with frequent placement moves are likely to need significant help to catch up in school. This help may have to be provided outside of school hours by extra tutoring

or other out-of-school learning and should be paid for by children and young people's services rather than relying on in-school provision. Care plans should automatically consider this if the child has been moved frequently.

• The same should apply to children who change schools in Years 10 or 11.

If these recommendations are implemented, looked after children will have a much better chance of achieving their potential. It is never going to be easy to close the achievement gap; by definition, looked after children have difficult backgrounds and often behavioural problems and other educational difficulties before they even enter the care system. However, these factors need not be compounded by the care system itself. Professionals implementing these recommendations will still meet many challenges but we must not lose sight of the fact that looked after children can and do achieve; some of the results from these cohorts are A*s. If these children are carefully tracked and supported throughout their education, their potential will be recognised and fulfilled and hopefully they will have a greater chance in life.

## Postscript: Closing the gap five years on

In the five years since the original piece of research was published we have seen a change of government, the end of Aim Higher funding, a tripling of university tuition fees and the publication of a number of relevant policy documents, such as the report of the All-Party Parliamentary Group, *Education Matters in Care* (APPG, 2012). The Way Ahead project continues, managed by a mainstream post funded by and based within the Looked After Service in the 18+ (leaving care) team of Leicester City Council (LCC). The project now has a broader remit covering education, training and employment for looked after children and care leavers. The manager continues to support the local authority in its reporting of academic achievement and identifying those in education, employment or training at 19, and promotes higher education to looked after children and care leavers.

The strong links formed with Higher Education Institutions (HEIs) during the early years of the project are now embedded in their outreach programmes. HE summer activity days are delivered annually by the three local universities in partnership with the local authority and the Way Ahead project manager. HE awareness training for carers and care professionals, in collaboration with local universities who hold the Buttle Trust Quality Mark (see footnote, p 137), is another example of the sustained success of the *Way Ahead* project. It has played a significant role in improving the opportunities available to care leavers, such as work placements and apprenticeships, and by developing and maintaining effective partnerships with post-16 providers, colleges and HE providers. A genuine ongoing success story.

## Progress on the longitudinal study?

The aim of the original study (O'Sullivan and Westerman, 2007), reproduced above, was to 'identify students from early SATs results who had the potential to achieve well at Key Stage 4'. The intention was to track the care and education records of these youngsters to see if pivot points could be identified that might be linked with failure to fulfil earlier promise. Unfortunately, the analysis of the SATs results was disappointing as many of the records were missing. Very few records tracked the children right through Key Stages 2, 3 and 4 and where these data were available no clear patterns seemed to emerge. Most of the children attained lower than average SATs results at all levels and made less than expected gains between Key Stages 2 and 3, but this was unsurprising considering that large numbers had SEN statements.

Making the best use of available data, a number of key variables were correlated with the number of GCSEs achieved at A*–G. The variables considered were: age of entry to care, total number of placement moves and length of time in care. We also looked at those who had moved more than 10 times, those moved more than three times within one academic year and the GCSE pass rate of their last school. When correlated with GCSE A*–G success rates, none of these variables appeared to have any predictable impact on outcome. Clearly, as McClung and Gayle (2010) also recognise, many factors contribute to the lower achievement of looked after children. However, further analysis of these data identified five factors that appear to be synergistically linked to such an extent that if all apply, a young person is likely to do less well than earlier SATs results would predict, or not even have the opportunity to sit GCSEs.

The key factors are:

- gender – boys in the study did less well at Key Stage 4 than girls;
- statement of SEN – not necessarily due to learning difficulties;
- a school move in Years 10 or 11;
- more than 10 placements during their time in care;
- more than three placements in any one academic year.

If *none* of these applied to an individual their chances of gaining up to 11 GCSEs A*–G appear to be higher. So despite the frustrating gaps in the data, some patterns started to emerge. However, in order for these to be investigated further and for effective interventions to be planned and implemented, much improved data management systems are needed. This point was made strongly in the evaluation of the Virtual School Head pilot (Berridge *et al*, 2009) and in the subsequent Ofsted report (2012a), which commented:

> . . . data management systems were of variable quality which meant that some local authorities were not able to monitor and report on the progress of looked after children and young people.

A local authority needs to monitor and track the attendance, exclusions, and the attainment and progress of those in its care so that, in collaboration with schools, carers, social care and other professionals, it can provide children and young people with support and interventions which will improve outcomes and life chances. If that local authority has, say, over 350 school-age children and young people in over a hundred schools and in 20 or more local authorities, then a high-quality information management system is critical; it is the bedrock of the virtual school (DfE, 2012; Who Cares? Trust, 2012).[3]

Enough local authorities now have systems and the capacity for systematic tracking of the educational careers of those in care. This would enable them to assess the relative impact on educational attainment of key variables such as: gender, ethnicity, duration of time in care, type and number of care placements, type of school, number and timing of school moves, and school-related factors like attendance and exclusions.

Of course, there are many less tangible factors that would be difficult to capture. Nonetheless, better longitudinal data collection would allow for a more informed debate on the priorities for practitioners and policy-makers about where resources need to be concentrated if a serious attempt is to be made to "close the gap" and ensure that those who have the potential to achieve are supported to do so.

The next longitudinal study to be undertaken by the *Way Ahead* project is underpinned by good-quality data systems and it is anticipated that its recommendations will go some way to ensuring that being in care actually enhances educational outcomes. There is a growing body of evidence that care can be a positive intervention for many young people (Hannon *et al*, 2010). It would be fantastic to hear more care leavers echoing the young person who told the Ofsted inspectors: 'If I hadn't been in care, I wouldn't have got such good grades' (Ofsted, 2012a).

---

3  See also *The Virtual School Head Toolkit* (DCSF, 2010).

# 6 Spare-time activities for young people in care: What can they contribute to educational progress?

*Robbie Gilligan*

*Earlier work by Robbie Gilligan has argued the case for the value of participation in spare-time activities for young people in care in terms of its potential to enhance their resilience (Gilligan, 1999, 2000). Here he focuses specifically on how it may contribute to their positive educational progress. First, evidence is examined as to what, if any, impact taking part in hobbies and other extra-curricular activities may have on the educational achievement of young people in general. Attention then focuses on the possible educational impact for more vulnerable young people, including those in care. This chapter was first published as an article in* Adoption & Fostering *(31:1, 2007).*

## Introduction

The approach taken in this chapter proceeds from a number of propositions:

- Educational attainment is linked to a young person's motivation for education and engagement with school.
- Such motivation and engagement are linked to a complex array of factors in the young person, in the school environment, and in the relationship between these and the surrounding context.
- Motivation and engagement in the case of young people in care are also influenced by a range of additional factors, including issues that pre-date, or contributed to reasons for, admission to care.
- Given the often depressing evidence about educational progression and attainment among young people in care, it is important to pay attention to factors that may have a positive effect on educational outcomes and that may lie within the influence of the concerned adults in the young person's life.
- One such set of factors involves spare-time activities, such as in the areas of sport, arts and culture, care of animals, community service and work.
- Spare-time activities are one of the means open to carers and other concerned adults in terms of influencing the educational progress and motivation of young people in care.

The review below examines some recent international (mainly US) evidence on the association between spare-time activities and positive educational progress. It also looks at some of the means by which such activities may serve to influence positively educational progress. The heavy reliance on US material merely reflects the fact that most of the work on exploring this relationship seems to have been undertaken there. It cannot, of course, be assumed that evidence from one country or cultural context necessarily holds true elsewhere, but the insights offered by this material at least provide a starting point for considering the issues from this different vantage point. The chapter also draws on a range of qualitative case material to illustrate how spare-time activities may have an impact on young people's education-related progress. These have been garnered by the author from a range of sources (carers, social workers, young people in care and others who have been participants at workshops, conference courses and other activities in which the author has been involved). In such instances, the nature of the source is indicated.

## Research studies reporting on extra-curricular activities and educational achievement

Broh (2002) analysed data from the National Educational Longitudinal Study of 1988 in the US to explore possible relationships between participation in school-based extra-curricular activities and academic achievement. The author claims that this data-set was the most recent then available in the US and the most suitable for the purpose. Broh found particular academic gains and benefits accruing to students taking part in "interscholastic sport" (competitive sporting events including other schools) (involving 42% of boys and 21% of girls) and, to a lesser degree, to those students participating in music groups (15% of all students), or in within-school sport. Results for participation in other forms of activity tended to have academic effects ranging from limited, positive to negative. It should be noted, however, that the only form of activity that led to improved scores on reading tests was participation in a drama club. Broh argues that his findings suggest that the key ingredients of activities that are linked to academic achievement are 'structure, adult supervision, and parental involvement'. He notes that 'interscholastic sport' may strengthen student (and parental) ties to the school and thereby have an impact on the student's educational performance. The implication of these findings would seem to include the importance of carer involvement or interest in school-based extra-curricular activities, and the possible impact of gender differences in participation in competitive sport.

Barber *et al* (2005) undertook a longitudinal study of the activity participation of 1,800 youth and young adults in Michigan, a piece of research that involved eight separate waves of data collection over periods of time. From their findings, they argue that:

> . . . *making diverse clubs and activities available to a wide range of students is important. At a time [adolescence] when identity formation is a central concern, the opportunity to embed one's identity in multiple extracurricular contexts and to experience multiple competencies facilitates attachment to school and adjustment.* (p 206)

In their multiple-wave New Zealand longitudinal study of child and youth development based in Dunedin, McGee *et al* (2006) found that the young people's participation in clubs and groups was 'significantly related to adolescent attachment to parents, friends and school/workplace, as well as self-perceived strength'.

Mahoney *et al* (2003) report on findings from an intensive longitudinal study in the US state of North Carolina. They found that for both boys and girls 'consistent participation in extracurricular activities across early and middle adolescence was positively linked to educational status at young adulthood' and to growth in interpersonal competence, especially for those with poorer interpersonal competence at the outset.

Fredricks and Eccles (2006) report on a longitudinal study in Maryland (N = 1,480 in Wave 1 in seventh grade to N = 912 in Wave 5, one year after participants had completed high school). One of the principal findings was that 'participation in both high school clubs and sports predicted academic adjustment [grades and educational expectations] at eleventh grade . . . [and ] educational status two years later'.

Darling (2005) studied an ethnically diverse sample of Californian young people's participation in school-based extra-curricular activities (N = 3,761). She found that those who took part were 'more likely to perform better in school, have a more positive attitude to it, and believe that they will remain in school longer'. The study also identified an association between participation and stronger academic aspirations. The author observed that her study 'like others [has] provided some evidence that participation may be particularly beneficial to higher-risk adolescents'. She cautions that the effects on educational outcomes that can be attributed directly to participation may be 'small'.

The findings from these six studies (one national and four regional in the US, and one regional in New Zealand) generally lend support to the claim that taking part in extra-curricular activities has a positive effect on educational engagement and attainment. But it is clear that the message has to be more complex and nuanced. Many factors come into play in this process of how activities influence educational progress, including, it would seem, the nature of the activity, the quality and duration of the young person's engagement, the quality of adult commitment in relation to the activity within the school or other setting, and the interest of the parent figure/carer. It should also be noted that the US studies focus heavily on extra-curricular activities *within* schools.

The studies reviewed above relate to general populations of young people, not to samples of young people in care. A recent Irish study (Daly and Gilligan, 2005) provides some evidence on possible relationships between participation in activities and education for young people still in long-term foster care. In a national cohort study of *all* 13- to 14-year-old children in long-term foster care (N = 205) based on telephone interviews with carers, a response rate of 83 per cent for the relevant population was achieved. The researchers found a statistically significant (that is, not due to chance) relationship (of correlation rather than causation) between the young person experiencing 'social support from friendships and participation in hobbies/ activities' and 'positive educational and schooling experiences' (p<0.05). (It should be noted that this is not proven to be a causal relationship in either direction.) The friendship/participation measure was based on a composite measure of the young person having 'an established friendship network . . . at least one close peer friendship . . . [and involvement in] hobbies/activities outside the home'. This suggests that the US and New Zealand findings of how leisure/spare-time activities may impact positively on educational progress may also have some relevance for young people in state care.

In addition to quantitative findings such as those reviewed to this point, it is also important to attend to qualitative evidence as to how different forms of spare-time activity may have educational impact. The accounts tend to complement well some of the findings from the studies above, such as those in Broh (2002).

## A range of activities

### Commitment to music

A young woman growing up in foster care was helped to keep up her interest in learning the flute by her foster carers, her school and her social worker over 10 years. As she became a better musician, she needed more expensive instruments but the adults involved ensured that she secured them. Today this young woman is a university graduate and working as a qualified music teacher (source: workshop participant).

For another less academically able or motivated young woman, participation in her beloved school choir served as an important incentive for her to remain in school beyond school-leaving age. The choir may not have helped her achieve better results but delaying exit from school may have assisted her to develop important social skills and assets (source: professional colleague).

### Sport: an example from skiing

Involvement or attainment in sport may influence positively a young person's attachment to school or the project of learning. It may enhance their sense of competence not just in relation to the specific skills required by the techniques of the sport but also more generally. A young girl of 10 years of age in foster care had a reputation for being clumsy and under-performing in school. Nothing the foster carers did could persuade the school otherwise. The carers enjoyed skiing and decided that this would be a positive experience and distraction for the increasingly demoralised child. The young girl proved a natural at skiing. Her morale was transformed and when she returned to school she was a different person and was eventually recognised as such by her teachers. Success in skiing led the girl and her teachers to see her as competent (source: professional colleague).

## Sport: an example from football

Laura Steckley (2005) writes about her experience as a residential child care worker in Scotland and describes the case of Ewan, a boy in the residential school where she worked. She relates how Ewan's interest in, and ability at, football was a 'vital component' in helping him to develop 'a stronger sense of competency – not just on the football pitch but in other areas as well'. She argues persuasively that football offered a rare opportunity for at least some of the boys in this unit to experience "progressive achievement", something very precious in lives which had seen little success or sustained involvement in anything. This point has clear implications in terms of the wider educational significance for a young person of such initial "progressive achievement" in even the limited sphere of football.

## Caring for pets

An isolated and depressed 10-year-old boy in care joined his new foster family. Inspired by his foster father's hobby, he took up an interest in tropical fish. Soon this boy, who previously had no friends, was forming a tropical fish club in school, had tropical fish penpals abroad and had secured summer work in the local petshop because of his "know how" (source: professional colleague). While there are no data regarding the impact on his educational attainment, it seems safe to assume that his involvement with the fish enhanced his social integration and general sense of competence based on the evidence presented here, and that this in turn at the very least positively affected his identification/engagement with the school community, an important precursor of educational progress.

## Part-time work

While certain literature or commentary may regard work experience as problematic for young people of school age (distraction from study, premature exposure to risky opportunities due to additional income, etc – McKechnie *et al*, 1998), it is also the case that the workplace may offer opportunities for social and psychological gains to vulnerable young people. A French study found that the workplace offered disadvantaged young people a way of enlarging their otherwise comparatively diminished social network (Bidart and Lavenu, 2005). In their study of foster care alumni (young adult care leavers) of the Casey Family Program in the US, Pecora *et al* (2006) found that having employment experience while still at school raised the odds of the young person in foster care completing high school (which is accepted as a good indicator of 'future well-being and successful transition to adulthood' for young people in foster care (p 46). Those young people in foster care with 'intermittent employment experience' were over twice (2.1 times) as likely to complete high school, compared to a young person who had no such experience. For those with 'extensive employment experience', the odds of completing high school were even higher: 4.3 times more likely than for a young person in foster care with no such work experience.

Dworsky (2005) examined the economic progress of care leavers (leaving care post-16 years of age and in the period 1992–98) in the US state of Wisconsin (N = 8,511). She reports that those who had experience of being employed prior to discharge fared better in terms of gaining employment and securing better earnings on leaving care.

Experience in the world of work for the young person in care may thus deliver potential educational and economic benefits. But the gains may be wider still. This comment from an Australian care leaver serves to underline the social and psychological benefits that may flow from workplace experience for a young person who has grown up in care:

> The [work] traineeship made me feel really happy. Before that, my spirits were really down about getting a job. Like it was like 'I was no good' and then something like this pops up and you're in such a good mood. Makes you feel like you're wanted. (Cashmore and Paxman, 1996, p 147)

Overall, one of the key features of structured spare-time activity is that it may often bring the young person into positive contact with well-disposed adults who may go on to serve a mentoring role in the young person's life, often assisting their progress on educational or workplace pathways.

## The contribution of mentoring to educational progress

Mentoring by a committed adult may be an important support and influence in a young person's participation in spare-time activities. While formal mentoring programmes that match adolescents with specially recruited volunteers have become very fashionable in policy terms, it should also be acknowledged that mentoring relationships may also arise organically in the lives of young people. The value of such naturally occurring informal relationships for those in care has been argued in an earlier paper (Gilligan, 1999).

DuBois and Silverthorn (2005) studied the experience of having had a natural mentoring relationship at some point while growing up in a representative national sample of 18- to 26-year-olds in the US. Almost three in four respondents reported having had such an informal relationship, with 40 per cent of mentors being non-parental immediate or extended family members, and 26 per cent teachers or guidance counsellors. Other categories of mentors (roughly in 5% or less of cases in each instance) were sports coaches, religious leaders, employers, co-workers, neighbours, friends' parents, doctors or therapists, and others. Young people reporting a natural mentoring relationship 'were more likely to exhibit favourable outcomes in the area of education/work (i.e. completing high school, college attendance, working 10 or more hours per week)' and to have better psychological well-being and physical health. Importantly, the average length of relation-ship was nine years. Not only was longevity a feature of these relationships, but so also was daily proximity in many cases, as may be judged by the categories above. Of additional note is the fact that the researchers emphasise that natural mentoring is valuable for at-risk youth, but that it must also be seen as only one part of a multi-faceted approach to meeting need.

Considering mentoring in all its forms (formal or "natural"), Rhodes *et al* (2006) propose that mentors may contribute to the social and emotional, cognitive and identity development of the young person, and that the quality of the relationship may be influenced by factors such as the young person's previous attachments, the level of sensitive 'attunement' to the young person achieved by the mentor in the relationship, and the duration of the relationship.

In a study of one of the best established formal mentoring schemes, *Big Brother Big Sister* in the US, Rhodes and colleagues (2000) found that the mentoring scheme had a direct positive effect, among other things, on 'perceived scholastic competence' (and through that on grades achieved) and on school attendance, and indirectly on the value young people placed on school, through positively influencing the young person's relationship with parents affected.

In the case of residential or foster care, it should be noted, of course, that mentoring may represent a significant proportion of the constituent elements of the relationship between carers and young people in their care. It also needs to be recognised that not all education happens in school, nor is it all stimulated by teachers. Carers in residential and foster care settings may use seemingly mundane opportunities presented by daily living to support and stimulate learning, as in the example below.

## Mentoring of practical skills by carers

Carers may play an important part as mentors in the acquisition of practical skills by the young person. They may do this as work-related role models themselves or in supporting the young person in care to access such role models.

A young American woman in care underlines the significance of her carer as a role model in assisting her progress in the arena of work:

> I have someone to look up to and model myself after . . . Like he's [the caring adult] training to be a computer technologist, and he can teach me what I need to do to be a computer technologist. He can teach me the skills. (Quoted in Laursen and Birmingham, 2003)

Another key role for carers may be in relation to modelling and encouraging interest and skill in reading. There is evidence that strong literacy skills may be protective in conditions of adversity. In their analysis of data from the UK National Child Development

Study, Buchanan and Flouri (2001) found that high reading skills at 11 were one of the factors that may contribute to recovery from emotional and behavioural problems at age seven.

The following example, also from the UK, neatly illustrates how a carer may use spare-time interests to build motivation to learn. It concerns a young boy, John, in a residential unit who loved nothing more than to spend time in the kitchen helping to bake cakes. He had interest and ability and also thrived on the one-to-one attention involved in his baking with the particular care worker. John was not a star at school and still struggled to read. But as he got more interested in baking and cooking he saw that his mentor used cookery books a lot and he soon wanted to be able to read the recipes so that he, too, could deliver successful results. With this stimulus, John quickly became a more motivated student and a more proficient reader. In this case, the apparently incidental interest in baking sparked by a warm relationship with a care worker helped to lay the groundwork for recovery in reading deficits, a step important in itself but which may also yield wider benefits (source: conference contributor)

Mentors who play an educational role may also emerge from other parts of the social network of the young person in care. A young man in a residential unit was inducted informally into the trade of french (fine) polishing of furniture by his grandfather, a retired french polisher, thanks to the loan of a shed by the head of unit in which the activity could take place. The boy earned money from occasional commissions to polish furniture for people in the orbit of the unit and eventually took up a career as a french polisher (source: professional colleague).

## Conclusion

A key feature of spare-time activities is that they may entail engagement with committed adults who, it is suggested, may play their role most effectively when they 'provide an appropriate balance of structure, challenge, enjoyment and support' (Rhodes *et al*, 2006). There is evidence that such 'connectedness to non-parental adults' may offer adolescents the prospects of 'better outcomes in terms of scholastic success, social-emotional well-being, connections to social capital, and risk-taking behaviour' (Grossman and Bulle, 2006). In making these points, it is important to heed the cautionary note sounded by Roth and Brooks-Gunn (2003), who warn against giving educationally vulnerable young people yet more schooling in out-of-school time. Spare-time activities may be more likely to yield educational benefit with this group of young people precisely because they are *different* from schooling. Anxiety about levels of educational attainment should not lead us to ignore this critical issue.

In broad terms, the evidence reviewed is positive, while not euphoric, about the educational benefits of participation in spare-time activities. While Broh's (2001) findings about intensive involvement in sport might not be entirely unexpected, the findings about the positive educational effect of participation in music groups and the literacy-enhancing value of drama clubs are of special interest. On the other hand, while his study has a strong design and dataset, it should be borne in mind that the findings come from a single US study and await corroboration in that and other national and cultural contexts.[4]

Overall, the evidence reviewed suggests that there are things that adults can do, as carers, parents, social workers, teachers and policy-makers, which can harness the potential benefits of spare-time activities in relation to educational progress. It is important that they receive training and encouragement to do these things. These include:

- valuing opportunities for carers/parents to stimulate, support and affirm engagement by young people in spare-time activities (Broh, 2002);
- seeking to use shared engagement in leisure-time interests as a basis for modelling and stimulating interest in more general learning (Laursen and Birmingham, 2003);
- seeking to maintain continuity of activities across placements by, for example, alerting new carers to previous patterns and arrangements and ensuring that they appreciate the developmental value and significance of such continuity (Fong *et al*, 2006);
- seeking to use leisure activities to link young people in care to peers with strong educational aspirations, or at least open up opportunities for mixing with such peers (Rhodes *et al*, 2006);
- seeking to offer or nurture experiences through spare-time activities that offer 'supportive peer and adult relationships, youth empowerment, and expectations for positive behaviour' (Roth and Brooks-Gunn, 2003);
- seeking, where mentoring relationships emerge or are encouraged, to ensure that they endure long enough to have value for at least a year, according to some US researchers (Grossman and Rhodes, 2002);
- recognising the value of involvement in a range of activities, for various reasons, including ensuring that no negative experiences occur in any one activity (Fredricks and Eccles, 2006);
- avoiding all participation in activities being linked to school in case the young person is forced to leave that school because of any placement change (Clarke, 1998);
- seeking to open opportunities for work experience for young people in care, based on the findings of Pecora *et al* (2006) and Dworsky (2005).

---

4 But see Hollingworth (2012), who provides support for these findings from a cross-European study [ed].

# 7 Improving foster children's school achievements: promising results from a Swedish intensive study

*Eva Tideman, Bo Vinnerljung, Kristin Hintze and Anna Aldenius Isaksson*

*This chapter, reprinted from* Adoption & Fostering *(35:1, 2011), reports on the results from a Swedish project aimed at improving foster children's school achievements. Standardised psychological and pedagogical instruments were used for assessing each individual foster child's potential, her or his educational service needs, and for tailoring the individualised educational and psychological support that was provided for two years. After this period, the 25 children included in the project were re-tested with the same instruments. Post-intervention test results were compared to pre-intervention scores for assessing outcomes. Results showed significant gains in IQ (as measured by WISC-III), reading and spelling skills, but weaker, non-significant improvements in maths skills.*

## Introduction

For several decades, research from most western countries has consistently reported that children in out-of-home care tend to be low achievers in school and are at high risk of entering adulthood with a low level of education (e.g. Bohman and Sigvardsson, 1980a, b; Festinger, 1983; Dumaret, 1985; Runyan and Gold, 1985; Stein and Carey, 1987; Barth, 1990; Weiner and Weiner, 1990; Christoffersen, 1993; Veland, 1993; Cheung and Heath, 1994; Cook, 1994; Jackson, 1994; Cashmore and Paxman, 1996; Vinnerljung, 1996; Blome, 1997; Courtney *et al*, 2001; SEU, 2003; Pecora *et al*, 2006; Egelund *et al*, 2008; Clausen and Kristofersen, 2008).

Vinnerljung and colleagues (2005) used Swedish register data for eight national birth cohorts to examine the educational attainments of over 31,000 former child welfare clients and almost 750,000 majority population peers. Compared to majority population peers with low educated mothers (only compulsory schooling), young people who had been in long-term stable foster care had a two to three-fold elevated relative risk of reaching adulthood with only a compulsory education – that is, after controlling for influence of the birth mother's education. Majority population peers with low educated mothers were, at the age of 25, between two and four times more likely to have a post-secondary education degree when compared to former foster children who had been in long-term care. A decade earlier, the British researcher David Berridge had concluded that the compensatory long-term effects of care on education seemed, at best, to be neutral (Berridge, 1994, 1997). In a US doctoral dissertation, Deborah Matthews (1997) examined 293 children using various standardised measurements and related the results to the length of time spent in out-of-home care. She found that reading achievement, mental development and overall behaviour problems were negatively correlated with the duration of care, but found no association between time in care and intelligence scores or achievements in maths.

This large body of research is based on cross-sectional data. We know less about foster children's progress – or its absence – in school during their time in care. The UK Social Exclusion Unit (SEU, 2003) found that the gap between looked after children's school achievements and that of their peers tended to widen with age. However, it measured educational outcomes for different age groups at the same point in time and studies based on longitudinal designs, although fewer, show less uniform results. Fanshel and Shinn's classic *Children in Foster Care* (1978) found that foster children's school achievements actually deteriorated during the first two-and-a-half years in care, but improved during the subsequent 30 months. After Fanshel and Shinn, several US longitudinal studies employing matched comparison designs concluded that out-of-home care does not seem to facilitate children's cognitive or academic development (cp. Doyle, 2007; Berzin, 2008; Berger *et al*, 2009; Stahmer *et al*, 2009). In the UK, Heath and associates (1994) followed 49 foster children through three years of care and reported a lack of educational progress compared with national age standardised norms, even for those who were in stable long-term placements.

Poor academic performance in primary school seems to be a robust predictor for future psychosocial problems for all children and adolescents (Jablonska *et al*, 2009; Vinnerljung *et al*, 2010). A series of recent national cohort studies by Vinnerljung and colleagues (2010) showed that Swedish children who grow up in foster care had substantially lower performance in primary school than their peers with similar cognitive ability. Foster children in long-term care also displayed higher risks (RR = 6-10) for future suicide attempts, serious criminality, substance misuse, long-term dependence on public welfare and several other negative outcomes. This increase in risk was reduced by roughly half after adjustment for school failure (cp. Zingraff *et al*, 1994). Sonia Jackson in the UK has for decades argued that poor school performance and low education are the strongest risk factors for looked after children's futures (Jackson, 1994). The Swedish cohort studies strongly support her hypothesis.

The dismal educational performance of looked after children has been explored in numerous UK studies during the last two decades (see, for example, Jackson *et al*, 2001, 2007c). But, in spite of all these research efforts, there are few examples of evaluated attempts to do something about the problem, even when using a wide definition of the concept "evaluated". The by-and-large successful US "emancipation programmes" include educational support, but are limited to foster children in their mid- to late teens (e.g. Montgomery *et al*, 2006).

We have come across only three examples of interventions aimed at primary school age foster children that have been evaluated with regard to their effects. In Olisa and colleagues' pre-post intervention study from London (undated report), 10 foster children were given extra literacy and numeracy training over a 20-week period outside of the curriculum. Five children did not receive any such interventions. All participants were tested with standardised instruments for cognitive capacity and literary/numeracy skills at the start and at the end of the project. The results suggested that the training sessions had some effects: the children who had received extra training had made progress and were catching up with their peers in reading, spelling and maths.

A literacy-focused intervention in Kent, UK, was evaluated by Wolfendale and Bryans (2004). In this project, 58 foster children were provided with books, a hand-held computer and other tools to stimulate their interest in reading books. A comparison of pre- and post-scores on a standardised literacy test showed significant gains in reading accuracy, spelling and comprehension. The intervention seemed most beneficial for children with low pre-test scores. In an ongoing Canadian randomised field trial, foster carers were trained to be adult tutors to their 77 foster children. Recently reported results from the first year follow-up are promising. Children who had received foster carer tutoring had significantly better results on several measures of academic performance (e.g. numeracy skills) than peers in the control group (Flynn *et al*, 2010).

In this chapter, we report on the results from a Swedish intensive project aimed at improving foster children's school achievements. By employing standardised instruments for baseline and follow-up measurements, it shares some common ground with Olisa *et al* and the Kent studies. However, in this project baseline test results were also used for assessing individual potential and educational service needs, and for tailoring interventions to meet the needs of individual children. After a two-year period, the same tests were used for assessing post-intervention outcomes.

## Method

### Sample

The project was launched in Helsingborg, a town in southern Sweden with about 125,000 inhabitants. We included all 30 children aged 7–11 in foster family care whose placements were perceived by case workers as likely to last another two years. From this sample, we excluded five children who either had been diagnosed with a neuropsychiatric disorder or were placed in special education schools due to very disruptive behaviour. This left us with 25 children. Their median time in care since birth was 3.5 years with a median of more than two years in their present foster family. Subsequently, the large majority of the children can be characterised as placed in long-term foster care. At the start of the project, the children's median age was ten years. The majority were already in care when they started primary school (age 7). Compared to all children in Swedish out-of-home care, the children in the project were younger as two out of three children entering foster or residential care are teenagers (Vinnerljung *et al*, 2007).

Most children (13 of 23; data were unavailable for two children) had experienced more than one placement in out-of-home care since birth and 10 out of 23 had been in three placements or more. But most had experienced reasonably stable schooling. About two-thirds had not changed school at all since they started primary education or had changed school only once; a third had changed two or three times.

## Design

At the start of the project (baseline/T1), a psychologist assessed each child's cognitive ability. The results of the cognitive tests were compared to results on standardised tests for reading, spelling and numeracy, administered by a special education teacher, and also to achievements in school, as perceived and reported by the teachers. Standardised tests were also used to assess baseline psychological well-being and behaviour, as well as the child–teacher relations.

The psychologist and the special education teacher were employed in the project and henceforth became external resource people for the schools. Both had long experience in their fields and were well suited to pursue the intentions of the project. The psychologist worked part time in the project but had a flexible schedule and could adapt her working hours to the needs of the children at their respective schools.

The results from the tests were communicated to the children, their foster carers and teachers, and to the case workers by the psychologist and the special education teacher at meetings with all parties present. This approach was chosen in order to create a good working relationship among all those concerned, but also to demonstrate that the child was not a person with problems but rather a member of the team. Potential for school achievement, strengths and obstacles were identified in co-operation with children, teachers and carers, resulting in a written individualised plan (limited to one sheet of paper) for each child, indicating his or her needs for educational support and other kinds of interventions (as described below). During the 24 months intervention, the psychologist and the special education teacher were key players, as one fundamental principle of the project was that they should constantly motivate and tutor the teachers in how to assist each child to attain the goals set. They did less work on a one-to-one basis with the children and worked mostly with and through the teachers. Also, they closely monitored the individual progress and difficulties of each child, as perceived by children and teachers. This information was used in planned meetings every three months, with all parties present. This model made it possible to evaluate continuously the interventions and support provided. The head of each school was also informed on a regular basis about the progress of individual children in order to enable her or him to support the teachers.

Two years after the initial intervention, all children were re-tested by the psychologist and the special education teacher with the same instruments as at T1. Post-intervention test results were then compared to pre-intervention test scores to assess the outcomes.

## Psychological instruments

The psychological assessment was performed using standardised psychological tests with adequate psychometric properties. The WISC-III (Wechsler Intelligence Scale for Children [3rd edition], Wechsler, 1999) is an individually administered clinical instrument for assessing intelligence among children aged six to 16. It provides standardised measures of a variety of abilities that reflect different aspects of intelligence. The WISC-III consists of one verbal and one performance scale, of which each one comprises five regular subtests as well as three optional subtests. Four factor-based index scores can also be calculated (verbal comprehension, perceptual reasoning, freedom from being easily distracted and processing speed). As children's abilities develop along many dimensions during growth, the age norms are divided into six-month intervals.

The VMI (Beery and Beery, 2004) is a paper-and-pencil test that screens for visual-motor deficits and helps to assess the extent to which the child can integrate visual and motor abilities.

The Beck Young People Inventories (Beck *et al*, 2004) consist of five self-report scales assessing anxiety, depression, anger, disruptive behaviour and self-concept among children and adolescents aged between seven and 18. Each scale contains 20 statements about thoughts, feelings and behaviours associated with emotional and social impairment. The respondent marks how often each statement is true for him or her (never/sometimes/often/ always).

The SDQ (Strengths and Difficulties Questionnaire) (Goodman, 1997; Smedje *et al*, 1999) is a short behavioural questionnaire completed by parents and teachers. It consists of 25 items divided into five scales: emotional symptoms, conduct problems, hyperactivity/inattention, peer relationship problems and pro-social behaviour. Each scale receives a score, each of which then contributes to a total difficulties score. There is also an impact supplement which asks the respondent whether the young person displays problems, and if so, further enquires about their duration, distress, social impairment and burden to others.

On a VAS-scale (Visual Analogue Scale) (Badia *et al*, 1999), each child and teacher separately rates their perception of the emotional quality of their relationship on a scale of one to 10 (distance–closeness).

## Pedagogical instruments

Standardised tests, frequently used in Swedish schools, were selected for this part of the project. In order to assess potential reading skills, the test Letter-Word Chains (Jacobson, 2001) was used, as this test taps the child's visual and motor speed regarding recognition/identification of letters and words. The task is to separate as quickly as possible letters or words that are written without interspaces.

In order to assess reading speed, the test DLS Reading Speed Test (Jarpsten and Taube, 1997) was used. The child is asked to read silently a text in which three words at certain intervals appear in brackets. The task is to mark the word which is in accordance with the context. Spelling skills were assessed by administrating the DLS Spelling Test (Jarpsten, 1999), whereby the child is asked to spell correctly a total of 36 words of increasing complexity.

To assess different aspects of numeracy skills and mathematical reasoning, the Magne Math Diagnostic Test (Engstrom and Magne, 2003) was used, in which a series of different calculation problems of increasing difficulty have to be solved.

In addition to these tests, classroom observations of the relationship between the child and his or her main teacher, as well as with peers, were carried out by the special education teacher. She also interviewed the main teacher regarding the child's "school competences", such as the ability to change topics, to receive guidance and control anger.

## Outline of working model in the project

The intervention started when the results of the mapping of each child's prerequisites were communicated to the children, teachers and foster carers. In order to adapt interventions to each individual's needs, potential for school achievement, strengths and obstacles were identified by all the parties, resulting in a written individualised plan. This consisted of specified educational goals to be reached within a certain time period, such as being able independently to solve mathematical problems using all four methods of calculation. Also incorporated were the support needs of each individual, the pedagogical methods to be used and what responsibility each party had in the process. Children with the greatest needs, detected in the initial assessments, were initially offered separate sessions with their teacher (who was tutored by the special education teacher) for one-and-a-half hours a day for eight weeks. This procedure was chosen in order not to stigmatise the children, which would have been a risk had they been transferred to a special education class. Parallel to this process, the special education teacher sought to motivate the in-school teachers into thinking, 'I have not yet found the right way to help this child, but I am working on it' in order to encourage them to find the best way of supporting each child to reach the desired goals. Furthermore, the foster carers were instructed in how to assist the child with the homework. The special education teacher also inspired the teachers to use new, validated teaching methods (e.g. Chance, 2008).

The psychologist used the Caplan consultee-centred consultation method, emanating from the International Child Development Programme (Caplan and Caplan, 1993), to give the teachers and foster carers new tools to tackle the children's psychological problems. Every three months or so, the psychologist and the special education teacher visited the school in order to meet the head, the respective teacher, the foster carers and the child. The current situation was analysed, new goals were set and a plan of how to reach them was designed. Special computer programmes for improving reading or maths skills were introduced to the child in some cases. Each meeting ended with a mutual decision regarding a date for the next.

### Attrition

One child returned to the birth parents during the two years of the project and was unavailable for re-tests. The analyses comparing pre- and post-intervention measures are therefore based on 24 children, but for two of them some data were missing (see Table 3).

### Statistical analysis

Differences in means between pre- and post-intervention were examined with T-tests. The sample was too small to allow for multivariate analyses that could explore the influence of background and mediating factors. All statistical analyses were performed in SPSS 16.0.

## Results

In accordance with the project design, the results are presented in the following order (see Tables 1, 2 and 3): first, the results from psychological instruments (i.e. cognitive test results); second, results regarding psychological well-being; and third, the child–teacher relationship. After that, the results from the reading, spelling and numeracy tests are summarised. Under each heading, results from the baseline assessment (T1) are compared with those post-intervention (T2).

### Psychological instruments

At baseline (T1), all children scored within the normal range on the WISC-III Total IQ scales (range 73–115, mean 94.4, median 95.0), except for two who scored below this (see Table 1). Results were similar for the Verbal IQ-scale (range 79–116, mean 96.6, median 95.0) and for the Performance IQ-scale (range 67–121, mean 93.2, median 91.5). All in all, the foster children scores were moderately, but significantly, below average compared to age standardised norms. Two years later, when all children were re-tested with the same instruments (T2), the total IQ scales ranged from 80 to 124 (mean 100.1 and median 101.0). These changes were highly significant (p<0.001). More than half of the children showed a marked improvement in their cognitive functions and among these were the five children with the lowest scores at T1. At T2 all these children performed within the normal IQ range. In addition, several of the best performers at T1 showed improvements at T2. No tendency of regression towards the mean was found.

*Table 1*
**WISC-III at pre-intervention (T1) and post-intervention (T2) 24 months later, and comparisons of T1/T2, N = 24**

| WISC III IQ/index scales (Mean = 100, S.D. = 15) | T1 | | T2 | | T-test (T1/T2) |
|---|---|---|---|---|---|
| | Mean | S.D. | Mean | S.D. | p |
| Verbal | 96.6 | 10.1 | 100.8 | 12.3 | * |
| Performance | 93.2 | 14.2 | 99.0 | 13.1 | ** |
| Total | 94.4 | 11.9 | 100.1 | 12.6 | *** |
| Verbal comprehension | 97.3 | 8.9 | 103.3 | 13.7 | ** |
| Perceptual reasoning | 93.2 | 13.0 | 97.9 | 13.0 | * |
| Freedom from distractability | 96.1 | 12.0 | 95.8 | 12.4 | n.s. |
| Perceptual speed | 92.3 | 14.8 | 101.0 | 15.3 | ** |

* p<0.05;  ** p<0.01;  *** p<0.001;  n.s. = non-significant result

The improved test scores on the WISC-III total scale were equally distributed between the Verbal and the Performance scales, but the improvement on the Performance scale was stronger (p<0.01) than on the Verbal scale (p<0.05). On the Verbal scale, five out of the six pupils with lowest performance at T1 had improved their results at T2. As processing speed is an important ability in the learning process, it was satisfying to note that the results on this scale had improved significantly at T2 (Table 1).

Results from the VMI-test were at T1, all within the normal range (not shown in tables), and yielded no signs of specific visual-perceptual disabilities. This test was therefore not used at follow-up (T2).

At T1, scores from the Beck Young People Inventories scales showed, somewhat surprisingly, that most of the children scored within the normal range, only four being above a clinical cut-off on every sub-scale. At T2, a small but not significant portion of the children showed increased ratings, indicating some degree of emotional and/or social impairment (not shown in tables). In a normal group, the expected incidence of this type of impairment would be 25 per cent of the group (Beck *et al*, 2004), roughly the same as in the study sample.

At T1, both the foster carers and the teachers rated the children low on the four problem scales of the SDQ (see Table 2). In fact, the ratings were similar to the total mean scores of the scores found in the general populations in Sweden and the UK (Smedje *et al*, 1999; Meltzer *et al*, 2000). On the fifth scale, measuring pro-social behaviour, ratings from both foster carers and teachers were remarkably high, indicating that most children's behaviour was good. At T2, the ratings of the foster carers and teachers on the four problem scales of the SDQ remained the same (Table 2), with the exception of peer relationship problems where significant improvement was found (see Table 2).

Assessments of the interpersonal relation on a VAS-scale (1–10 distance–closeness) between the child and his or her main teacher at T1 showed that the children scored highly (mean 8.4, range 3–10; not shown in tables), with the teachers' assessments of their relationship to the pupils only slightly lower (mean 6.9, range 2–8).

At T2, the positive ratings continued. The pupils still scored highly (mean 8.3, range 3–10), as did their teachers (mean 7.3, range 1–10), in spite of the fact that for 10 pupils a new teacher had taken over their class (not shown in tables).

*Table 2*
**SDQ parent and teacher ratings at pre-intervention (T1) and post-intervention (T2) 24 months later, and comparisons of T1/T2, N = 24**

| SDQ | T1 | | T2 | | T-test (T1/T2) |
| --- | --- | --- | --- | --- | --- |
| | *Mean* | *S.D.* | *Mean* | *S.D.* | *p* |
| *Parent ratings* | | | | | |
| Total difficulties score | 8.33 | 6.43 | 8.71 | 6.42 | n.s. |
| Emotional symptoms | 1.40 | 1.58 | 1.67 | 2.26 | n.s. |
| Conduct problems | 1.44 | 1.61 | 1.54 | 1.61 | n.s. |
| Hyperactivity/inattention | 3.88 | 3.06 | 4.33 | 2.94 | n.s. |
| Peer relationship problems | 1.56 | 1.71 | 1.17 | 1.95 | n.s. |
| Prosocial behaviour | 7.33 | 2.26 | 7.67 | 2.46 | n.s. |
| *Teacher ratings* | | | | | |
| Total difficulties score | 7.52 | 6.52 | 6.52 | 4.23 | n.s. |
| Emotional symptoms | 0.96 | 1.30 | 1.17 | 1.56 | n.s. |
| Conduct problems | 1.35 | 2.29 | 1.30 | 1.64 | n.s. |
| Hyperactivity/inattention | 3.87 | 3.43 | 3.52 | 2.73 | n.s. |
| Peer relationship problems | 1.52 | 1.56 | 0.52 | 0.85 | ** |
| Prosocial behaviour | 6.83 | 3.00 | 7.52 | 2.15 | n.s. |

** $p < 0.01$;   n.s. = non-significant result

## Pedagogical instruments

When comparing individual results on the cognitive tests with those of the reading skills tests and the maths test at T1, the majority (around 75%) were clearly below what could be expected from their cognitive competence, as assessed with WISC-III. This discrepancy was reduced at T2. As seen in Table 3, both the results for reading skills (Letter-word chains) and the speed of reading (DLS) significantly improved (p<0.05), including the 11 pupils who had the lowest result at T1.

Table 3
**Age standardised pedagogical tests at pre-intervention (T1) and post-intervention (T2) 24 months later, and comparisons of T1/T2**

| Test | N | T1 | | T2 | | T-test (T1/T2) |
|---|---|---|---|---|---|---|
| Stanine scale, Mean = 5, S.D. = 2 | | Mean | S.D. | Mean | S.D. | p |
| Reading skills Letter-word chains | 22[1] | 3.9 | 2.2 | 4.8 | 1.6 | * |
| DLS reading speed | 11[2] | 4.1 | 1.4 | 5.2 | 1.9 | * |
| DLS spelling skills | 24 | 5.1 | 1.6 | 5.8 | 1.8 | * |
| Magne Maths Diagnostic Test | 24 | 4.1 | 2.1 | 4.2 | 2.1 | n.s. |

[1] 22 children had reached the lowest age at which this test is applicable, according to the manual.
[2] 11 children had reached the lowest age at which this test is applicable, according to the manual.
[3] 2 children were not available for testing at T1, consequently their results at T2 were excluded.
* p<0.05;  n.s. = non-significant result

This positive trend was also found in relation to spelling skills. Nine pupils had clearly improved their results on the DSL Spelling Test at T2 compared to T1 (Table 3 and Figure 1).

The pupils' results on the Magne Maths Diagnostic Test also improved over time. At T1, 10 pupils scored very low, 10 pupils were in the average range and two scored high. The mean for the whole group tended to rise from T1 to T2. However, the difference did not reach a significant level (see Table 3) although seven out of the 10 pupils scoring very low results at T1, had improved their results markedly, as shown in Figure 2.

*Figure 1*
**Reading skills at T1/T2 for the 11 index children with the lowest results at T1**

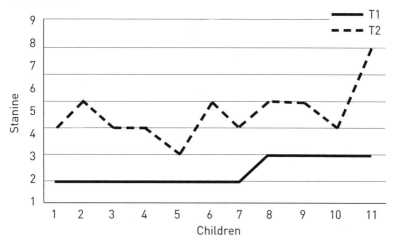

*Figure 2*
**Maths skills at T1/T2 for the 10 index children with the lowest results at T1**

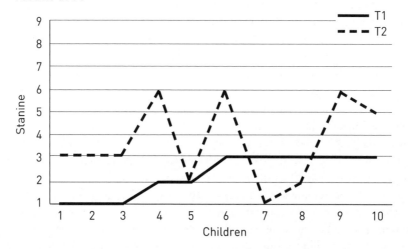

## Special interventions

In addition to all this testing and support, some children received specialised interventions. The special education teacher identified five children as showing signs of having visual impairments. Consequently, these children were tested and all were provided with spectacles. Four children were given individual help to improve their homework, eight were counselled by the school psychologist in order to improve their social interaction skills and in five cases both foster carers and teachers were given counselling by the project psychologist, aimed at strengthening their ability to handle the child's difficult behaviour.

## Discussion

In this project, a battery of standardised tests was used to map each child's potential, strengths and difficulties at school. The assessment tools provided a base for the clinical work of the psychologist and the special education teacher. The test results enabled them to work with each child's teacher, foster carers and the child him or herself when tailoring individual support and when accessing special education support – in theory, available to all children but never systematically used for those in foster care.

After two years, the young participants had significantly improved their average scores on the IQ-tests on reading and on spelling tests, while the improvements of their numeracy skills were weaker. During the early school years children are mostly taught how to read. Later, they are supposed to transfer from "learning to read" towards "reading to learn". Therefore, the significantly improved reading speed at T2 in the group is an important part of the results, being a favourable prognostic indicator for future school performance. All in all, the results from the project are hopeful, even though the study design does not allow any conclusions about causal inference.

Yet a fundamental question remains: Why did so many of the foster children perform below their potential at the start of the project when the results on the SDQ clearly indicate that they did not have excessive behavioural or psychological problems? The conclusion from the project is simple: the reason was *gaps in knowledge*, often accumulated over several years. For the project, this was good news. Lack of basic cognitive abilities are very difficult to repair, as are psychological traumas or learning difficulties caused by early childhood neglect or abuse (Lansford *et al*, 2002; Boden *et al*, 2007; Stone, 2007). But gaps in knowledge can be filled through educational support and targeting the children and their carers (Durlak, 1997; Ferrer-Wreder *et al*, 2004). Interestingly, the interventions also seem to have enhanced the foster children's capacity to engage socially, as their peer relations in school had significantly improved by the time of follow-up.

The story of mathematics is different. Weak improvements for the foster children indicate that stronger interventions than those available in this project are necessary. Given the strong predictive power of early numeracy skills for future school achievements (Duncan *et al*, 2007), our results point in the same direction as the conclusions from several US early developmental programmes: namely that numeracy and literacy training for vulnerable children should be promoted at an early age (Currie, 2000; Duncan *et al*, 2007; Manning *et al*, 2010).

The process by which the psychologist and the special education teacher told the foster carers and teachers that the child had normal cognitive ability and had the potential to profit from the education in school is the major salutogenic element of the intervention (Antonovsky, 1999). Many foster carers and teachers had low – or even pessimistic – expectations of the foster child's school performance at the start of the project. Before the assessments were done, no less than six of the 25 project children were assumed by their foster carers and teachers to have a very low cognitive capacity or even to be learning disabled. When the assessments proved that these children performed cognitively within the normal span, the expectations of both foster carers and teachers radically changed, making them far more optimistic about the child's capability to do reasonably well in school (Rosenthal and Jacobson, 1992; Caplan and Caplan, 1993).

The acquisition of basic knowledge in reading, spelling and maths is a prerequisite for further learning (eg Barber and Mourshed, 2007) and therefore is a strong predictor of reasonable success in school. As demonstrated in this study, filling knowledge gaps through educational support for foster children helps them to achieve scholastic goals, thereby improving their future prospects.

School performance is of course influenced by many factors – individual (e.g. cognitive capacity), familial (e.g. poor support at home) and school related (e.g. the competence of the teachers; see Hattie, 2009). A report from a Swedish longitudinal research project sends an alarming signal with regard to the education of looked after children. Children's peer status in primary school was found to be strongly related to future educational outcomes, more or less independently of socio-economic background (Almqvist *et al*, 2010). In addition, a Danish national cohort study reported that children in care had threefold augmented risks for being victims of bullying (a strong indicator of poor peer status), even when possible confounding variables, including experience of different types of maltreatment, were taken into account (Christoffersen, 2010). Like Jackson (2007b), we disagree with those who claim that we can expect little from these children, considering their damaging early childhood experiences (e.g. Berridge, 2007).

## Methodological issues

There are three obvious limitations of this study. The first is the small (and geographically selected) sample. Successful replications in other locations are needed before we can generalise the results. The small sample size also prevented us from analysing confounding and mediating factors. At present (summer 2010), the project is being replicated in Norrkoping, a town of similar size to Helsingborg. Several other local authorities in Sweden are planning to follow and the project will also be replicated in Norway.

The second is that the pre-post intervention design does not enable us to infer any causal conclusions about effects of the intervention. However, since most other studies have failed to detect positive development of cognitive and academic performance in looked after children, the results suggest that the project has made a difference. At the start, we concluded that there were considerable ethical problems linked to a traditional randomised controlled trial (RCT). It seems – in our opinion – hardly defendable to stage a clinical situation where assessment results would not be communicated to case workers and teachers, and not used for improving the children's school situation *with regular services*. This project was not based on new untested methods; it was founded mainly on a model for systematic assessment to help children access services that are already available but not used systematically for foster children. These are services which the children, by law, have a right to receive. Some children in the project also seem to have benefited from simply having the test results communicated to them:

> What? Is my intelligence normal? Even better than normal? God Almighty, they have always told me that I am stupid . . . (Quotation from a child in the project, who shortly afterwards started for the first time to get good grades in maths tests)

Before the project, another child was believed by the foster carers, the case worker and the teacher to have learning disabilities but scored high average in the WISC-III pre-intervention test. This was a shocking revelation for the foster carers, who radically changed their attitude to their foster child's future prospects.

Finally, the relatively short follow-up time is also a limitation. We do not know whether these results are sustained over the teenage years, a troubled time in primary school for many children. The project is now a part of the regular child welfare services in Helsingborg, and has been extended to older children. Hopefully, new follow-ups and replications can shed light on this question.

## Conclusions

Standardised tests of foster children's cognitive ability, reading, spelling and numeracy skills seem to provide a sound base for tailoring individualised support for foster children in school, probably far more than unstructured assessments by teachers and social workers. The results further suggest that the poor educational performances of foster children can be improved through systematic work by foster care agencies and schools. This is a hopeful message.

### Acknowledgements

Financial support was provided by the National Board of Health and Welfare, the Skåne County Administration, and the Children's House Foundation (Allmänna Barnhuset). Thanks to all teachers, principals, social workers, and foster parents who participated in the project. Last – but not least – our sincere thanks to the 24 children who gladly and patiently guided us towards a better understanding of their school situation.

# 8 Improving the educational outcomes of looked after children in Scotland

## Graham Connelly

*Graham Connelly examines whether the distinctiveness of the Scottish political landscape has the potential to lead to improvements in tackling the deficits in the educational experience and attainment of looked after children and young people, clearly acknowledged by the authors of two reports:* Learning with Care: The education of children looked after away from home by local authorities *(Her Majesty's Inspectors of Schools and Social Work Services Inspectorate, 2001) and* Report on Educational Attainment of Looked After Children *(Scottish Parliament, 2012).*

## Introduction

The generally low attainment of looked after children in Scotland has in recent years been a matter of considerable concern for politicians, education journalists, academics and front-line practitioners. The history of this concern dates from an inspection report of educational provision for children in residential homes (Her Majesty's Inspectors of Schools and Social Work Services Inspectorate, 2001) and the issues came under significant further scrutiny more recently as a result of an inquiry conducted by the Education and Culture Committee of the Scottish Parliament, begun in the autumn of 2011 (Scottish Parliament, 2012).[5]

Scotland received considerable administrative autonomy as a result of gaining devolved powers in 1999, although its separate legal system was maintained following the Union which created the UK in 1707. The legacy of these distinctions and the fact that arrangements for education, social services and health are the province of the Scottish Parliament mean that there are contextual differences between Scotland and the other nations that make up the UK, though the substantive issues concerning the experiences of looked after children in the education system are not much different from those being addressed in many countries.

This chapter provides some background to the particular Scottish context, summarises what we know about the educational outcomes of looked after children, considers the implications for an improvement agenda and discusses the role of carers in providing

---

5   A full account of the inquiry is available on the Scottish Parliament website at www.scottish.parliament. uk. Navigate to Committees, then to Education and Culture Committee, and then to Inquiry into the Educational Attainment of Looked After Children.

support and encouragement for children's progress in education.

## The Scottish context

In Scotland a child or young person becomes "looked after" when the state intervenes to address significant concerns about his or her safety or welfare. The intervention usually involves a children's hearing (a panel of three trained volunteers) or a sheriff (judge) making an order for compulsory measures of supervision.[6] The supervision order stipulates the place of residence and also the conditions of the supervision. It is the duty of the local authority to make the arrangements to ensure that supervision requirements are carried out.

At 31 July 2012 there were 16,248 children looked after by Scottish local authorities, a 0.1 per cent increase on the previous year, the smallest increase in numbers since 2001.[7] Looked after children represent almost two per cent of the 0–18 population, a proportion that is higher than in the rest of the UK. The explanation for this difference lies principally in the inclusion within the definition of a "looked after child" of children who would be recorded in youth justice statistics in other legal jurisdictions. In Scotland children can be looked after "at home" (about one-third of all looked after children), where they remain living with their family under a supervision requirement, and "away from home", in foster, residential and kinship care settings. The use of community placements such as foster care has increased in recent years (up by 4% between 2010–11 and 2011–12), while there has been a consequent fall in residential placements (accounting for only 8.8% of the looked after population in 2011–12).

The primary responsibility for providing support for the child and the family has been with social workers, but in recent years the principle of multi-agency collaboration has been advocated in relation to supporting children and their families. In particular, the *Getting it right for every child* (*GIRFEC*) framework, whereby all representatives of the local authority and its key partners (e.g. health agencies) are regarded as sharing the responsibilities of parents, has implications for professionals working with children (Scottish Government, 2008). Teachers and other children's services professionals have always had duties to co-operate in the children's hearing system, for example, in the provision of reports, but the newer arrangements imply a greater degree of responsibility to initiate action, monitor arrangements and call partner agencies to account. All looked after children should have a care plan (known as the Child's Plan), which should specify actions and responsibilities and arrangements for review. School staff should have

---

6  More information about the children's hearing system is available, including links to information packs aimed at primary and secondary schools at www.chscotland.gov.uk. Follow the links at the 'Publications' tab.

7  Scottish Government children's statistics are available at www.scotland.gov.uk/Topics/Statistics/Browse/Children

contributed to the plan, particularly in relation to educational aspects, and should be active in monitoring progress. Teachers are also expected to voice concerns if, for example, a child's plan has not been shared with the school, or if it does not sufficiently address the child's educational needs and indicate responsibilities for ensuring that these are looked into.

---

**Contents of the Child's Plan**

The format of the documentation varies between local authorities but all have common features, including:

- a summary of reasons for having a Child's Plan;

- assessment, based on the My World Triangle (How I grow and develop, What I need from the people who look after me and My wider world). A teacher should be contributing to aspects concerning educational development;

- A summary of needs, including a clear Action Plan. A teacher should be contributing to this aspect too, aware that the schools provide opportunities for meeting needs beyond the educational/intellectual domain;

- explicit arrangements for reviewing the plan.

---

Despite the good intentions contained in the *GIRFEC* policy, it is clear that there is much work still to be done to ensure that the educational aspects of children's lives are prominent when making decisions about their care. A study of the reports, plans and children's hearing decisions of 250 children aged between three and 17, with supervision requirements in 10 of Scotland's 32 local authority areas, found that in virtually all cases the lead role was taken by social workers, despite official expectations that in many circumstances it would be appropriate for a teacher to have this "lead professional" responsibility. The research audit also found that only 68 per cent of plans contained a reference to the child's education and less than half included specific actions. Plans were also more likely to identify problems than talents. For example, only 17 per cent of children who were achieving educationally had plans to support their potential and continued achievement, and none of the children who were described as talented had plans to support their abilities. Few plans recorded the child's views or aspirations and only six per cent of plans contained actions to support the child's ambitions. Less than a quarter had educational goals beyond the current school year (Henderson and Whitehead, 2013).

## The educational outcomes of looked after children in Scotland

An assessment of Scotland's performance in relation to the expressed desire of its politicians and professionals to raise the attainment of looked after children needs to be set within a broader context of the country's success in education in comparison with other nations. The report of the Commission on School Reform (2013) concluded that 'although the system generally performs well and enjoys a good reputation both in Scotland and elsewhere, it is no longer a world leader' (p 36). In considering Scotland's position as judged by various international surveys of school performance, the Commission concluded (p 37) that 'Scotland's performance puts it among the world's higher achieving systems, but its position is relatively weaker than it was when surveys began'. One reason for this slippage relative to other countries is the failure to make a significant impact on the negative educational consequences associated with multiple deprivation. The Commission (p 42) noted that:

> About one in five or one in six of Scotland's young people experience some important degree of educational failure at school. Furthermore this proportion has not significantly altered over decades.

Despite the existence of universal comprehensive education for at least 30 years, with only a very small private school sector, except in Edinburgh and Glasgow, local authority-managed schools in more affluent areas achieve significantly better in terms of examination results and post-school destinations than those in areas of social and economic deprivation. Looked after children tend to have poorer outcomes than their peers, even those living in communities with high levels of deprivation. For example, in 2010–11, while 36 per cent of looked after young people were unemployed nine months after leaving school, the comparison figure for all school leavers was considerably lower at 10 per cent.

School attendance is a useful simple proxy for monitoring progress in educational outcomes, simply because there is *inter alia* a direct relationship between attending school and gaining qualifications. Unfortunately, it is also virtually the only measure that is available across the age range in Scotland since the decision was taken to abandon national testing of all children in favour of the Scottish Survey of Numeracy and Literacy, first conducted in 2011. This survey, while valuable overall, includes too few looked after children in the sample to provide any useful data about this specific group. Table 1 shows the average percentage attendance for looked after children (all LAC) compared with all pupils in two successive years.

*Table 1*
**Average levels of school attendance (%)**

|  | 2009–10 | | | 2010–11 | | |
|---|---|---|---|---|---|---|
|  | *All pupils* | *"at home"* | *All LAC* | *All pupils* | *"at home"* | *All LAC* |
| Primary | 94.9 | – | 93.5 | 94.8 | – | 93.6 |
| Secondary | 91.2 | – | 80.5 | 91.1 | – | 82.8 |
| All schools | 93.2 | 78.7 | 87.8 | 93.1 | 79.1 | 88.6 |

First, it can be seen that looked after children as a group have considerably below average attendance. If the attendance rates of pupils from socio-economically deprived backgrounds, or those receiving free school meals, was substituted, similarly lower figures would be noted. Second, and more positively, the table shows a small improvement in the attendance of looked after children, a pattern that is evident over a longer period than the two years shown here. Third, attendance is poorer among all secondary school pupils, as well as those looked after. Underlying this particular observation is a much more complex picture, which highlights the disadvantage experienced by some pupils who do not fare well in the transition from primary schools, with their typically more intimate learning environments, to secondary schools with different teachers for each subject in the curriculum.

As the Commission on School Reform report points out, Scottish school education is characterised by a high degree of uniformity. In a country which has taken standards in education seriously, and which was apparently the first in the world to have a General Teaching Council to register teachers and specify graduate-level qualifications, the unintended consequence has been a rigidity which has created barriers to flexible arrangements that could benefit individual children. There are, however, signs that both attitudes and practices are changing and, for example, primary-trained teachers and youth workers are working alongside secondary teachers in some schools. Fourth, but not shown in this table, when looked after children are stratified into different care settings, considerable differences are noted. Children in foster care have had average attendance marginally higher than the average for all pupils in recent years, perhaps evidence of the value foster carers place on education and their skill and persistence in liaising with schools. The lower overall average attendance of looked after children is found to be attributable to lower rates of attendance among children living in local authority children's homes and, more significantly, on "home supervision". The latter group presents a particular challenge for schools, which have tended to respond somewhat procedurally to truanting. Teachers find it easier to intervene quickly when problems start if they can talk to a carer, while in the case of parents who do not respond to informal approaches by phone and text, the more formal, and drawn-out, methods of official letters

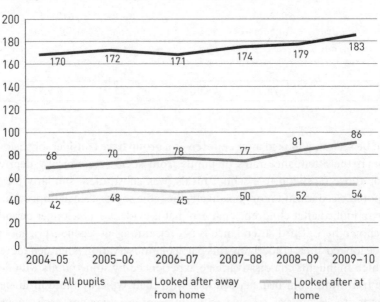

*Figure 1*
**Average tariff score of Secondary 4 pupils, 2004–05 to 2009–10**

and visits by an attendance officer (sometimes known as education liaison officer) tend to be used. This observation has the merit of indicating where effort needs to be deployed, although not which approaches are likely to be successful.

Inspection of attainment statistics, in terms of qualifications accredited by the national examination agency, the Scottish Qualifications Authority (SQA), shows the dramatic "gap" between looked after children and all school pupils. Figure 1, which charts average tariff scores (a measure which allows comparison of different types of SQA qualifications) of pupils in the fourth year of secondary school (age 15-16) for six successive academic years, shows the gap graphically. The gradient of each line is similar, indicating modest improvement, but the attainment of looked after children is, on average, significantly lower than for all pupils at the minimum school-leaving age. Given what we now know about the poor attendance of children looked after at home, it is not a surprise to note that this group has the poorest attainment.

Two further facts are particularly disturbing. First, the average tariff score for looked after children is boosted by the inclusion of very basic, so-called "access" and "foundation" level qualifications. These are intended to recognise the very real achievements of pupils who have additional support needs and for some they will be stepping stones to more advanced qualifications. On the other hand, they do not represent a currency valued by potential employers and by aspirant parents. One feels conflicted in drawing attention to low attainment because of the danger of stigmatising children, their teachers and carers, yet it is important to advocate for much higher ambitions for children in disadvantaged circumstances. Second, very few looked after children gain the minimum level of education required for gaining access to higher education, at least in part because most tend to leave school at the minimum age of 16, typically at least a year before pupils take the "Higher" examinations needed for university entrance. In this regard, Scottish looked after pupils appear to be more disadvantaged than their counterparts in, for example, Nordic countries (Connelly and Matheson, 2012).

Destination statistics, compiled by the government agency, Skills Development Scotland, show that only between one and two per cent of looked after school leavers progress directly to higher education, based on a very small number of young people. This appears to compare unfavourably with statistics for England (6–7%), although the more encompassing definition of the term "looked after" in Scotland contributes to this apparent difference. Further education (FE) colleges represent a more significant initial destination for looked after school leavers. Many are on low-level courses and the drop-out rate is worryingly high. On the other hand, for others, FE provides an important access route to higher education. For example, for 57 applicants to one Scottish university in 2012 who declared their looked after status through the UCAS process, 47 were not at school and were studying in some form of post-school education. Of the 2,542 young people eligible for aftercare services on 31 July 2012, with known economic activity, four per cent were recorded as being in higher education, while 63 per cent were not in any form of education, training or employment. The latter statistic is truly shocking and highlights the risk to well-being that is a consequence of being looked after for many young people, particularly those who do not experience stable foster or residential placements.

## The implications for teachers and other educationalists

So, faced with the somewhat bleak evidence outlined above, what is to be done? Perhaps it is important to acknowledge that there has been progress, even if it is modest and the rate of advance in terms of educational outcomes is slow. This slow pace is frustrating for politicians who want quick results and of course there is also a terrible human cost in terms of life chances for individual looked after young people. As has been described in detail elsewhere (Connelly and Furnivall, 2013), there is also arguably evidence of considerable infrastructural development, both at the strategic level (as evidenced by a Scottish Government-led strategic planning group and the existence of a national Centre for Excellence for Looked After Children in Scotland (CELCIS) – www.celcis.org) and also at practitioner level (as evidenced in the development of high-quality training materials and support for continuing professional development (CPD)). Teachers, social workers and carers would need to confess to having lived on another planet to use the excuse that they had not been exposed to, at the very least, basic information about looked after children and the risks they face in education. During the past decade the extent of statistical monitoring data has improved significantly, from a few tables within the children's social work report, based on an annual census, to the position where there is a separate, detailed educational outcomes report based on data for individual children looked after for the preceding 12 months. Still more statistical data would be helpful, such as better-quality information about disabilities and additional support needs. Scotland, unlike the other countries of the UK, does not publish data on the health of looked after children. The lack of published attainment data for primary-age looked after children is a serious disadvantage, which could be partially ameliorated were the Scottish Government to introduce assessment using, for example, the Strengths and Difficulties Questionnaire (SDQ), as is the case in England. However, lack of information available nationally should not preclude local authorities from analysing data locally about the attainment of younger looked after children in the core skills of reading, writing and mathematics.

The report of the inquiry conducted by the Education and Culture Committee of the Scottish Parliament (2012) identified several themes emerging from the written submissions and oral evidence received in response to their wide consultation. In particular, the politicians identified the need for looked after children to be "ready to learn". The awareness that some looked after children risk being excluded from school, sometimes on frequent occasions, and that others have poor attendance as a result of placement instability, illness or the fear of being bullied has led to calls for teachers to have better understanding of the psychology of attachment and its implications for the classroom. Since a child with attachment difficulties learns that adults behave inconsistently, it is important that teachers do not lower their expectations for appropriate behaviour in the classroom, and attitudes to learning in school and at home, while at the same time being understanding and supportive when difficulties arise. The child may expect teachers to give up on them, to be relieved when they are absent, and to be tempted not to follow this up diligently. In an attempt to respond to this CPD need, CELCIS has developed a short course on understanding attachment and its relevance to looked after children, supported by a monograph aimed at practitioners (Furnivall, 2011).

The logical consequence of the evidence of the research conducted by the Scottish Children's Reporter Administration, outlined earlier, indicating that decision-making about children's care is unlikely to be influenced by a detailed understanding of their progress in education, is that gaps in learning, and support for special needs and aptitudes, are likely to be addressed too late, if at all. There is, however, general recognition in Scotland of the need for earlier identification of difficulties and quicker intervention. This is exemplified in the Scottish Government's Early Years Framework,[8] which includes

---

8   See www.scotland.gov.uk/Topics/People/Young-People/Early-Years-and-Family/ Early-Years-Framework.

indicators of readiness to learn, such as 'the percentage of children displaying age-appropriate communication skills', and 'the percentage of pre-school children who have been read to on four or more days in the past week'.

Another theme highlighted by the politicians is that of support for looked after children at school. Head teachers are expected to nominate a "designated" manager to have a co-ordinating role for looked after children within the school. In reality the nominated individual is likely to be performing several other roles, particularly in a secondary school, and enthusiasm for performing the tasks implicit in the role varies between individuals. The Committee highlighted two particular qualities of supportive schools: the need for children to experience good relationships with teachers and excellent leadership shaping the ethos of the school. The Commission on School Reform report also noted that the quality of relationships is crucial to success in education, and recommended that more attention should be focused on the personal and social development of young people. The Commission considered that this would be achieved by changing the role of schools, both by providing a greater range of learning experiences to counteract disengagement with education and also by seeking out opportunities provided by a range of agencies, and by actively 'ensuring that young people are made aware of them and, if necessary, assisted to take part' (Commission on School Reform, 2013, p 50). This point is particularly important in the case of looked after children who often experience a narrow curriculum, in particular, missing out on opportunities to participate in drama, music and extra-curricular activities, opportunities which can be crucial in helping to develop confidence and personal efficacy (see, Gilligan, Chapter 6).

It is ironic that the extent to which a particular school is likely to provide a welcoming and nurturing environment for a child in turmoil is often a matter of common knowledge locally, yet this intelligence is very unlikely to be deployed when making decisions about placing a young person in school. One of the recommendations made in the Commission's report seems particularly relevant in this respect:

> *The allocation of support for pupils and schools experiencing disadvantage should be reviewed and needs to be better targeted. More of the available support should follow the individual disadvantaged learner.* (Commission on School Reform, 2013, p 44)

A further theme explored by the Education and Culture Committee of the Scottish Parliament (2012) was, perhaps unsurprisingly, the old chestnut of the need to achieve better joint working between the many different agencies involved with the child and the family. Evidence given to the Committee highlighted the early years and the transition from primary and secondary school as specific points where efforts directed at more effective collaboration are needed. The charity, Children in Scotland, in its submission, noted that services are often delivered too late, fail to deal with the problems in a holistic way and are triggered by behaviour or performance becoming difficult for teachers to manage rather than at the point when a child starts to struggle. This at least gives a clue to possible remedies. The *GIRFEC* approach emphasises collective responsibility for children in crisis, rather than expecting social work services always to take the lead role, but its implementation across Scotland is acknowledged to be patchy. Several local authorities have emphasised the value in having monthly joint assessment and planning meetings for the education of looked after children. In one authority this meeting takes the form of schools' designated managers giving case presentations on children where there is a cause for concern and using the range of professional expertise in the group to identify potential actions, which are then reviewed at subsequent meetings. This approach replaced the previous practice of talking about all the looked after children in the schools in a more general and unfocused way.

Two further ideas contained in evidence presented to the Committee contain important messages for improved inter-agency working. The Care Inspectorate submission observed that the local authorities that do particularly well are those in which there is a strong ethos that emphasises the belief in getting the best for children. This strong "corporate parenting" culture is evident in the leadership of chief officers and elected members, and is also demonstrated in the approach of front-line services. The second idea is the observation of the Association of Directors of Social Work in Scotland that good inter-professional relationships are important: facilitated by having opportunities to work together regularly and getting to value the contributions of different professions.

## The role of carers in supporting children's educational development

The importance of all caregivers in supporting the educational development of children, both as primary educators themselves and also as partners with early education providers and schools, is undisputed. There are of course particular demands made of carers and parents of looked after children, such as attending children's hearings and reviews, and advocating on behalf of children who need additional support, or who face school exclusion. The then Scottish Executive's (2007) *Looked After Children: We can and must do better* report identified four "common themes" in relation to a child's or young person's right to experience a stable, safe and nurturing home environment:

- A stable, safe and nurturing home setting is essential for looked after children and young people to feel both safe and nurtured and to realise their potential.
- A supportive home setting which promotes education is essential for looked after children and young people to improve their educational outcomes.
- Young people require good-quality accommodation; accommodation that meets their various needs, both when in care and also when living independently.

- 'Young people need to be better supported during the transition to independent living.' (Scottish Executive, 2007, p 50).

The Regulation of Care (Scotland) Act 2001 introduced the National Care Standards,[9] a series of detailed guides to the rights of users in particular care settings. The standards for foster care and family placement services include the statement quoted below, indicating the general entitlements of a child to support for education in a foster placement. A similar statement appears in the standards for residential care:

*You know that the agency makes sure your foster carer:*

- *provides you with an educationally-rich environment;*
- *helps to meet your educational needs; and*
- *helps you to develop the skills, ability and knowledge that you will need when you become an adult.*

The first of these expectations refers to the quality of the home environment, whether foster, kinship or residential care setting, in providing appropriate physical space and support for school homework and in providing activities that are themselves cognitively stimulating. The 2001 *Learning with Care* report (Her Majesty's Inspectors of Schools and Social Work Services Inspectorate, 2001) was highly critical of the residential care homes inspected in this respect. Since that time, many residential carers have engaged in CPD in relation to their role in supporting education. Local authorities that have built new residential homes have considered educational needs in the design process, for example, ensuring that bedrooms have space for study, there is a stimulating play environment inside and outside, and that there are appropriate facilities for visiting teachers who support children in completing homework and to catch up when they have missed schooling. Children's homes are now more likely to have internet connection and educational software provided by the council's education or library services. Much of what we know about improvement, however, is anecdotal and a comprehensive inspection to assess the educational richness of children's homes in Scotland is arguably overdue. A report on residential care for children by Audit Scotland concluded that: 'Not all children in residential care receive the best quality of care and support' (Audit Scotland, 2010, p 16). The auditors assessed twice-yearly inspection reports by the Care Commission and found that one in 10 residential homes or schools in 2010 had been classed as "adequate" or "weak", amounting to a total of 18 establishments caring for around 160 children. The auditors also quoted from a study of case files carried out by the Care Commission between 2006 and 2008 which found that 'care plans were not fully addressing the care,

---

9   See www.nationalcarestandards.org.

well-being or educational needs of young people in 17 per cent of the 224 providers registered at the time' (Audit Scotland, 2010, p 15).

A perusal of the inspection report for a residential school, which was graded either "very good" or "excellent" on all measures, highlights important features in providing a good educational experience for looked after children. Unsurprisingly, these include: strong leadership; commitment of staff to improving services; high-quality relationships between staff and pupils that make young people feel safe, valued and respected; personalisation of the curriculum to meet individual needs; and "outstanding" personal support for young people. A positive development within the sector is that residential schools appear well placed to benefit from curriculum reforms in Scotland (Curriculum for Excellence), which broadly speaking emphasise the need for education to be relevant to the world in which young people find themselves, and the creativity of teachers to make learning relevant and interesting. The education press has featured some articles about ways in which residential schools have responded to curriculum reforms and these have contrasted with the more prominent coverage of the burden of the changes on teachers in mainstream schools.

The second expectation quoted earlier underlines the important contribution carers can make as educators by role modelling enthusiasm for learning, coaching and providing varied cultural and educational opportunities. One important role of parents and carers is to support children's literacy development through the mutual enjoyment of reading. The importance of reading to and with young, and even older, children is emphasised in training for foster carers, such as BAAF's *Supporting Children's Learning* programme (Pallett *et al*, 2010), though it is much less likely that there is easy access to this kind of support for kinship carers and parents of children looked after at home. A number of activities have sought to encourage the development of looked after children's reading skills. Among these is the *Reading Rich* programme for foster and residential care settings provided by NCH Scotland and the Scottish Book Trust. The formal evaluation reported promising findings, including the inspirational outcomes that arose from involving authors in the programme, and also the variable degree to which carers felt equipped to encourage children to read:

> Some reported inadequate knowledge of children's books, some were unsure of how to share reading, and some felt vulnerable by becoming involved in the programme because they did not have a reading habit of their own. (Finn, 2008, p 8)

A disadvantage of such schemes is that they are typically set up by third-sector agencies and it is not clear how much activity is sustained once the specific grant funding ends. More recent activities in Scotland, about which no evaluations were available at the time of writing, include book-giving schemes specifically targeted at looked after children, such as the Letterbox Club and the Dolly Parton Imagination Library.

An interesting by-product of the considerable amount of in-service education for residential care staff, who require qualifications for obligatory registration, has been the opportunity for intergenerational learning, whereby young people and adults become more attuned to each other's studies and use their skills to support each other's learning. Anecdotes abound of staff benefiting from the computing skills of young people and there is an opportunity here for researchers interested in exploring these experiences.

Parents and carers often express concerns in relation to their contact with schools. A pilot study by St Andrew's Children's Society, aimed at informing the agency's planning of training for adoptive parents and foster carers, identified three sets of concerns with education services expressed by families:

- *... concerns regarding the quality of communication systems between home and school, particularly in relation to how the needs of the child were being met;*
- *concerns regarding the lack of a coherent frame of reference within the school for the management of behaviour presented by the children who were experiencing attachment or related difficulties;* and
- *concerns relating to the social development of the child in the wider community setting and also within the social and recreational facilities of the school.* (MacLullich, 2012, p 80)

Among these concerns, those related to communication were regarded as being particularly problematic. These included delays in transferring records when a new placement means an unavoidable change of school, lack of information about progress in education and attainment provided in the transfer documentation, delays in arranging assessments and dissatisfaction with the assessment process, and lack of awareness by some members of teaching staff in relation to attachment difficulties. The study distinguished between "new parents" and "experienced parents", finding, for example, that new parents:

> *... spoke about their difficulties in negotiating access to additional support for the children – they described themselves as unfamiliar with procedures and legislation and were sometimes reluctant to enlist support ... fearing that their competence as parents would be questioned if they elicited help.* (MacLullich, 2012, p 81)

Support for the parents of children looked after at home is also a problematic area. This ought to be a priority since children on home supervision orders have the poorest outcomes in education. Yet provision is patchy and services, particularly those employing specialist teachers and nurses, have typically been set up for children looked after away from home. Teachers in mainstream schools do not always have the knowledge and skills needed to work with parents, especially those who appear unwilling to engage with schools. Families can also be reluctant to engage with social workers and therefore the extent to which "supervision" leads to support, which can make a real impact on a child's education, is often very limited.

The third bullet point from the care standards quoted above ('helps you to develop the skills, ability and knowledge that you will need when you become an adult') refers to the kinds of support that most parents aim to give their children, often over an extended period, as the young people develop increasing degrees of independence. But, as a report by Scotland's Commissioner for Children and Young People (2008) pointed out, looked after children tend to have independence thrust on them at a much younger age than is common for most children today. The Commissioner reported a tendency for young people to leave care at 16 and variability between local authorities in the quality of throughcare and aftercare services. Pressures on funding and a lack of precision in the legislation about local authorities' statutory obligations are blamed for the situation. Foster carers and residential services complain that supervision requirements tend to end at an age when young people need continuing support with relationships, managing money, college courses and finding employment. At the time of writing, the Scottish Government was consulting on the provisions of the Children and Young People (Scotland) Bill, which includes the power of young people to request assistance from the local authority up to age 25, though many respondents argued that the proposal should be strengthened to give local authorities a duty to provide support.

## Conclusion

Scotland woke up later than its larger neighbour, England, to the shame of admitting that children in its care system were not faring well in education. But having identified the problem, there was a flurry of activity, directed by two major reports in 2001 and 2007. The inquiry instituted by the cross-party Education and Culture Committee of the Scottish Parliament was set up in response to politicians' frustration at the slow rate at which activity was turning into actual improvement in outcomes. It would be hard to sustain a charge of complacency in facing the problems and, despite the failure to see a dramatic up-turn in outcomes for school leavers, it would be harsh to conclude that progress has flat-lined since it is too soon to see results of, for example, the increased emphasis on earlier intervention.

As the Education and Culture Committee pointed out, there is no shortage of legislation and official guidance, and so scarce resources should not be deployed in creating more, without good reason. There are also many examples of innovative practice across Scotland, such as the mentoring scheme in Glasgow aimed at supporting ambitions for higher education and the emphasis on reading, but too many looked after children face significant barriers to getting a first-class education. The conditions for improvement are likely to lie in having good strategic leadership from local authority senior managers, and empowering school staff and their community partners to develop creative approaches to supporting their looked after pupils. In particular, it is important to acknowledge the vital role of parents and carers in supporting looked after children in their education and to provide resources to help them to do this well. In this regard, there are particular challenges in supporting kinship carers and the parents of children looked after at home and responses to these challenges need to be important elements of the strategy for improving the educational outcomes of all looked after children in Scotland.

# 9    Paired reading as a literacy intervention for foster children

*Cara Osborne, Julia Alfano and Tanya Winn*

*Research suggests that education is sometimes viewed as a low priority by carers in comparison with other aspects of a foster child's life. The aim of the study reported here was to address this issue by directly involving carers in supporting their child's literacy skills through the use of a "paired reading" literacy intervention. Thirty-five carers and children took part in the project over a 16-week period. The results revealed an average improvement in reading age of 12 months during this time, suggesting that the programme offers a constructive way of enhancing foster children's literacy skills. Feedback from carers supported this view and suggested that the impact of the project may extend beyond the realm of literacy per se, resulting in improvements in confidence and motivation as well as reading ability. This chapter is updated from an article first published in* Adoption & Fostering *(34:4, 2010).*

## Introduction

In spite of increasing interest in the education of looked after children, the academic performance of these children still remains poor compared to the general pupil population (DCSF, 2009b). The impact of this extends beyond the realm of school, with care leavers more likely to be unemployed by the September after leaving school (DCSF, 2009b) and less likely to go on to higher education than the general population (Jackson and Ajayi, 2007, reprinted in this volume). In some senses, such findings are unsurprising. The early experiences of looked after children are often marked by neglect or abuse (DCSF, 2009a) and once in care, these children may continue to lack stability in their home and school placements (Fletcher-Campbell and Archer, 2003a), all of which are likely to affect educational achievement. This is not to suggest that poor academic outcomes are inevitable for looked after children, rather that special attention might be needed to ensure that they are properly supported during their school careers (Jackson, 1998b; Jackson and McParlin, 2006). The current study examined the impact of a literacy programme set up in schools, but supported by foster carers. Reading can be considered the foundation of learning, insomuch as it offers a gateway to success in other academic areas (Jackson, 1987, 1998b); it therefore offers a useful starting point when seeking to enhance the education of looked after children.

## Factors contributing to the education of looked after children

Research suggests that two of the key factors needed in order for a child in care to succeed academically are placement stability and a supportive home environment that encourages studying (Stein, 1997; Martin and Jackson, 2002). Unfortunately, placement stability of children in care is often poor, both in terms of care and education placements. For example, Fletcher-Campbell and Archer (2003a) found that a quarter of the young people in care in their study had had six or more care placements, while a third had had three or more education placements during their time at secondary school.

A further difficulty is that there is often limited contact between the key adults involved in supporting the education of looked after children, such as social workers, carers and teachers, and a lack of training on the value of education (SSI/Ofsted, 1995). Perhaps as a result, education is sometimes considered a low priority by foster carers. For example, in a study by Barnardo's (2006), 39 per cent of children in care reported that no one attended their school parents' evening; this was in contrast to four per cent of parents of children who were not in care. Similarly, 47 per cent of children in care reported that they had never been praised for doing well at school, while just three per cent of the parents of children not in care reported the same. Sinclair (1998) suggests that such findings may be exacerbated by placement instability; turnover of carers and time pressures on social workers mean that looked after children may not have a consistent key adult in their life who will take an interest in and support their educational progress (Jackson and Thomas, 2001).

The low priority ascribed to education may consequently result in low expectations on the part of the children concerned (Firth and Horrocks, 1996). Harker *et al* (2003) interviewed 80 children in care and found that nearly a quarter felt that their educational progress was below average. When questioned about the barriers to their academic achievement, a number of children reported a lack of interest by residential or foster carers. Children highlighted a general absence of support, for example, in terms of encouraging attendance at school, providing help with homework or attending school events. Deficiencies in more practical areas were also flagged, with some children bemoaning the absence of reading material and access to a local library.

Martin and Jackson (2002) took a slightly different approach to this issue and examined the views of a group of care leavers who had attained good levels of education (a first degree or postgraduate degree). These individuals came from disadvantaged families and had similar pre-care experiences to a comparison group of care leavers with either no or very few qualifications. It therefore seemed that something within the high-achieving individuals' care experiences had promoted their educational achievement. In line with this, three-quarters of the high-achieving sample emphasised the importance of carer interest in their education, citing the positive effect of encouragement to do well and achieve. In particular, it was felt that foster carers needed to value education, as well as hold an understanding of the best ways of helping a child to achieve a good education.

## Promoting carer involvement

Carer interest and involvement in their foster children's education therefore appears to be a fundamental part of supporting these children's academic progress. One sensible approach to enhancing the education of foster children might, therefore, be to encourage all carers to take a direct role in supporting their child's education. The current study was particularly concerned with facilitating carer involvement in supporting looked after children's reading ability. Reading was focused on for two reasons. First, it has been suggested that looked after children are most likely to be behind in literacy as a result of a lack of adult involvement (Jackson, 1987; 1994). Indeed, research suggests that parents and carers can play a key role in helping children to learn to read (e.g. Lucey and Walkerdine, 2000), thus this seems a skill which is particularly likely to benefit from carer involvement. Second, early reading ability has been linked to future educational success (Jackson, 1987; 1998b), implying that the establishment of good levels of literacy may facilitate success in other areas.

## Literacy interventions for looked after children

In recent years, a number of initiatives aimed at improving the literacy of looked after children have been launched, particularly through voluntary agencies. As Fletcher-Campbell and colleagues (2003) have highlighted, there is limited published (ie peer-reviewed) research on these initiatives, although a number of unpublished reports are in the public domain. Family learning projects, in particular, have been carried out in a number of authorities (Fletcher-Campbell *et al*, 2003; Ofsted, 2009). Such projects are aimed at increasing foster carers' participation in their child's learning. However, they tend to involve a wide range of participants (of which foster carers are just one) and a wide range of skills (of which literacy is just one), meaning that it is difficult to identify the precise impact of such interventions on looked after children's literacy *per se* (e.g. Ofsted, 2009).

Other initiatives have focused on increasing looked after children's access to books and, in turn, their motivation for reading. Examples include the *Right to Read Fund* set up by the Paul Hamlyn Foundation (cited by the DfES, 2007, as an example of good practice), the *A Book of my Own* initiative set up by John Bald, and the *Letterbox Club* (see Griffiths, Chapter 4), a joint initiative between the Booktrust and the University of Leicester. The Letterbox Club has recently been the subject of two evaluations (Griffiths *et al*, 2008; Dymoke and Griffiths, 2010). The project offers looked after children the opportunity to receive a monthly package of books and stationery over the course of six months. The results have been encouraging, revealing a significant improvement in reading ability following the six-month programme (Griffiths *et al*, 2008) and positive feedback from most children and carers involved (Dymoke and Griffiths, 2010). One difficulty acknowledged in the most recent report, however, is the lack of involvement on the part of some carers. Although not a requirement of the programme, nor explicitly suggested to participants, it was hoped that carers would participate by reading with their children. Feedback from those involved suggested that some of the children did indeed read the books they received alongside their carer; in other instances, though, carers were unclear on their role in the project, and did not appreciate that they could have read the books alongside their child. Consequently, the authors highlighted the need to provide additional support for carers in order to help them support their child's reading.

One intervention that offers a structured way of engaging both child and carer in the reading process is "paired reading" (Morgan, 1976), a literacy intervention that involves both the pupil and a partner reading together. The technique involves a number of key elements, outlined succinctly by Topping (2001). The first stage involves both pupil and partner reading together, so that the pupil is provided with a model of competent reading. As the pupil becomes more confident, they are given the option of reading alone. If the pupil subsequently makes a mistake which they are unable to correct themselves, their partner repeats the correct word and begins to read together with them again. Thus, paired reading involves a cycle, moving from reading together to reading alone, ensuring the child receives as much help as necessary. The process is designed to be interactive; the child selects their own reading material and is supported by their partner through discussion, questioning and correction, where necessary. This method enables the child to gain extra practice in reading, receive feedback on their performance, and also experience modelling of correct reading by their partner, thereby promoting reading fluency and comprehension (Topping, 1985; 2001). Thus, as well as providing an opportunity for the child to participate in regular reading sessions, it also offers a way of including the carer within this process.

A number of studies have found support for the use of paired reading in improving literacy (see Topping and Lindsay, 1992; Brooks, 2007, for reviews), although only one (Menmuir, 1994) has specifically examined its use with looked after children. Unfortunately, the findings of Menmuir's study were based purely on the basis of weekly monitoring records kept by foster carers and residential staff, and not actual reading ability. The responses were very positive, and suggested that the intervention had been helpful, but the lack of an objective measure of reading ability means that such findings must be interpreted with caution.

The current study aimed to improve upon this methodology by taking pre- and post-measures of reading ability. The objective was to examine whether actively involving carers in the learning process – through the use of a paired reading intervention – would enhance the literacy levels of their children. Such a project builds upon past research by offering a structured method for including the child's carer within the reading process.

## Method

### Design

The reading ability of the children was assessed in terms of (1) reading age before and after the intervention and (2) ratio gain (change in reading age/change in chronological age). Feedback from carers was also used to illuminate any improvements found.

### Participants

The project was open to all looked after children, even those with good literacy skills, as it was felt that all children could benefit from reading alongside their carer. In total, 68 primary school-aged children currently looked after by foster carers were identified by schools to take part in the project. Ultimately, evaluation data were only provided for 35 children. The reasons for the missing data varied. In some cases, the school simply did not return the requested evaluation data. Often, however, the specific circumstances surrounding the care of the child meant that the school had not been able to put the intervention into practice; for example, a number of schools reported difficulties engaging the child's carer, while others reported that the child had changed placement (either home or school) during the course of the programme and this had prevented the intervention from continuing.

The mean chronological age (CA) of the children at the start of the evaluation was 9 years 4 months ($SD$ = 1 year 9 months; range = 5 years 10 months to 11 years 6 months), while their mean reading age (RA) was 8 years 0 months ($SD$ = 1 year 8 months; range = 4 years 3 months to 10 years 2 months). Thus, most of the children had reading ages considerably below their chronological age. There was, however, some variation in this, and seven of the children actually had a reading age above their chronological age.

### Materials

Children were allowed to select their own reading material during the course of the intervention. Reading age was assessed by teachers using the Salford reading test. Additionally, a weekly monitoring sheet was used to track the progress of the work. This requested information regarding the number of sessions that had taken place that week and any difficulties the carers had encountered. The final monitoring sheet included some additional questions for carers regarding whether they and their child had enjoyed taking part in the programme, what its positive aspects were, whether anything could have been done differently and whether they perceived the programme to have had a positive impact on their child's reading ability. Thus, the aim of the monitoring sheets was not only to ensure that schools were liaising with carers and helping them to "keep on track" with the project, but also to yield some feedback from carers regarding their perceptions of the project.

## Procedure

Training workshops for foster carers, school staff and social workers in the use and delivery of paired reading were undertaken by the lead area co-ordinator for the programme and the educational psychology service. Foster carers subsequently took part in the paired reading programme with their child for 16 weeks. Carers were advised that paired reading should take place at least three times a week, for a minimum of 20 minutes each session. Schools liaised with carers on a weekly basis, and this contact was formalised through the completion of the weekly monitoring sheets.[10]

Each school was asked to collect a baseline measure of reading age using the Salford reading test immediately before the paired reading began, and again immediately after the intervention finished. Salford is the most commonly used reading test in schools in this local authority, thus staff members were familiar with its use and application. The same person in each child's school carried out the pre- and post-tests, ensuring consistency in the administration of the two tests.

## Results

### Quantitative analysis

The average reading age of the children at the outset of the intervention was eight years ($SD$ = 1 year 8 months). During the course of the intervention, the reading age of all the children improved, rising to an average of nine years ($SD$ = 1 year 7 months) by the end of the intervention. On average then, each child made one year's progress in just over four months[11] ($SD$ = 8 months, range = 1 month to 31 months). This increase was statistically significant ($t$ (34) = 9.32, $p < 0.001$).

Ratio gain was also calculated in order to assess the children's rate of progress across time. Ratio gain is defined as the number of months' progress made in literacy, divided by the number of months the intervention has been running; it therefore refers to the average amount of progress made for each month that the child has participated in the intervention. Overall, the mean ratio gain was 2.96. Thus, on average, for every month spent on the intervention, reading age increased by just shy of three months.

There was some variation in the amount of progress made. For example, one child made just one month's progress, while another made 31 months. Further examination of the data revealed that level of progress was related to initial reading ability, such that children with reading ages considerably below their chronological age at the outset of the project revealed greater gains than those with reading ages closer to it (see Table 1). This

---

10  Analysis of these sheets confirmed that carers took part in an average of three sessions during each week of the project.

11  On average, the length of time between the collection of pre- and post-scores was just over four months (mean = 4.24 months). The ratio gain was calculated based on this, rather than the length of the intervention itself.

relationship was statistically significant ($r$ (33) = –0.52, $p < 0.001$). Thus, while all children showed some form of improvement following the intervention, poor readers showed the greatest gains. This finding may, in part, be driven by a ceiling effect and will be considered in more detail in the discussion.

*Table 1*
**Mean increase in reading age according to initial reading ability**

| Initial reading ability | Mean increase in reading age |
| --- | --- |
| More than 36 months behind (n = 3) | 1 year 3 months |
| 24–35 months behind (n = 10) | 1 year 4 months |
| 12–23 months behind (n = 11) | 1 year 2 months |
| 1–11 months behind (n = 4) | 6 months |
| RA better than CA (n = 7) | 7 months |

## Feedback from carers

Feedback was provided by some of the carers following completion of the project (N = 16). All carers reported that both they and their child had enjoyed taking part in the programme and, with the exception of one, none reported experiencing any difficulties:

> *[Child] took until week 13 to begin to enjoy paired reading. Until that point it was a struggle with lots of tears and sulks.*

As might be expected given the positive improvements found in reading age, all but one carer agreed that there had been a positive impact on their child's reading ability (this was the same carer who reported struggling to engage their child until week 13). Carers cited a range of examples, highlighting increases in reading fluency and comprehension:

> *Now reads with plenty of expression, not monotone.*

> *It has given [child] time to think about what she has read and therefore helped with comprehension.*

> *He can recognise more words independently.*

Carers also reported increases in their child's confidence and interest in reading following the intervention:

> *[Child] definitely shows more of an interest in books. Her confidence has grown enormously and she has enjoyed the one-to-one reading.*

*[Child] is trying to read a lot more on her own.*

*He now enjoys reading.*

In addition to improvements linked specifically to reading, carers also reported that taking part in the programme had enabled them to share valuable one-to-one time with their child. This was considered as important as the improvements in their child's reading ability:

*Spending quality time one-to-one and getting to know more about her reading ability . . .*

*[Child] enjoys looking at books together and discussing the story and topics covered.*

*Spending time with [child], seeing him enjoy books so much . . .*

## Discussion

The results of the paired reading study were encouraging, demonstrating a marked increase in the reading age of the foster children who participated. On average, reading age improved by three months during each month that they participated in the project. Thus, in four months, each child made an average of one year's progress. Such findings meet both Brooks's (2007) and the Department for Education and Skills' (DfES, 2003b) criteria for effective literacy intervention. While it must be acknowledged that progress might not be expected to continue at this rate, the results suggest that paired reading offers a useful and effective short-burst intervention for enhancing the literacy of children in foster care.

The project was offered to all foster children, even good readers, as it was considered beneficial for all to spend time reading with their carers regardless of reading ability. Perhaps unsurprisingly, poorer readers showed the greatest gains in reading age. This finding may in part be driven by a ceiling effect – those children with good initial literacy skills had less "room for improvement", and so might not be expected to show such dramatic increases in reading. Nevertheless, while poor readers showed particularly impressive gains, even those with an initial reading age above their chronological age showed an average gain of nearly double the length of the intervention. Additionally, feedback from carers suggested that the impact of the project may extend beyond literacy skills alone, and have a positive benefit on the child's confidence and enthusiasm for reading, as well as the relationship between carer and child. This suggests that all readers – even good ones – may have something to gain from taking part in such a project.

## Impact on literacy skills

It is important to view these findings in context; looked after children often come from backgrounds of abuse or neglect (DCSF, 2009a), are likely to have experienced turbulence in their home and school placements (Fletcher-Campbell and Archer, 2003) and may lack consistent adult support in their education (Jackson, 1998b; Sinclair, 1998), all of which are likely to have affected their educational achievement. It is therefore extremely heartening to see that a short-term intervention such as paired reading can have a significant effect on these children's reading ability and development beyond reading *per se*.

The rationale behind the study was that looked after children often lack a key adult who will take an interest in and support their education (Barnardo's, 1996; Jackson, 1998b; Sinclair, 1998; Harker *et al*, 2003). The fact that the results show that carer support can have a considerable impact on these children's reading ability is important because it suggests that the negative effect of certain factors such as past trauma and changes in school and home placements on educational progress can be ameliorated with carer support. The current study focused on primary-aged children, but future work is planned to examine the impact of paired reading on those of secondary-school age. Older children are most likely to suffer from the care experience, simply by way of the fact that they are likely to have spent more time in care (Jackson, 1994), and so carer involvement may be all the more important for them.

## Impact on other areas

A by-product of the paired reading work was that it facilitated links between carers, teachers and social workers. Social workers attended training sessions with carers, and teachers liaised with carers to complete the weekly monitoring sheets. Thus, such work offers a useful way of raising the profile of educational achievement of looked after children, at the same time encouraging the key adults in these children's lives to work together to support them. Additionally, the results reinforce the need to encourage foster carers (and social workers) to value education and support their child with this.

The improvements found in reading are particularly important given that early interest and ability in reading have been associated with positive outcomes later in life (Jackson, 1987; 1994). The feedback from carers certainly indicated that the benefits of the project extended beyond reading ability. Carers commented on increases in their child's confidence and motivation when reading, as well as their own enjoyment at being able to share one-to-one time with their child. Such comments raise two important issues. First, perceived changes in the children's reading confidence suggest that, in addition to improvements in reading ability, the children's self-esteem and motivation for learning may also have improved. This in itself may have important implications for other areas of learning. Second, the quality time shared between carers and children during the paired reading may have additional benefits. One possibility is that this shared time might lead to a closer relationship between the child and carer, and ultimately a better and more stable placement.

Plans are currently underway to examine these issues more extensively. The paired reading project is being rolled out across more schools in the authority and additional measures are being collected with a view to probing the wider-reaching consequences of the project – in particular, the impact on the children's views of themselves as learners and on carers' views of their relationship with their child. Additionally, future work aims to examine National Curriculum levels at the end of Key Stage 2 for those children who took part in the project, with a view to establishing a potential link between participation in paired reading and other academic achievement. Such work will help to ascertain the impact of paired reading on other areas, outside of literacy *per se*.

## Limitations of the findings

While the results of the current study are encouraging, it is important to acknowledge the limitations of the findings. First, although very good progress was made by those children who completed the intervention, the mean reading age of most still lagged behind their chronological age at the end of the study. This raises the question as to whether continuation of the project beyond 16 weeks might offer an even greater benefit, and potentially allow these children to "catch up" with their peers. A useful avenue for future research might be to extend the length of the current study, in order to see whether the improvements observed continue with further input. Equally, a follow-up study of the current cohort would show whether the present improvements were maintained, or indeed extended, following cessation of the project.

A second issue is that a number of schools did not return evaluation data. While such difficulties are common in most research studies, it may be that the particular nature of these children's lives exacerbated the problem in this instance. Indeed, a number of schools reported that children taking part had either moved school or carer, preventing the intervention from continuing. In some circumstances, schools made concerted efforts to liaise with new carers, with a view to continuing the project. Often, however, the intervention simply ceased. Consequently, the results of this study are based only on those children who completed the whole intervention and whose school returned their evaluation data.

Although beyond the scope of the current study, in future it would be worthwhile to examine the specific factors involved in preventing some children from finishing the paired reading intervention and, conversely, the factors which enable other children and carers to complete it. In particular, it would be helpful to gather further data concerning the experiences of carers during the course of the intervention – for example, what they found to be helpful or worked particularly well, and vice-versa. This would serve two purposes: it would allow additional support to be offered to future participants, with a view to reducing drop-out during the course of the intervention; and it would allow consideration of the factors that are associated with the best outcomes on the project. Together, these would provide valuable information on when paired reading is most likely to be followed through by carers and children, and also when it is likely to work especially well.

It is important to express some caution here, however, and acknowledge that paired reading may not be a singular process and what "works well" may vary from participant to participant. As Topping (1997) suggests, the intervention may offer a number of pathways to improving reading, such that 'different components of the technique might be most potent for different subjects, reducing the probability of finding a few process factors which are omnipotent for all' (p 84). This suggests that trying to attribute particular actions to particular outcomes on the project might not be the best approach, for as Topping argues, 'it would be naïve to seek a uniformly and ubiquitously "best" technique' (p 84). Instead, it may be more appropriate to consider the practical issues faced by carers and how these were overcome, with a view to using these insights to guide future participants in the project on how best to approach paired reading with their child.

## Conclusions

In summary, the paired reading project revealed a positive impact on the literacy skills of the children who took part. Such work is in its infancy, and it is hoped that follow-up research will provide further understanding of the impact of this work in supporting looked after children. Critically, the current work serves to highlight that poor educational progress in looked after children is not inevitable. With focused support from all those involved in supporting these children, substantial improvements can be observed. Such findings are encouraging and offer a useful way for schools, carers, social workers and educational psychology services to support children in foster care.[12]

---

12 Editor's note: BAAF's training guide, *Supporting Children's Learning: A training programme for foster carers* (Pallett *et al*, 2010) includes two sessions on paired reading which is also demonstrated in the accompanying DVD.

**PART 3**

**THE SCHOOL EXPERIENCE**

## 10  Is inclusion always best for young people in care? A view from the classroom

*Maria Poyser*

*Maria Poyser grew up in care but went on to qualify as a teacher and be awarded a PhD for her research comparing the education of children in care in Canada and the UK. In this chapter she questions whether the prevailing ethos of inclusion is always the best option for looked after children with social, emotional and behavioural problems.*

### Introduction

The proportion of looked after children who are identified as having special educational needs (SEN) has remained remarkably constant at around 27 per cent over many years. SEN covers a number of different conditions but in the past it has been assumed that children with this label have little chance of educational achievement. In this chapter, based on my experience as a teacher and parent as well as many years of research, I want to challenge this assumption and look at how far the educational settings offered to such children provide opportunities to overcome difficulties or simply compound them. Are their real needs being recognised or addressed?

In secondary schools within the UK children with social, emotional and behavioural difficulties (SEBD) represent the largest proportion of children with SEN. Fifty per cent of children and young people in some socio-economically disadvantaged populations have speech and language skills that are significantly below  those of others of the same age (Bercow, 2008; Ripley and Yuill, 2005). These are often the populations from which young people in the care system are drawn (Berridge *et al*, 2008). A disproportionate number of looked after young people and young people with SEN end up in pupil referral units (PRUs). Usually they have been excluded from schools, but not always for disruptive behaviour. Among the 13,000 pupils attending PRUs, a high proportion suffer from a range of psychological problems such as panic attacks, school phobia, depression, obsessive compulsive disorders and substance misuse (Thambirajah *et al*, 2008). Some also cater for pregnant schoolgirls and school-aged mothers, among whom young people in care are greatly over-represented. The fact that being taken into care is a deeply traumatic experience in itself is seldom taken into account (Reimer, 2010; Ashcroft, 2013).

According to Steve Howell's review for the National Children's Bureau, most studies of PRUs are highly critical. One report described them as 'overstretched, underfunded dumping grounds for difficult pupils unwanted elsewhere' (Howell, 2011). There are too few teachers in PRUs equipped to provide the 'imaginative and personalised curriculum' that might re-engage disaffected young people in learning. Almost all studies reported on the failure to address the severe mental health needs of young people attending such units, with the few units rated by Ofsted as good or outstanding characterised by staff trained and skilled in the use of education as a therapeutic tool. Finney (2009) pointed out that specialist mental health services such as CAMHS (Child and Adolescent Mental Health Services) cannot hope to meet the scale of need and that mental health training for teaching staff is therefore essential.

## Getting stuck

I have spent most of my 17-year teaching career in SEN and the last six years in pupil referral units. The formal aim of PRUs is to reintegrate the young people into a mainstream setting, although there appear to be no statistics on how often they are successful. Alternatively, they may contribute to an assessment to obtain a Statement of SEN and a placement in a special school. But what often happens is that the young people get stuck in a bottleneck.

In the units where I worked there were some pupils who only stayed six to eight weeks and were quickly found a new school. This tended to be where the exclusion had been a one-off incident and their behaviour at the PRU had been exemplary. Others had had a double permanent exclusion. In other words, they had been to the PRU once before, had been reintegrated and then bounced back. These were often looked after children or sometimes "children in need", on the brink of care proceedings. A PRU is supposed to be a temporary expedient, but one boy I taught remained there for most of Key Stage 2 and was still at the unit in Year 7 before the local authority finally decided that the only way forward was to allow Statutory Assessment, so that he could go to a special school with a package of support. If that had been provided earlier he might have gone to a mainstream secondary school, been educated along with other children and received an education in line with his considerable ability, being quite capable of passing GCSEs. Another looked after child had entered the PRU in Year 7 and was still there in Year 9.

The reality of PRUs is that they do not prepare a child for reintegration, either socially or educationally. The young person does not arrive at the unit until 9.15am at the earliest. A mainstream school usually starts soon after 8.30. The PRU finishes at 2pm compared with around 3.30pm. Most PRUs only teach core subjects and lessons are in the morning, with the afternoons being taken up by enrichment activities such as swimming, horse-riding, go-karting, drumming, etc. In a mainstream setting a pupil is expected in lessons all day, every day. So for a young person who has spent any length of time in a PRU, returning to mainstream education can be a cultural shock, particularly if they never made the transition from primary to secondary school in the first place. At Key Stages 2 and 3, the staffing and numbers equate to those of a special school, with generally no more than six to eight pupils in a classroom with a teacher and teaching assistant in each. It is not surprising then, that attempts at return to mainstream are so often unsuccessful. At Key Stage 4 the majority are sent to "alternative provision" with no hope once there of gaining any meaningful qualifications.

## Can inclusion work for all?

So should all children in care be educated in a mainstream setting? Should social workers and carers be fighting much harder against the decision to consign them to pupil referral units, alternative provision and special schools? Many people would say yes (Mittler, 2000). Each case needs to be assessed, as with any child, on its own merits. But my own view is that a blanket policy in favour of inclusion is at best misguided; at worst it is an immoral and ineffectual cost-cutting exercise. The majority of looked after children can cope with and benefit from inclusion. But there are also many for whom it is inappropriate. Some people argue that every child should have access to the same curriculum, should have the chance to take public examinations and gain qualifications that will fit them either for further and higher education or the world of work. But a looked after child with special needs for emotional or behavioural reasons, who has gained some GCSE grades, won't necessarily be more employable as a result. Many looked after children have disabling difficulties with social interaction and, as already mentioned, poor language and communication skills. They need highly skilled help and intensive support if they are to benefit from formal education.

I have come across many bright young people within mainstream schools who spend their school days acting out their distress at being in care and end up refusing to go to school altogether. They spend their time truanting, hanging out with undesirable companions, or isolated in their residential care home, glued to their computer or iPhone. Social difficulties make the looked after child more vulnerable to bullying at school, particularly if previous "friends" know they no longer live at home. I have heard one child say to another, 'At least my mum wants me.' Looked after children are easy targets because they are often alone and unlikely to seek help. They may not necessarily identify bullying for what it is – when you have been abused, when you have never learned the norms, you sometimes fail to recognise behaviour that is unacceptable by ordinary standards.

## The problem of large schools

The typical secondary school can be a challenging environment even for children without the many additional problems faced by children in care. Mary Warnock (2005, pp 49–50) wrote: '. . . in a small school there is the possibility of real, experienced inclusion . . . Pupils know and are known to their teachers . . . Pupils can identify with and take pride in their school.' Similarly, James Wetz, formerly a comprehensive school head teacher, has argued strongly for "human-scale education" (Wetz, 2009). Children in care need to be guided and supported in the development of their social skills by patient and experienced adults who know them well. They need understanding, not blunt instruments like punishments and sanctions if they are to move on. Their needs are unlikely to be met in the anonymous environment of a large comprehensive school where the staff see hundreds of different children every week.

At the time of writing, I am managing a student referral centre where all the young people have been on School Action Plus with the major "special need" being identified as SEBD. The centre was set up for a core group of children who experienced a range of difficulties, whether or not they had a psychiatric label like ADHD or Attachment Disorder. The pupils who come to our unit have often chosen not to subscribe to the social norms demanded by society, and those who are looked after often cast themselves adrift at 14 or 15. For many looked after young people their life paths will have been punctuated by unhappiness and depression, and a sense of not quite fitting in wherever they may happen to be. For others, disengagement from education will have led to social marginalisation and offending, leading to a bleak path through the youth justice system, painfully described by Ben Ashcroft in his book, *Fifty-one Moves* (2013).

Currently in our unit is a boy of 11 who had tremendous difficulties adjusting to Academy life after leaving primary school. He erupted at the slightest comment, misinterpreted innocent remarks made by fellow pupils, shouted at rather than spoke to staff. The school was soon facing the possibility of permanent exclusion because his behaviour was so challenging, erratic and bizarre. Within just a few weeks of entering Year 7, he had exhausted all of the school's sanctions and the internal Learning Support Unit staff and so was sent to our external centre. As with many of the young people who pass through our centre, there may be little we can do to change the child, or the life circumstances that made him or her what they are. But sometimes, even if just for a short while, a child needs a safe environment, such as we provide, in order to build a level of resilience that will later allow them to engage with others in a mutually beneficial way and to leave the centre behind.

I often recognise in a looked after child a young person who is living in a hostile world which they cannot begin to apprehend. They are removed from a home life, which wasn't safe but at least was familiar, and then taken away by adults to a place and people they do not know. The adults around make huge assumptions that they understand what has happened and why the young person has been taken into care and all the negotiations, care reviews and interactions with social workers that occur afterwards. We then have the audacity to make moral judgements about their presenting behaviour, when instead we need to develop the analytical skills to explain why things went wrong and how we might set the child on a more promising pathway.

## Providing a supportive environment

In time, and after many ups and downs, things do settle and episodes of difficult behaviour, often provoked by a stressful event such as contact with parents, become less frequent. It is important for a school to liaise closely with social care in order to know when this type of event is happening so that key staff can support the child. Often a looked after child's future in a school continually hangs by a thread. Such children tend to straddle the gap between "normal" schooling and the need for more specialised provision. The average teacher usually does not possess the knowledge and skills fully to understand the difficulties such a child is facing since their training does not include learning about the care system (see Chapter 11).

For mainstream schools to work for looked after children it is the education system and not just the children that has to change. Teachers have to alter their perceptions and abandon the deficit model of the challenging learner. Schools need staff who have the insight to discern patterns in children's behaviour. They must be skilled and knowledgeable, but also willing to embark upon a significant reassessment of their own ingrained attitudes towards difficult pupils and behaviour in general. They have to offer unconditional support no matter how remote and unwelcoming the child may be, and in turn be given the same level of support by those in positions of higher authority within the school.

Many problems could be avoided by earlier intervention, for example, ensuring that young children in care and on the margins of care access good-quality pre-school education (Nutbrown and Clough, 2013). Admission to care should be recognised as a traumatic experience, to be addressed by provision of therapy and/or counselling at the earliest opportunity.

After pre-school and primary, the looked after group most poorly catered for by our education system is the academically able teenagers. Most special schools cannot provide a high enough level of academic teaching; most mainstream schools cannot offer enough social education and pastoral support. Our school's answer to this problem is the offsite student referral centre which provides a secure, supportive environment where one-to-one help can fill the gaps in social and other important life skills. Because the child is still on the school's roll, there is a greater chance of reintegration when he or she is ready as it avoids them being formally excluded and placed in a PRU with no hope of return. It is a therapeutic environment in which individual resilience can be enhanced and learning promoted. Effective learning requires confidence in who one is and where one is going. It means being prepared to take risks and sometimes to fail. Many looked after children are afraid to learn in case they fail. Fear underlies much of the challenging behaviour that characterises the looked after child.

We try to provide an environment in which children who would otherwise have been excluded can grow and develop as individuals. We do not shirk our responsibilities to challenge the young people, but do so with the skills needed when addressing the complex problems they bring with them. We try to ensure they are fully prepared for their return to the main site, however long that takes. The irony of school for many looked after young people is that emotionally they reach leaving-school age just as, in some senses, they are ready to begin their education.

## Conclusion

To sum up, the Government should greatly increase the amount of training on offer with regard to pupils with emotional and behavioural difficulties – for all teachers, not just specialists. For children in care or on the edge of care, it should invest in early intervention programmes. Pre-school places should be a priority, not an afterthought. Therapeutic support needs to be provided to a child taken into care in the same way as physiotherapy is given following a traumatic physical injury.

After working with children with emotional and behavioural difficulties for most of my teaching career, I have concluded that inclusion should be regarded as a goal for the majority rather than a dogma. Inclusive societies are healthier and more humane than those that discriminate against difference and disability, but we should also recognise that we have yet to arrive at a definitive ideal for what the inclusive school system ought to provide.

A great deal can be achieved in mainstream schools. They can employ staff with special skills and expertise for meeting special educational needs and specific learning difficulties, and they can liaise with other institutions that embody such expertise. But what they cannot do is offer the range of experiences that many vulnerable young people require for the full development of their capacities, and in particular, for the looked after child, their sense of self. Laudable as the drive towards full inclusion may be, the time has not yet come when the special schools should close their doors. Too many vulnerable children are still ending up consigned to a PRU due to the refusal of local authorities to issue Statements of SEN, priding themselves on being a "low statementing authority", while cynically allowing children to remain out of sight and out of mind, sometimes for most of their school career.

Badly handled, looked after children suffer infinite stress and depression, which contribute to low educational attainment and may leave them with mental health problems for the rest of their lives. It does not have to be this way, but to get things right requires time, effort, money and recognition that the term "looked after" should mean just that, instead of being the gross misnomer that it too often is.

## 11  In Care, In school: giving voice to children and young people in care

*Richard Parker and Michael Gorman*

*School is enormously important in the lives of children in care. It can be a haven or a place where they suffer further rejection and discrimination. This chapter describes a highly innovative collaboration between a university and a "virtual school" which engaged the local In Care Council to tackle the issue from the school side, designing materials to inform and change attitudes among schoolchildren, teachers and education students.*

## Background

The In Care, In School project originated from a conversation between Mike Gorman, Head of the Virtual School in Bath and North East Somerset (B&NES), and Richard Parker of Bath Spa University. The B&NES In Care Council (ICC) had told Mike that the greatest barrier they faced at school was a lack of understanding from other pupils and teachers, while Mike, as a former secondary school head teacher, was concerned at the lack of training available to help teachers understand the care system and learn about children and young people who are looked after away from home.

---

**The virtual school head (VSH)**

The role of the VSH is to support and improve the educational attainment of children and young people in care as if they attended a single school. The idea was first introduced in the Labour Government's White Paper *Care Matters: Time for change* (DCSF, 2007). A pilot scheme took place in 11 local authorities between 2007 and 2009 and was positively evaluated (Berridge *et al*, 2009). Following a report in September 2012 from the All Party Parliamentary Group on Looked after Children and Care Leavers (APPG, 2012), and an Ofsted (2012a) evaluation the following month, the present Government is legislating in the Children and Families Bill to make the post of VSH statutory for all local authorities.

---

---

### In Care Councils (ICCs)

ICCs were established following *Care Matters: Time for change* (DCSF, 2007), which set out an expectation for 'every local authority to put in place arrangements for a "Children in Care Council", with direct links to the Director of Children's Services and Lead Member. This will give children in care a forum to express their views and influence the services and support they receive.' Although this was never made a statutory requirement, ministers of all political parties have made clear their commitment to ICCs and the Department for Education (DfE) continues to publish a national newsletter on their behalf. A study undertaken on behalf of the DfE in 2011 found that 147 of 150 responding local authorities, or 97 per cent, had a functioning ICC by March 2011.

---

We consulted with a number of national organisations, including the British Association for Adoption and Fostering (BAAF) and the Who Cares? Trust, who confirmed that the gulf in understanding between social care and schools continues to present a major problem. In consultation with the ICC we began to develop two projects, one geared towards teacher awareness-raising and the other to develop Personal Social and Health Education (PSHE) materials and approaches for Year 9 secondary pupils.

As we developed our ideas, several key points became apparent. First, we needed to consider how we could influence attitudes and behaviours at a much earlier stage – in the primary school. Second, we realised that we had drawn a false distinction between teacher education and PSHE teaching. We needed to develop programmes of teacher training in order to use the materials effectively in the classroom; at the same time we could use those materials to promote teacher awareness of the issues involved.

Third, we needed to establish what sort of materials and classroom approaches we were promoting and what role members of the ICC could play. Should we, for example, develop a programme of visits for individual members to schools, supported by student peer mentors and an advocacy development programme for ICC members, or should we concentrate on developing stand-alone materials that could be used in any classroom?

Some core principles began to emerge. The main points were:

- The ICC should agree and determine the pace and direction of the project.
- The project should inform and involve as many children and young people in care as possible.
- Any materials/classroom approaches should avoid sensationalism and be rooted in children's and young people's everyday experience of school.
- The project should involve the next generation of those working with children and young people – students at all levels.

- The project should validate and accredit the contribution of individual ICC members
- The materials and classroom approaches must be useable within schools and designed to hold all pupils' interest.

## Partnership and governance

We clearly needed to establish a broad-based partnership to develop this work and each partner brought something different to the table. Alongside the ICC and the virtual school, colleagues from the Bath Spa University Widening Participation team had been awarded the Buttle UK Quality Mark[13] in 2010, and led the Aim Higher programmes for care leavers on behalf of the West Universities Consortium (Goldsworthy, 2012). The PGCE team were keen to promote, pilot and evaluate the project as part of student placements.

We established a steering group with representatives from all partners, reporting directly both to the Bath Spa School of Education Board and to the ICC. These partners included: the Who Cares? Trust, which brought expertise and experience of developing materials with young people in care; VisionWorks, an organisation with considerable experience in developing effective PSHE materials in local schools; and the National PSHE Association, which provided curriculum and teacher professional development perspectives. ASDAN (formerly the Awards Schemes Development Accreditation Network) brought not only curriculum expertise and national distribution networks, but also a qualifications framework that could recognise and accredit the personal development of the young people from the ICC and those using the curriculum materials in schools. The local teacher associations, represented by the National Union of Teachers (NUT), were highly enthusiastic about the project and provided much-appreciated reality checks as to the type of materials and support hard-pressed teachers might find useful, as well as an opportunity to showcase the work at their annual conference.

## Developing the project

Following protracted discussions, it was agreed that the initial aim of the project would be to produce a number of short film scenarios based directly on the experiences of ICC members. A professional film company was commissioned to undertake the filming and write the scripts, using professional and child actors, with classroom materials and teachers' guidance being produced by project team members. Funding for the filming was provided by a special B&NES Council Cabinet grant.

---

13  The Buttle UK Quality Mark is awarded to further and higher education providers that demonstrate their commitment to young people in and leaving care. It provides a framework for validating the quality of support the institution offers, and a basis for the assessment of retention and progression strategies, as well as encouraging young people from care to apply to these establishments. By 1 May 2013, 88 universities and 47 colleges had achieved the required standard.

The ICC was involved at every stage, drafting the scenarios in a closed session with only one adult facilitator present. Members were involved in interviewing four different film companies and made the final recommendation on selection to the project group. Individual members spent a day with the scriptwriter, again in a closed session, were involved in auditioning the actors and worked with the director over the two days of filming. We saw it as an important point of principle that the Council had first sight of the draft lesson plans and teachers' notes, and although they did not wish to go through them in detail, members did ask for an opportunity to observe them being used in the classroom.

The films themselves comprise 10 brief (1–2 minute) everyday scenarios – five primary and five secondary – based on the experiences of ICC members and illustrating different interactions that might happen in a school: pupil/pupil, pupil/teacher/other staff, inside and outside the classroom. They were deliberately left open-ended to encourage viewers to discuss possible motivations, outcomes and the issues involved.

By coincidence, an Ofsted inspection of B&NES services for looked after children took place soon after the films had been produced and several inspectors watched them as part of their meeting with the ICC. Their conclusions were:

> Looked after children have made an excellent contribution to the development of high-quality education materials for use in personal, health and social education programmes in schools across the authority and further afield. These materials include a DVD which is based on the experiences of children in care which are poignantly and powerfully re-told in a series of scenarios using professional actors. The DVD is designed to promote awareness of what life is like for looked after children and young people growing up in B&NES. (Ofsted, 2012b, p 33)

In addition to the lesson plans and classroom activities for each of the 10 scenarios, a background briefing sheet for teachers was produced, alongside two generic lesson plans, which could be modified for different age ranges. These were designed to promote discussion of different family arrangements, cover the factual background to being in care and to develop empathetic responses using poetry and other media. The films and lesson plans were piloted by experienced teachers in a primary, a secondary and a special school, and ICC members participated in the feedback sessions with the pilot schools.

All 420 Bath Spa PGCE students were briefed on the project and given access to the materials. Fifty-eight students volunteered to pilot the materials as part of their second placement and Council members were directly involved in their training. The materials were also used for teaching purposes with several undergraduate Education Studies programmes on inclusion and on multi-agency working, and again ICC members were directly involved in lectures and seminars. Members attended a number of conferences, including the NUT Easter conference, and met with other ICCs to discuss and showcase their work.

## Expanding and building on project activities

Evaluations undertaken by the PGCE students complemented the feedback from the pilot schools, confirming the effectiveness of the materials in the classroom but also the need to provide suitable training resources and support for teachers. At the same time, we became aware of a need to address some of the broader issues thrown up by the work, in particular the experience of those in care beyond the age of 16, in terms of sixth-form or further education college provision, independent living, access to careers advice and to higher education.

For these reasons we commissioned the same film company, again funded by a B&NES Council grant, to develop materials. This time, following discussions with the ICC, we asked a number of individual Council members and care leavers simply to talk about their experiences and aspirations. These were then edited into three four-minute films covering the young people's experiences of education, post-16 pathway planning and "what they did next". We also made a film about "why we made this film". While the primary audience for these films was intended to be adult professionals, especially teachers, the group writing the classroom materials did also produce outline lesson plans for older secondary students.

A further aim was to produce an accreditation framework for the young people involved and also to support the use of the materials in schools. Although our original idea of accrediting individual ICC members efforts via the ASDAN Peer Mentoring framework proved impractical, those who took part each received a formal certificate recording their involvement. Another scheme is currently being developed, building on informal relationships with other ICCs, to produce a "how to" guide to help other councils in developing their own empowerment schemes. ASDAN has also provided a qualifica-tion framework for both primary ("Stepping Stones") and secondary (Certificate of Personal Effectiveness – CoPE) schools, which is included in the teachers' pack.

Developing a training framework for teachers opened up other opportunities. A simple six-point training plan was devised, based on the detailed feedback from pilot schools and the PGCE students, and using the existing classroom materials and films, including the new post-16 elements. At the same time, a new project was established, involving colleagues from B&NES Education, Psychology, Early Years and Play services, with input from other specialist agencies, to develop attachment awareness across all schools in the authority.

## Producing the packs

Translating a series of films, lesson plans and background briefings into a commercially viable package proved very challenging. Our initial intention had been to seek sponsorship to distribute the packs free of charge to every school in the country, but this was rejected by the project group. Former head teachers suggested that a "free" pack would be viewed with suspicion and not be valued by schools, while ICC representatives were keen to recoup some costs to ensure that project development would continue. Bath Spa University commissioned a design team to work with the editorial group and the film company, while a website was established to publicise the project, act as a point of sale, and eventually to enable materials to be downloaded. We worked with our partners in the Who Cares? Trust to check the accuracy of our background materials and to establish an effective distribution mechanism for sales. Following considerable discussion within the project group, a DVDRom format, including films and text, was agreed for commercial sales; the text files were to be available as a free download from the website, with a charge for downloading video files.

The project received a considerable boost from the agreement by Baroness Walmsley, a strong supporter of ASDAN, to host a launch in the House of Lords as part of National Care Leavers' Week 2012. The project had already received a strong endorsement from the new Minister for Children, Edward Timpson MP, in his previous role as Chair of the All Party Parliamentary Group (APPG) on Looked After Children and Care Leavers, and from his predecessor, Tim Loughton MP. This was followed by a local launch, hosted by the Chair of B&NES Council, with some highly positive press and television coverage. The project was shortlisted for the 2012 Children and Young People Now Awards and two of the young people attended the formal presentation dinner at the Hurlingham Club on behalf of the group.

## What have we learned and what has been the impact on young people and others?

For the young people in care, the project has served to reinforce the status and importance of the ICC while the impact on their individual confidence, self-esteem and ability to present their views to a variety of audiences has been highly significant. These have ranged from other care councils, Bath Spa students, representatives of national organisations, leading local councillors, the Vice Chancellor of Bath Spa University, members of parliament and NUT delegates. In this latter case it was noticeable how several teachers were actually reversing roles and calling upon the ICC members to provide advice on how they should approach specific issues. This reflects the way in which children in care gained status from becoming the "experts" in a number of primary pilot schools. Given the relatively low base of self-confidence from which many young people start, having been let down by families and very often care professionals at several points in their lives, this recognition of their expertise was extremely important. As one member told a group of undergraduate students:

> We talked about these ideas for ages at the In Care Council, and now here I am talking to you guys. It's unbelievable.

One very positive feature of the project was the maturity of the ICC's decision-making processes, despite some variation in attendance that occasionally necessitated going over old ground. At one point we had encountered frustrating delays in getting the film commissioning process started, which in many adult groups would have led to bitter recriminations and blaming, but the Council merely expressed gratitude to us for our efforts and their confidence that we would resolve the issues.

Another impact has been on young people in general. In several primary schools where the materials were piloted, children in care gained considerable kudos by explaining care issues to their peers; one even brought in a photograph of her foster family. Several PGCE students reported similar responses:

> I asked the child in care if he minded me teaching this lesson . . . He was happy to remain in class. In fact he actively participated. This was really amazing; I thought he was really brave and what he said came over to the class a lot more powerfully than anything I did.

In the special school, which modified the age-related materials to better suit their pupils, the materials were seen as valuable but some concern was expressed by one highly experienced teacher as to how to involve those in care, who were in greater proportion than in other schools:

> All of these children have stories of their own, which after years of working with staff at the school they choose to tell in their own way and in their own time. The school has worked hard to help other pupils understand their positions and vulnerabilities and I think has done a good job. It is an important part of the recovery process.

> I understand that these videos are an attempt to give a tool to further this work. However, I think to show these videos in my class would be asking the most vulnerable children to talk about issues when they have not chosen the method, the content, the time, the audience or the place. And if they did not choose to speak, it would be asking them to listen to other children talking, which is the wrong way round. I think it is the teacher's job to inform other children of such issues and talk with awareness and deal with the situations that are brought up in the video.

> . . . I do, however, think the videos could be a useful tool for educating teachers.

Similar reservations were expressed by secondary-aged members of another ICC, and one student in a mainstream primary school did report an issue of flippant comments, which he felt might have upset more sensitive children. However, in another mainstream primary school, one PGCE student commented:

> Surprisingly, those children [in care] were not reluctant to talk about the issues with

*this film, nor withdrawn from any part of our discussion; if anything, it was more a question of my own confidence to explore the project without upsetting these children.*

On the whole, those using the materials both in and out of school described them as having a positive impact on students, although a more detailed and longer-term quantitative approach would be desirable to draw firm conclusions. Comments from one primary class included:

*I didn't know that much about care but now I have had the lesson I know more!*

*This lesson changed the way I feel about children in care.*

*This lesson really helped me to not be mean to people in care and that we should treat them like us.*

*I think bad rumours shouldn't be passed around about other people.*

*This made me think more deeply about people in care.*

*I understand how hard it is for people in care now.*

A further key group has been teachers. Despite the generally positive reception given to the films and lesson plans, there was a degree of resistance, even in the pilot schools. This included concerns about the impact on individual children in care and quibbles about lesson plan details as against the overall approach; for example, a science teacher stated, just before a planned PSHE session, that he could not deliver any of the lesson because did not know what a haiku was (composing a haiku was one of the suggested follow-up activities). There were also concerns that some of the scenarios gave too negative an impression of teachers. In this particular school, the local authority PSHE adviser subsequently worked directly with the staff group to model, support and deliver the lessons.

Some of this resistance was related to senior management attitudes in particular schools. One PGCE student was gently discouraged from actually trialling the materials in the classroom but asked to give a presentation to the management team instead. Conversely, where teams of teachers had seen the materials as having wider applicability to pastoral/PSHE themes, some highly creative approaches emerged, such as a large comprehensive school which adopted the materials for a whole term to support a "relationships" module in tutor time for all Year 8 pupils.

Discussions with wider groups of teachers at the NUT Conference appear to have identified a significant number of teachers with a strong desire to find ways of better supporting children and young people in care, linked to some innovative pastoral practice. For instance, another ICC piloting the approach is planning to use school-attached social workers as champions in disseminating the materials in individual schools. Again, it would be desirable to develop some measures as to the impact of the project on staff attitudes, school strategies and CPD programmes in individual schools.

In line with our aspiration to influence future generations of teachers, there have been impacts on both PGCE and Education Studies students. The engagement of both primary and secondary PGCE students in the briefing sessions, the enthusiastic response to the call for PGCE volunteers and the level of response from undergraduate students all suggest that the project has succeeded in raising awareness of the issues. One student concluded in her evaluation:

*Having had little knowledge of this area and its potential impact prior to this assignment, I am now much more aware of the issues and will strive to promote this project throughout my career, as the benefits are considerable, not only for LAC but for their peers and teachers in promoting compassionate and sensitive learners regardless of home life.*

## Where do we go next?

In the foreword to *In Care, In School* (2012) Naina Thomas of the ICC writes:

*From this pack I hope teachers can take a step back and start thinking about the young person's needs and feelings. I hope pupils will get a better understanding of something they might not fully understand. Overall, I would like my experiences to make a change within the schools, and to make people more aware about people in foster care.*

Our priority now is to get these materials used as widely as possible in schools, colleges and in initial teacher education, so much of our effort is going into publicity and marketing activities. As outlined above, we are also working with a broader range of colleagues in Bath and North East Somerset to develop our approach to attachment-aware schools, including a further set of film scenarios and training packages for teachers and children's services professionals. This project has achieved support from the National College for Teaching and Leadership, the Department for Education and a number of other virtual schools across the country, and we are now exploring the possibility of establishing a national quality standard for attachment aware schools. At the same time, members of the ICC are working with us on a support package for other such councils to help them get their views across in these and other areas.

We were considerably heartened by the publication of the All Party Parliamentary Group Report, *Education Matters in Care* (APPG, 2012). We had already begun discussions with existing foster care partners as to how we might develop the In Care, In School materials to support foster carers in becoming more effectively involved in children's education, including developing proposals for a Foundation Degree for foster carers. We also jointly hosted the 2013 National Virtual School Head Teachers' Conference at the university, which gave us the opportunity to discuss the implications and challenges of their proposed new statutory role with over a hundred virtual head teachers and a range of national experts, including Maggie Atkinson, the Children's Commissioner.

Finally, the profile of the In Care, In School project has highlighted the importance of the Widening Participation agenda for care leavers at Bath Spa. One of the young people involved in the post-16 films recently graduated from the university with the prize for Excellence in Fine Art Development, and the project is working with the student services team and a wider group of universities, both locally and across the country, to publicise the range of opportunities available for young people in care, along the lines of the Liverpool University "Superstars" programme[14] – which actually uses the In Care, In School materials to train its undergraduate mentors.

## Conclusion

We believe that this project has demonstrated a way in which, with appropriate support and modest additional resources, young people in care and care leavers can have an impact on their peers, teachers, future teachers and other professionals. We believe that the model is replicable and can be used to support other groups of children and young people in care in getting their views heard.

We can see that this approach has had measurable impacts on building the self-confidence and ability of individual members of the ICC to communicate with and to act as advocates for other looked after children. It has further enhanced the status of the ICC itself, by enabling it to demonstrate its impact to significant adults such as senior administrators, elected members and members of parliament.

Thirdly, the initial evaluations indicate that the project has impacted on classroom practice in schools, with some anecdotal evidence of improved relationships between pupils (Streeter, 2012). In some schools the project has enabled children in care to act as experts and lead lessons.

There has been a variable response from teachers, some of whom have responded enthusiastically to the materials and engaged with individual young people in care as potential experts. However, others have been more reluctant, partly from a fear of losing control in this very specialist area, but also because of the emotional and personal challenges that the subject matter has entailed.

Similar responses have been observed from school managers. Where the approach has been supported by the senior management team, the types of classroom outcomes and

---

14 See www.liv.ac.uk/educational-opportunities/superstars/index.htm.

involvement of young people in care outlined above have been observed and appropriate support given to staff expressing reservations. However, other management teams have been more resistant.

The project has also had a powerful impact on Bath Spa students, both at undergraduate and PGCE level. There has been an important interaction between this awareness-raising and the involvement of ICC members. There is scope for further development of the existing relationships between the project and access work with care leavers, as well as significant potential for expanding the project into other areas, such as attachment awareness in schools, working with virtual schools, and supporting and accrediting foster carers in engaging with their children's education.

We believe that In Care, In School has enabled a particular group of children and young people in care to have an effective voice, and to increase awareness of their particular issues among schools, teachers, trainee teachers and other professionals. The materials produced stand by themselves, but are influencing a wider range of initiatives. We also feel that we have developed a way of working that can be used by other ICCs in promoting their aims. However, we recognise that there is much more to do if we are to have a lasting impact on the education of children and young people in care.

### *Acknowledgements*
We would like in particular to thank all the members of the In Care, In School Project Group for their unstinting enthusiasm and ability to meet impossible deadlines. We are also hugely grateful to our colleagues and senior managers at B&NES Council and Bath Spa University for their moral and financial support, especially the special grant from B&NES Cabinet that enabled the initial films to be made. We would like to thank Corsham primary and secondary schools for providing authentic film locations, our three pilot schools, Wellsway, Three Ways and St Mary's Timsbury, and the 58 Bath Spa PGCE students who trialled the classroom materials. We are grateful to Baroness Joan Walmsley, Francis, Earl of Listowel, Tim Loughton MP, Edward Timpson MP and Don Foster MP, Michael Allured at DfE and Sue Egersdorff at the National College for Teaching and Leadership for publicising our work. We would also like to thank all those schools and other organisations who are using the pack and have given us feedback on it. Most important of all, we would like to thank Adam, Ashley, Dan, Emma, Kelvin, Naina, Nicolette, Rosie and Sophie, who were willing to share their own life stories so that others would be listened to in the future.

## 12  The effects of trauma on children's learning

*Kate Cairns*

*The intense stress of attachment deprivation, abuse and other childhood traumas causes brain and body injuries, which in turn give rise to physical, emotional, cognitive and behavioural signs and indicators of distress. Children can present difficulties that perplex and frustrate teachers and carers. Knowing about trauma does not solve the problems, but it does provide a robust theoretical model from which to develop more effective and appropriate ways of living and working with children who have suffered such harm. This is a revised version of a chapter first published in* Nobody Ever Told Us School Mattered *(Jackson, 2001).*

## First thoughts: a day in foster care

### A fictional account based on real experiences across 40 years of living and working with children

For children who suffer the disorders which follow infant and childhood trauma, nothing, absolutely nothing, is easy or straightforward. Today breakfast has come and gone and he has not appeared. Yesterday, our day of rest, he arrived in our room at 5am with mugs of coffee. 'I wanted to do something for you. Aren't you pleased?'

Struggling to sit up in bed, I remember when we used to sleep naked, limb against limb, the friendliness of it. Those days ended with fostering, which could be sponsored by the makers of flannelette nighties. Struggling, too, to find a calm voice, knowing he truly means well, has no access to the same basic understanding that most of us happily take for granted. 'It's a good thought, but we still need to sleep, Shane. You go back to bed, and we'll have a drink together later.'

Slam. Crash. Coffee and mugs meet wall and carpet. A meeting that will lead to a permanent relationship if I don't get up and do something about it. And I have to get him to help me, get him to stay connected and take responsibility for what he has done. At five o'clock in the morning. Please can I have an easier job in my next lifetime? Wrestling bears or breaking rocks come to mind.

This morning is a not-getting-up day, however. It is also a visit-from-my-social-worker and a finding-out-my-mum-still-doesn't-want-to-see-me day. Perhaps these things are connected. Tim offers to go and wake Shane. I think his usual method, as regularly applied to older brother David, of six ice cubes down the back of the neck, while effective, might not be quite what Shane needs today.

Stern compassion seems to be closer to the mark. 'Shane!' I yell from the bottom of the stairs, 'I've made your sandwiches, ironed your shirt, and if you're not up and about in five minutes there'll be consequences!' Sounds horrible, means nothing, and judged properly is nearly always effective. My father, a head teacher, used to threaten there would be 'blood on the moon', but I take after the less violent side of the family.

Brian puts his arms around me. 'Do I need to shout at him?' 'No, I think that will have done the trick,' I say, listening to the morning litany of swearwords moving towards the bathroom. 'Then I'll take the dog for a walk,' he says, matching the actions to the words as she enthusiastically endorses the idea. On a morning like this it would not do to leave Shane and the dog in the same space. He will fall over her, drop scalding tea on her, "accidentally" tread on her; in any case she will end up hurt and he will protest vigorously, and for all I know accurately, innocence of any intention to do harm.

David, ringing home at lunch time: 'There's been some sort of fight in the school yard. I think you might need to ring school and sort something out.' 'Do you know what's it about?' 'I think Shane might be in some sort of trouble.' Tactful, this one. Not about to drop anyone in anything they haven't stirred up for themselves.

I ring Janice, the school secretary, a regular contact after all these years. She won't make mountains out of molehills, I know I can trust her judgement. 'I'm glad you've rung. The head of year was wondering whether to bring you in or deal with it himself. I think he'd like you to come in.'

We meet in a classroom – the tutor, the head of year and Shane gathered around a table at the front of the room as I arrive. Shane is wearing his blank defiance look. Uh oh. This does not bode well. The story is that Shane has stolen a pencil case belonging to another boy. The boy demanded it back. Shane denied all knowledge of the theft, the pencil case and anything else relevant or irrelevant to the matter under discussion. A fight ensued.

Once the tutor became involved, he asked Shane to turn out the contents of his bag. There the missing pencil case was found. Shane, however, was adamant that the pencil case was his and that he had stolen nothing. Since the pencil case had the name of the other boy inside it as well as a dozen pens with his initials and a calculator with his name stamped on it, Shane's story sounds a little thin. Except that he is so convincingly certain that this pencil case belongs to him and so evidently bewildered that anyone else fails to believe him.

Thank goodness David rang me. The school staff, to their great credit, are patiently continuing to exercise reason and rationality with Shane. I know that they could do this forever and it will take them no further. I pick up the pencil case and look at Shane until I am sure he is making eye contact with me.

'Shane, this pencil belongs to . . .'; quick check inside to get my facts right. 'Daniel. It is blue. Your pencil case is red. Where is your red pencil case, Shane?'

'I think it's on my dressing table.'

'Right. You can put it in your bag tonight and make sure you have it for tomorrow. Now we'll give this one back to Daniel and you can say sorry. Then perhaps Mr Johnson will lend you a pen for today.'

I look at the teachers. They look surprised but seem prepared to go along with the solution. The "fight" was really a scuffle and no one has been hurt. Shane gives the pencil case back to Daniel and apologises so pleasantly that I should think I am the only one who knows he still has no real idea of what he's done.

Shane arrives home cheerful. 'Have you had a good day?' I ask, interested. 'Yeah, great. We watched a video in English.' He looks back at me with a face innocent of all guile. He genuinely has construed this as a good day and that is how he will remember it. We have some work to do on this – I make a mental note – but not right now.

His social worker is due to arrive at any moment. I suggest we put the kettle on to make tea and biscuits for him, and Shane takes up the task with enthusiasm. He likes seeing his social worker. This is one of his most successful and comfortable relationships. He is central to it and is clearly the focus of care and concern within it, yet it remains occasional and therefore superficial and, most importantly for Shane, it is a relationship in which his actions do not have evident consequences.

I am grateful for this on his behalf. Grateful, too, that here we have a local authority still able to provide some service to the children it looks after.

After they have gone off to the burger bar, or pizza palace, or wherever else is serving its turn as a social work office, the rest of us gather for the evening meal. These occasional breaks allow us to eat together without the continual jolting reminders of the painful gaps in Shane's understanding of the most basic things about the ways human beings relate to one another. He is intelligent and sensitive and loving. And at some very early stage of his development he missed out on vital and fundamental learning.

Day by day, he makes us aware of the basic relational skills which otherwise we would take entirely for granted. Non-verbal signals and simple relational sensitivities are nearly all missing for him. Trust is missing. Fun and playfulness are missing. Curiosity and interest in the world around him are missing.

In place of all these he is left with a massive defensive egocentricity and a divided self, which simply cannot take responsibility or make plans since the left hand has no idea what the right hand has done, is doing or may be going to do. Yet with strangers he appears open and friendly and trusting. His beautiful spaniel eyes gaze adoringly at anyone who might let him call them his friend. We, who love him, are afraid for him.

Now he arrives bouncing and spluttering with excitement. He has, by agreement, gone on from his meeting with his social worker to play in the park. There he has met up with a friend. Wants to go back to his friend's house. Wants us to lend his friend a bicycle to make the journey easier.

'Who is your friend, Shane?'

'Oh, he lives the other side of the estate. He's in my class at school.'

'What's his name?'

He looks at me blankly. 'I forgot to ask him. Oy!' he shouts towards the front door 'What's your name? The old dear wants to know!'

'Shane,' I begin, thinking I ought at least to try, 'friends are people we know well. People we like and trust. Not just…' I give up. This is a time for decision not explanation. 'No,' I say, 'the answer's no. But you can bring him in and introduce him to me, and he can stay here for a while if you like.'

Happy enough with this, he brings in a bedraggled waif, and proudly introduces him, having checked his name afresh in the hallway. I give them both drinks and biscuits, and Brian takes them off for a game of snooker.

Bedtime brings tantrums. The social worker had brought news of fresh rejections, as we knew he would. Now, at last, in the peace and quiet of the ending of the day, the message sinks in. 'Come on, Shane, time you were thinking of bed,' I suggest. 'You shut your face,' he explodes, 'leave me alone. You're not my mum. I hate you. Just leave me alone.' Brian steps in, his quiet voice almost always effective in this situation. 'That's enough, Shane. Go to your room. We'll talk about it later if you want to.' Shane stamps upstairs, slams one door, two doors, turns on his radio at full volume. We wait, look at one another, wait a little longer. Sigh thankfully as the music is turned down. Now Brian will go and see if Shane wants to talk. 'Remember to make sure he packs his pencil in his bag,' I say, as I wander off to find my own quiet corner of the household.

## The nature and effects of traumatic stress

Any threatening or demanding event will cause us to generate stress hormones. The instant physiological response to our recognition that demands are to be made upon us enables us to function most efficiently and to survive in a difficult environment. The stress hormones thus produced tone up our brains and bodies to respond rapidly and effectively to challenging stimuli and increase our capacity to notice and engage with and respond to others of our kind, who may be enlisted as allies in our struggles. Moderate amounts of stress heighten our effectiveness physically, psychologically and socially (Goleman, 1996).

Traumatic events generate stress of quite a different order. These are events which are, or are perceived to be, so threatening to the life or physical integrity of self or others that the person confronted with them reacts with fear, helplessness or horror (Kinchin, 2004). Horrific events in our environment produce an intense stress response in us. This automatic response to terrifying events, known as traumatic stress, is so intense that the levels of stress hormones produced are toxic. Under the impact of traumatic stress we are poisoned by our own physiological survival response. The brain and body are injured at this level of toxicity, producing alterations in physical, psychological and social functioning.

Traumatic stress causes serious injuries to brain and body. In the developing child these injuries are even more serious and pervasive in their effects than in mature adults. Most children who suffer trauma, however, will recover spontaneously. To do so they need three conditions to be met. They must be in a safe place with people they trust and to whom they are securely attached; that allows for the first phase of recovery – stabilisation. Then they must be able to communicate what has happened to them, and the distress it causes them – integration. And finally, they must be able to experience the joy and delight of social reintegration – the phase of post-integrative development or adaptation.

Children in public care are very likely to have suffered traumatic stress. In infancy, separation from the primary caregiver may in itself be enough to constitute trauma. Developmentally the infant is utterly dependent on the care of adults, and will be forming the attachment relationships which are the foundation of so many vital structures for the adult personality by placing trust in those adults to provide nurture and comfort. If the adults disappear, the bereft child suffers severe stress, even though new adults step in to fill the gap and even if the first attachment figures were not in fact meeting the needs of the child.

Many children in care have also suffered some form of abuse or serious neglect. Children may be abused physically, sexually or emotionally, or they may suffer neglect which is also life-threatening to the dependent child. All these abuses are traumatic experiences for children. Often they suffer more than one form of abuse, and often these abuses are repeated over long periods.

Unfortunately the events which bring children into public care also indicate a high probability that the children will have lacked the conditions necessary for spontaneous recovery from trauma. They may have spent a long time in chronically unsafe environments. They are unlikely to have experienced secure social networks with well-formed attachment relationships. They may have had little opportunity to develop good communication skills through play or through conversation.

When people are unable to recover from traumatic stress, they may adapt to their chronic state of arousal, learn to live with some symptoms of disorder, and thus develop a reasonable level of social functioning. In these situations, the natural amnesia for the trauma often persists and the person establishes a lifestyle in which the trauma is locked away in a corner of their lives, with the rest of life being relatively untroubled. Although unstable, this is a tolerable situation. Others who are subject to more of the vulnerability factors develop stress disorders.

## Post-traumatic stress disorders (PTSDs) and child development

When the victim of traumatic stress lacks the social and personal conditions for recovery from, or containment of, symptoms the solution becomes the problem. The normal process of recovery is an alternating cycle of intrusive re-experiencing of fragments of the traumatic events, and periods of rest and integration in which all reminders of the trauma are avoided (Joseph *et al*, 1997, pp 69–86). Since this is an entirely automatic process of recovering health it tends to be set in motion even when important bits of the recovery equation are missing.

These abortive attempts at integration and recovery, for that is what they seem to be at the beginning of the disorder, lead to disaster instead of health. The brain is automatically triggered to release a fragment of traumatic memory for processing and transfer, as it were, to the safety of narrative memory; but the victim, unable to deal with this still overwhelming bit of recalled trauma intruding into everyday life, becomes terrified. Now the trauma memory has become a new trauma event. The victim is beginning to be retraumatised by their own memories. The avoidance part of the recovery cycle also comes adrift. Stress hormones are never really dropping to levels less than toxic, so that avoidance generates phobic behaviour and compulsive thoughts and activities accompanied by denial and minimisation. These symptoms of intrusive re-experiencing and avoidance are among the defining criteria for PTSD.

Children will respond to all this pain by becoming locked into a state of frozen terror from which they cannot escape without help. In this state of terror, and the uncontrollable rage which often accompanies it, they will begin to develop patterns of behaviour which the rest of us will find difficult to accommodate. Nightmares, night terrors, disorders of sleeping and eating, learning difficulties, memory problems, aggression, violence, hyperactivity, inattentiveness, phobias, compulsive behaviours, self-harm, and later, self-medication through abuse of drugs and alcohol are all common symptoms of post-traumatic distress.

If there are associated attachment difficulties, we could add in a long list that would include, for example, stealing, meaningless compulsive lying, destructiveness, cruelty to animals, self-stimulating behaviours such as head-banging or masturbation, self-soothing behaviours such as rocking or thumb sucking, and so on (Fahlberg, 1994). These are all indicators of the pain and distress suffered by children whose brain and body development has been interrupted and harmed by stress injuries.

What happens to these vulnerable, troubled and troublesome children will then depend on when they come to the notice of a professional service, and which service notices them. In general terms, boys are more likely to suffer from hyperarousal and thus to act out, while girls suffer more from dissociative conditions and are more likely to be seen as at risk and in need of protection or mental health provision following traumatic stress. These differences combine with different societal expectations about gender to result in boys being more likely to end up being looked after and less likely to find permanent carers through adoption than girls, and boys being more likely to enter the criminal justice system. Young children who act out sexually are likely to be seen as in need of care and treatment, while older young people sexually acting out are more likely to be seen as offenders (Farmer, 1998). Disabled children are both more vulnerable to abuse and more likely to be overlooked as victims of trauma, and services they receive are more likely to be health based than services offered to their peers.

Broadly speaking, it is fair to say that the results of the response of our community to children who have suffered trauma are at present exclusion rather than inclusion. Children in the care system are more likely to be excluded from school than their peers, and less likely to go on to further education. As young adults they are much more likely to be unemployed, to be homeless, to be in prison, or to be recipients of mental health care than other people of the same age. Victims of trauma, locked in the grey and terrifying world of stress disorders, feel themselves cut off from others; our social structures seem only too ready to make the self-image a reality.

## The effect of traumatic stress on learning

The functional changes produced by stress disorders are extensive and are even more global in effect following childhood trauma than for people already adult when first traumatised; 'The [DSM-IV][15] field trials confirmed that trauma has its most profound impact during the first decade of life' (van der Kolk *et al*, 1996, p 202). Brain and body functions, emotional functioning and social functioning are all likely to be seriously impaired. Cognitive processing will be distorted and the sufferer will be preoccupied with trauma-related affect and cognition.

Out of the global harm caused by unresolved trauma, each victim will generate a unique constellation of symptoms and responses. The complex interactive system of individual and social networks, which is the locus of response to traumatic stress, creates an intricate interplay of vulnerability and resilience which will determine the outcome for the course disorder. Children who have suffered or are suffering much the same precipitating trauma may attract very different assessments of need.

Let us consider some of the functions which may be impaired and the learning difficulties which may occur as a result.

### Brain
*Language*: areas of the brain in which several language functions are located are significantly altered under the impact of traumatic stress. Language and the symbolic representation of events and feelings are central to the functioning of human intelligence. Impairment in this area of functioning will lead to a range of learning difficulties.

---

15 DSM IV: Diagnostic and Statistical Manual of Mental Disorders (APA, 1994)

*Memory*: victims are likely to suffer partial or complete memory disturbance for the traumatic events. This may take the form of amnesia or hypermnesia, in which the victim is unable to forget – the trauma, or fragments of it, endlessly replay in the victim's awareness. Changes in the brain also lead to significant short-term memory loss or distortion. Children with impaired memory find it difficult to learn.

## Physiology
*Autonomic hyperarousal*: the permanent arousal of the autonomic nervous system which controls bodily functions and physiology, and kindling of the limbic system which provides regulation of emotional states leave the child unable to concentrate or to string thoughts together cohesively. Preoccupation with trauma-related affect and cognition, and the pressing need for a permanently high stimulus environment, will lead to inattentiveness and disruptive behaviour.

*Hypervigilance*: perpetually scanning the environment for threat, interpreting neutral stimuli as traumatic stressors, subject to exaggerated startle responses so that they jump to every sound, these children are exhausting to be with. When not distressed and hyper-active, they will also be exhausted themselves. There is no middle ground at this level of arousal.

*Altered perceptions*: perceptual fields alter under the impact of traumatic stress. Peripheral vision sharpens, scanning the environment, and concentration on focused visual tasks such as reading becomes very limited. Auditory field selection changes, as the innate preference for the human voice is superseded by the need to notice danger. Non-threatening sounds are tuned out and children may be thought to be deaf. They will certainly be regarded as inattentive.

## Physical functioning
*Lack of co-ordination*: hyperarousal of the long muscles leads to problems with physical co-ordination and clumsiness, as well as stiffness and pain in the joints. This has an impact on many educational activities, and also contributes to the poor self-image which follows traumatic stress and again reduces educational attainment.

*Numbness*: overloaded with self-generated pain relievers (endogenous opioids) which are part of the traumatic stress response, the child cannot experience pain appropriately and is at risk of injury. These endogenous opioids are addictive, and this may lead to self-harming behaviour which positively seeks out injury to generate an added dose.

*Psychosomatic conditions*: stress hormones alter many bodily functions. Persisting over time, these alterations in digestion, breathing, heart function, circulation and muscle tone are likely to give rise to problems. The immune system is also challenged by the toxic levels of stress hormones. Moreover, children who are unable to experience feelings, but instead experience physical changes of function (somatisation), are often subject to illnesses when other children would experience emotions. Poor health may cause absences from school and inattentiveness when in school.

## Emotional functioning

***Numbing***: it is very difficult to engage with children who are suffering emotional numbing, or to engage them in any activity requiring emotional responsiveness. Aesthetic appreciation, a vital part of learning, is absent or impaired.

***Extreme reactiveness***: the same perpetual arousal that produces numbing also produces a hair-trigger reactivity to neutral or trivial emotional stimuli. The reaction will be one of terror or rage or both combined. This has a significant impact on the capacity to learn. Schools often find it difficult or impossible to contain the behaviour, which may be actually dangerous to self and others.

***Somatisation***: the inability to experience feelings as anything other than alterations in physical functioning, and the absence of language for feelings, may severely limit the capacity to understand concepts, or participate in activities, that require emotional sensitivity and recognition.

***Anhedonia***: the loss of the capacity to experience joy will severely circumscribe all educational activity which relies on appreciation, wonder and awe.

## Social functioning

***Loss of the ability to relate to others***: preoccupation with trauma-related constructs and affect means that other people are at best largely irrelevant to the child thus affected. At worst, other are misinterpreted as threatening and treated accordingly. Since trauma victims are uncomfortable to be with, this social exclusion is likely to be two way. Group learning activities are difficult for children in this situation, and social interactions in and out of school are likely to be impaired.

***Loss of social intentionality***: a key element in the development of social accountability, which Shotter (1984) suggests is crucial in human development, is the recognition that intentions and not just actions are central to human interaction. The victim of PTSD is 'trying to survive. This supersedes all other intentionality' (Cairns, 2010). Motivation to interact with others is severely limited when the child cannot generate social intentions.

*Loss of ability to perceive or construct meaning*: traumatic stress destroys central constructs of meaning (Janoff-Bulman, 1992), leaving the victim of PTSD unable to discern connections or make sense of their universe. Since connectedness is at the heart of sound education, this functional impairment critically damages the ability to learn either extensively or intensively.

## The basis of effective treatment programmes

PTSD affects body, mind and society. It is a bio-psycho-social condition and effective treatment must address all three dimensions of the disorder simultaneously. The victim needs to learn to manage their own physiological and biological stress reactions, to bring the autonomic hyperarousal and kindling of the limbic system to a level of tolerability, and to recover or create some conscious control over autonomic processes. They also need to process and come to terms with the horrifying traumatic memory fragments, and to restore or create personal constructs of meaning and intention. At the same time they need to recover or discover social connectedness and the possibility of joy.

They also need the disorder to be recognised, of course. This hardly happens at all at present. One possible reason for the profound silence around stress disorder is that it is difficult for any discipline to address itself to a disorder that requires connections across several professional disciplines – even to recognise its existence. Yet once it is recognised, there is an increasing body of knowledge about how to treat it effectively, provided that the various disciplines can get their heads, and their budgets, together.

The need for treatment to be three-dimensional has led to the recognition that every practitioner involved with the child needs to be part of the treatment programme if it is to be effective. The disorder is global and treatment must therefore address every aspect of the disordered functioning. Trauma experts generally agree that this is most elegantly and effectively achieved by 'phase-oriented' treatment which 'divides the overall trauma treatment into discrete phases . . . of treatment' (Brown *et al*, 1998, p 437). Three stages or phases are recognised: stabilisation, integration and post-integrative self and relational development (or adaptation). Each of these phases in turn needs to be addressing the three dimensions of the disorder: biological and physiological, cognitive and emotional, and social and spiritual functioning.

Children who are victims of PTSD need safety, stabilisation, therapy, secure social attachments and the possibility of joy (e.g. Siegel, 2011; Joseph, 2012). Many children in the public care system are receiving none of these and very few receive all of them. Yet this is not a list from which options may be selected. For the child to recover, all of these elements – stability, appropriate therapy, lasting social connectedness and restitutive emotional experience – must be present, and the whole healing process must be based on effective treatment of PTSD.

## In conclusion

Consider Article 39 of the UN Declaration on the Rights of the Child:

> *States Parties shall take all appropriate measures to promote physical and psychological recovery and social reintegration of a child victim of: any form of neglect, exploitation, or abuse . . . Such recovery and reintegration shall take place in an environment which fosters the health, self-respect and dignity of the child.*

We now know what such child victims need in order to recover and reintegrate. They need a safe, stable, loving home; they need access as and when required to therapists who understand the root problems; and they need a social milieu in which schools, doctors, police officers and the criminal justice system all recognise the effects of childhood trauma, and work together to provide appropriate treatment and prevent further deterioration into disorder. Only when these needs have been met will we be coming close to honouring our commitment to uphold the rights of the child.

# PART 4

# IN CARE AND BEYOND

# 13  Foster care and higher education

*Sonia Jackson and Sarah Ajayi*

*This article, reprinted from the special edition of* Adoption & Fostering *(31:1, 2007) on education, reports findings from the first UK study of young people in care who go to university. They suggest that foster care could play a major role in enabling more looked after children to access higher education and complete their courses successfully.*

## Introduction

It is still an exceptional achievement for a young person in care to go to university. There are no reliable figures but the most optimistic official estimate is that six per cent of care leavers now continue into higher education. This represents an improvement on the one per cent estimate of the Social Exclusion Unit (SEU) in 2003, but still compares very poorly with the figure of 39 per cent for the general school population. Two retrospective studies found that some care leavers who have had little success at school return to education in their 20s and 30s, but they are almost certainly a small minority (Jackson and Martin, 1998; Mallon, 2007).

This chapter draws on the findings of a prospective longitudinal study of university students who had spent all or part of their childhood in care and were still looked after by a local authority at the age of 16. The research aims were to find out how these young people achieved an educational level so much higher than most looked after children, how they fared once they entered university and how effectively they were supported by their local authorities. The study, known as *By Degrees*, was commissioned by an educational charity, the Frank Buttle Trust, and funded by a consortium of other charities and the Department for Education and Skills (DfES). The findings of the research are reported in more detail elsewhere (Jackson *et al*, 2003; 2005). This chapter focuses on the role of foster care, both in helping young people to achieve the academic results required to apply for university entrance and in continuing to provide emotional and practical support during their time at university. We conclude by considering how foster care might be used more purposefully to widen participation in higher education by young people in and leaving care.

## The *By Degrees* study

Participants in the study were all volunteers, referred by local authority lead officers for the education of looked after children or by leaving care teams. All local authorities in

England and Wales were contacted repeatedly, asking them to put the researchers in touch with any young people in or leaving care who were known to have applied for places on degree-level courses. Despite expressing support for the objectives of the research, many local authorities responded that they knew of no care leavers proposing to enter higher education, and a few admitted that no young person in their care had ever gone to university. So although we cannot know if the volunteers were typical of all children in care who go to university, it seems probable that they represented a high proportion of this very select group. Over 90 per cent of those contacted by the research team agreed to take part in the study.

The criteria for inclusion were that the young person had been looked after for a year or more, was in care at the age of 16 and had been offered a place to study at degree level in a higher education institution. Three successive cohorts of university or college entrants were tracked through their university careers, the first group up to the first year after graduation, the second for two years and the third group for their first year only. All participants were interviewed face to face on the first occasion and on two or three further occasions, in some cases by telephone.

Despite initial doubts as to whether it would be possible to recruit an adequate research sample, over 50 individuals volunteered to participate in each year. However, not all were eligible, some failed to take up their university places and others could not be contacted for interview so that the final achieved samples were 46 for the first cohort, entering university in September/October 2001, 37 for the second, and 46 for the third. One hundred and twenty-nine participants were still in contact with the research team when the study ended in 2005 and several of them are continuing to collaborate with the researchers to disseminate the findings.

To date this remains the only UK study of higher education students with a back-ground in care but there is increasing interest in the US in the barriers to college attendance for "foster youth" and the problems they experience, and a growing body of research-based literature. Despite the very different context, the findings of the limited available research are remarkably similar to those of the *By Degrees* study (Casey Family Programs, 2003; Wolanin, 2005). Initial participation in post-secondary education by young people leaving care is much higher in the US than in this country (around 50%) but very few stay the course, with some studies reporting drop-out rates of up to 80 per cent (Elze *et al*, 2005). In most European countries drop-out rates from university are higher for all students than in the UK, but there are no figures available for participation of young people from a background in public care.

## Characteristics of the participants

Basic information about young people who volunteered to take part in the *By Degrees* study was obtained by means of a short postal questionnaire which was followed up for those who qualified for inclusion by a semi-structured interview in which they were asked to tell the researchers the story of their lives so far in their own words. This covered their birth family, the reasons why they had come into care as far as they knew them, their placement history, educational attainment and school experience, sources of financial and emotional support and what it was like to be a university student with a care background. We wanted to know if and in what way they differed from other children in care and to document their experiences of university life.

*Table 1*
**Ethnicity of By Degrees participants**

|  | Cohort 1 | Cohort 2 | Cohort 3 | All LAC 31 March 2004 |
| --- | --- | --- | --- | --- |
| White British | 24 (52%) | 14 (38%) | 23 (50%) | 80% |
| Mixed | 1 | 5 | 0 | 8% |
| Black African | 8 | 9 | 11 | no % given |
| Black or Black British* | 5 | 2 | 3 | 8% |
| Asian or Asian British+ | 4 | 3 | 5 | 2% |
| Other | 3 | 4 | 4 | 2% |

*includes African-Carribbean
+includes Indian, Bangladeshi and Chinese

Comparing them with the care population in general, we found females were over-represented, particularly in the third cohort, of which 70 per cent were women. As Table 1 shows, the participants also included a high proportion of young people from a minority ethnic background. Overall, 16 per cent of the research participants had come to the UK as unaccompanied asylum seekers (see Chapter 15). This may partly account for the relatively large number (60%) who had entered the care system late, aged 14 or older. However, there were also some individuals (almost 20%) who had been looked after since early childhood.

Asylum seekers often differed in important respects from indigenous children, not only in race and ethnicity. They tended to be much more educationally ambitious than UK-born care leavers. Their birth parents were much more likely to have educational and professional qualifications and to have given the children a sense of the vital importance of education. Therefore it is possible that the more promising figures for children in care continuing into higher education being reported by a few local authorities may be artificially inflated by their presence.

Not surprisingly, the *By Degrees* participants had done much better at school than most looked after children, although, with some exceptions, their achievements were unremarkable compared with the general population. The average number of GCSE passes was nine for females and eight for males; 70 per cent in Cohorts 1 and 2 and 91 per cent in Cohort 3 achieved five or more passes with A*–C grades, compared with six per cent (at the time) for all looked after children.

*Table 2*
**Educational attainment of *By Degrees* participants**

The average number of GCSE passes among all three cohorts was 10

| | Cohort 1 | Cohort 2 | Cohort 3 | All care leavers aged 16+ 31 March 2004 |
|---|---|---|---|---|
| 5+ GCSE A*–C | 32 (70%) | 27 (71%) | 42 (91%) | 6% |
| 1+ CCSE A*–G | 45 (98%) | 37 (100%) | 45 (98%) | 42% |
| 5+ GCSE A*–G | 41 (89%) | 37 (100%) | 38 (83%) | 29% |
| 1+ A level A–E | 24 (52%) | 22 (59%) | 28 (61%) | not known |
| 1+ A/S level A–E | 6 (13%) | 14 (38%) | 17 (37%) | not known |
| 1+GVNQ pass | 14 (30%) | 7 (19%) | 10 (22%) | 3% |
| 1+ BTECH pass | 4 (9%) | 3 (8%) | 9 (19%) | |

* Source for national figures: *National Statistics Bulletin* (January 2005) based on 61,100 children looked after; 53% of young people who ceased to be looked after aged 16+ had no qualifications.

It is interesting to note that only four of the 129 research participants had attended high-ranking secondary schools (defined as 90% of pupils achieving five GCSE passes at A*–C grades) and many told us that they had been allocated to schools with poor academic records which had empty places. This point is addressed in the government Green Paper, *Care Matters*, which states that in future local authorities will be encouraged to 'navigate the system' as parents do to place children in care in top performing schools (DfES, 2006a).

The academic difficulties of looked after children are often attributed to the short-comings of their birth families and to pre-care traumatic experiences (Aldgate *et al*, 1999; Schofield *et al*, 2000; Berridge, 2007). There was no shortage of these in the histories of the *By Degrees* participants. The reasons why they had come into care conformed very closely to those given in government statistics for all looked after children. For almost exactly the same proportion – 61 per cent – abuse or severe neglect was the main reason why they were living away from home. Over 80 per cent said they had experienced some form of

*Figure 1*
**Reasons for coming into care**

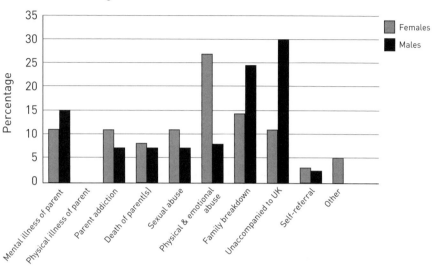

abuse. Other important reasons were alcoholism, drug misuse and mental illness, particularly of mothers. Many of those who came from overseas had been caught up in violent conflict and experienced extreme privation in the process of escape. Several gave us graphic accounts of travelling to the UK in the backs of lorries, arriving cold and hungry, only to be quickly abandoned by their escorts, and in some cases left destitute.

## Placement experiences

Students entered university from a variety of different living situations. Sixty per cent were in foster care or supported lodgings. Of the rest, most were living independently, usually in local authority flats, and a few were staying with friends and relatives. Only one participant went on to higher education directly from residential care. Most residential units still expect young people to leave at age 16, so even if, unusually, they were doing well at school at that point, their opportunity to continue in education was severely limited. Almost a third of the participants had spent time in children's homes, mostly for brief periods, and only one reported a positive experience. Others commented how difficult it was to study in the residential environment. Colin told us:

*I was the only child in the home who went to school. I had work to do and the other kids would be kicking off, sometimes all night, and I had to go to school in the morning. The others had no motivation. The staff didn't push them. One of the boys was doing well at school until he came into the home. He was really bright. But within five months he had given up going to school, had started smoking and was using drugs. The only person who helped me was the only educated one, the one with a degree ... The location was half the problem. They should put children's homes in a respectable area, not one where there's scallys hanging round every corner.*

Other accounts were less extreme, but almost all commented on the lack of opportunity to read or study and the absence of any interesting or stimulating activities in the home. This is a sadly consistent finding dating back to the 1970s (Berridge, 1985; Jackson, 1987). Our respondents told us that staff showed little interest in their school experience beyond occasional enquiries about whether they had done their homework. Asked to what she attributed her academic success, Samantha said, 'I was lucky. I've never been in a children's home. That's like being thrown on the educational scrapheap.'

By contrast, most of those who had a relatively long-term foster placement (two years or more) spoke very warmly of their foster families and the support and encouragement they had received from them. In some cases this was a late placement after a series of less successful ones. Boris and his brother were in and out of care for several years as a result of their mother's alcohol problem, culminating in her death in particularly traumatic circumstances. They had seven different foster homes before their final placement, from which both went on to university.

Most of the participants had not attended school regularly until they came into care and reported that their attainment was well below what was expected for their age. The majority attributed their educational recovery partly to their own motivation but also, in large part, to the remedial efforts of their foster carers and the feeling that there was somebody who really cared about what happened to them at school and wanted them to succeed.

Stacey came into care when her mother had a breakdown. She always wanted to do well at school:

*I didn't want to be a drop-out and just settle for a job. I always wanted to go to university from an early age . . . I had this weird drive even though I had things on my mind.*

She looked back with gratitude to her foster home:

*Marian would do word games with me. I think that helped a lot. She was really encouraging and all for education.*

Dahlia was fortunate to have the same social worker from the age of four and a stable foster placement throughout her childhood. Owing to her mother's mental illness she never went to school before coming into care:

*. . . we used to ride around on the buses all day . . . So when I arrived with my foster carers when I was almost seven I couldn't even read or write. And my foster mum, Monica, she read with me every night and every moment possible, so eventually I got to the same level as the children in my class.*

Later Dahlia went to a Catholic secondary school, the same one that her two elder foster sisters attended, and can't remember a time when she didn't want to go to university like them, 'the natural sort of step to take next':

*Monica and Martin didn't have the opportunity to go to university themselves but they've encouraged all three of us to work hard and make ourselves into something.*

Many of the research participants referred to the structure, discipline and consistency that they experienced in their foster homes, in contrast to the chaotic conditions in their birth families. Dahlia's foster carers knew how to create an environment that harnessed the educational interest and success of their children:

*Martin and Monica are quite strict as foster parents . . . like I couldn't go out on a school night; I had to stay in and do my work. I couldn't watch telly like my friends were doing. At the time it does seem a bit annoying, but she just treated me the same way as her own daughters. I'm thankful to her because it just is a hard slog getting all the work done and then there was netball and orchestra to fit in as well.*

Sandra was placed with her grandparents after several episodes when her mother, who had an alcohol problem, left her alone in the house and she was severely neglected:

*Nothing is too much for them if it is to help my education. My granddad would always drive me around, and if there was hockey or netball tournaments he was always willing to help transport us or pick me up late from school if I was doing after-school classes. I was a bit disappointed with my A-levels, because I thought I would disappoint them, but they said nothing I did could disappoint them.*

Fenella said of her foster mother:

*She's lovely, my mummy. She's a great person, funny and entertaining. She was the best thing that could have happened to me. Her main ethic is 'education, education, education'. She used to make me learn similes and metaphors, long division, fractions and decimals. She used to leave me sums to do when she went to work.*

When she was 16 her (foster) mother told social services that Fenella would be going to university. She felt that her (foster) mother was behind her '150 per cent'.

Damien was born in Uganda and came to England when he was 13. He was placed with temporary foster carers because of conflict with his mother and the temporary placement turned into a very supportive long-term relationship:

> Well, when I first got there, you know, I was really keeping to myself most of the time. But they kind of gave me my space. They gave me my room, they got everything I needed to study. You know, they didn't say, 'As long as you study we'll support you.' They just cared. I was given advice but not told what to do. They are really nice. And when they got paid they gave me some of the money to do the kind of adventurous activities I like to do, which tend to cost a lot . . .

> I mean, they are proud of me, you know. They've come to presentations when I was getting awards and everything else. And they're pleased.

Asked why he chose the university he attended, he said:

> I looked in The Times and this is one of the top universities, so... It's far enough away from home for me to be able to do anything I want to do and close enough for me to go home and have Sunday dinner.

In his second year Damien was still phoning his foster carers every week and turned to them or his foster brothers whenever he had a problem. Although they had helped him financially, it was their emotional support that he valued most.

It is noteworthy that in over a third of the foster families one or both parents were graduates, a much higher proportion than among foster carers generally, of whom only five per cent have a qualification equivalent to NVQ3, and most left school with no GCSEs or O-levels. There were also likely to be older children in the family who had gone to university and could provide practical advice as well as acting as role models. Even carers who did not have educational qualifications themselves were said by their foster children to value education highly and consider school very important. Many paid for educational equipment, such as books and computers, when the local authority was unwilling to do so, or fought for extra support in school or private coaching for children who had fallen behind due to interruptions in their schooling.

However, not all foster carers were in a position to help financially; many were dependent on welfare benefits or very low earnings (Triseliotis *et al*, 2000). A recent report by the Fostering Network found that three-quarters of foster carers are paid less than the minimum wage and 40 per cent only receive the fostering allowance with no element of payment, even though only 12 per cent work full-time outside the home. Nearly 20 per cent are dependent on income support or jobseeker's allowance (Fostering Network, 2007).

Some local authorities operate a policy, driven by their financial departments, of cutting off the fostering allowance on the young person's 18th birthday, irrespective of the point they have reached in their educational career. It is perhaps too easy to feel critical of foster carers like the single woman whose allowance was abruptly ended on Stephanie's 18th birthday, a few weeks before she was due to sit A-levels. Stephanie had been in this placement for seven years but she was told she would have to leave at once to make way for a new foster child, for whom the local authority would pay. Stephanie experienced this as a devastating rejection. Not surprisingly, her A-level results fell far below her predictions and she was fortunate that her social worker found her supported lodgings with a landlady who strongly encouraged her to persist with her educational aims and even persuaded the university to hold a place for her. Nevertheless, it was a year before she recovered sufficiently to start her course.

There are still some authorities where foster placements are ended even earlier. One young woman, aged just 17, was told that she would have to find her own accommodation at the start of her A-level course because the placement was needed for a younger child. However, foster carers did not always fall in with local authority plans: some protested vehemently when inappropriately timed moves were suggested and succeeded in continuing to provide a home for the young person they were looking after.

Participants who were able to remain in established foster placements up to the point where they started their university courses had a much more "normal" experience than those who left care earlier. Often foster carers would drive them to university and help to settle them in, just as most parents do. However, there were some sad accounts of ex-care students who had to struggle to transport their possessions on trains and buses, and described how lonely and isolated they felt as they watched their contemporaries unloading fridges and television sets from the family car.

## Staying the course

Foster families were named as an important source of support, particularly during the first year, by almost all of the participants who had experienced a good foster placement. Some of the research participants found it very hard to settle into university life and often said they might have dropped out without the encouragement and support not only of foster parents but also of older foster siblings. Many, like Damien, went home to their foster families every weekend in the early stages, as well as in the vacations. By the second year they had usually made friends and moved out of university accommodation into shared houses and flats, but continued to keep in close touch with their former foster carers by telephone and, increasingly, email. In the final interviews with Cohort 1 participants, four years after they started their courses in 2001, foster carers were still likely to be placed high on the list of the five most important people in the young person's life.

## Picking up the pieces

Despite their success in obtaining university places, many of the students struggled to cope with the academic demands of their chosen courses. They tended to attribute this to the frequent interruptions to their education caused by the volatility of their birth families, changes of placement and periods out of school. In addition to gaps in their knowledge, many of them referred to a lack of basic study skills and difficulty in organising their work. This showed up particularly after the first year when longer and more complex assignments were set. Being a slow reader was a problem that was frequently mentioned, sometimes attributed to lack of encouragement to read and limited access to books in childhood. One student, despite having done very well in the early part of his course, was so daunted by the prospect of a third-year dissertation that he decided to opt for an HND (Higher National Diploma) instead of a degree. Among the first cohort only half passed all their assessments at the first attempt and those who had come to university by the "non-traditional" route – GNVQ or BTech – seemed to have the most difficulty. Some students became discouraged and considered dropping out. In these cases the foster family often played a crucial role in encouraging them to persevere, and almost all did so. For the few who gave up the struggle, support from a foster family was even more important in enabling them to overcome the experience of failure and maintain their self-esteem.

Students with a close, continuing relationship with a foster family were less likely to leave university prematurely than those living independently before they started their courses. This is perhaps surprising, since the latter group would have had more experience of managing everyday living and budgeting and might have been expected to be more competent at managing the practical aspects of university life. However, it illustrates the great importance of the emotional support offered by foster carers.

Being able to return to a foster home during vacations significantly reduced the stress of college life. Students who lived independently were inclined to use the holidays to work full-time in order to reduce indebtedness or save money for the following year. As a result, they sometimes returned for the new term already tired, leaving them less able to cope with the next tranche of academic work.

## Problems in foster care

It would be misleading to suggest that foster care, as experienced by the *By Degrees* participants, was problem free. Foster placements were reported as varying widely in quality. Muddah was a refugee from the war in Liberia. He twice asked to change placement because his foster carers showed so little concern for his education and there was nowhere in the house where he could study, but his first move was out of the frying pan into the fire:

*I went to a second foster carer, she wasn't very nice; she wasn't support at all in my education side, she don't know how good I am in school, what is my homework; she never asked so always I feel very bad. It's like they don't care, it was just about giving your pocket money, your bus fare, your lunch money; they don't know what's going on with me with my education, what I'm finding difficult, whether there is any help and support available for me . . . because I know if there was I could do even much better in my GCSEs.*

He contrasted this strongly with his third foster placement, where the children of the family were all at college or university and spent a lot of time talking to him about it. This reinforced his ambition to continue in education as far as he could go:

*I'm not clever; I find studying very very difficult. I just work hard because I want to get somewhere, and my foster carer was very interested in my education. It was part of everyday life. Five days a week, Monday to Friday, every day she need to know my homework, she need to see my books, she need to speak to my teacher.*

By the time of his final interview Muddah was speaking fluent, grammatical English and flourishing socially and academically, with continuing support from his former foster carers.

Abby, a young black woman of outstanding academic ability, who eventually achieved 10 GCSEs with As and A*s and three A-levels with top grades, had two very unsatisfactory short placements and was then placed with a single woman who looked after several younger children. Because the foster carer was white, social workers repeatedly tried to move Abby to a black family, including a week before her GCSEs. She resisted, not because she was happy in the placement, but to avoid disrupting her exam preparation. The foster carer took no interest at all in her achievements and made her eat by herself in a separate room from the rest of the family. Her main support came from a school friend's mother, who gave her a computer to work on for her A-levels, and her Further Education college tutor, who encouraged her to apply to a top university, which offered her a place to read law.

Having no contact with her birth or foster family and inadequate financial support from her local authority, Abby found university life a struggle. The university prohibited paid work during term time and her social worker's idea of contributing to her academic expenses was £15 a term for books, about a tenth of what she needed. As a black woman in an overwhelmingly white environment she felt very much alone and at one point was depressed to the point of needing hospital treatment.

A few carers, perhaps because they had had bad experiences of school themselves, ridiculed educational aspirations and actively undermined the young person's efforts to do well, for instance by playing loud music or turning up the sound on the television when they were trying to revise for exams. They usually did not see it as their business to attend parents' evenings or school events. Many foster homes were very busy, noisy places, with people coming and going all the time and little opportunity for reading or concentrated study. Shared bedrooms, especially with a younger child, were unsatisfactory places to do homework. Most problems were reported as having occurred in earlier placements, in contrast to a final successful placement, which provided the launchpad for the young person to apply for a university place.

## The local authority as corporate parent

The possibility that children in care might continue into further and higher education was envisaged as far back as 1946 by the Curtis Report (Curtis, 1946; Jackson, 2006), and their right to do so was firmly stated in the Guidance to the Children Act 1989 (DH, 1991b). However, when this study began, there were still wide variations between local authorities in the extent to which they had taken this responsibility on board. Some provided generous support for accommodation, educational expenses, field trips, study visits abroad and computers; others appeared to begrudge every penny (Jackson *et al*, 2003). The two local authority surveys conducted as part of the study found an improvement following the implementation of the Children (Leaving Care) Act 2000, but that still left many students struggling to make ends meet, and often working long hours in low-paid jobs to cover their basic living costs, leaving too little time for their academic work. They were rarely able to put anything aside for contingencies, with the result that any unexpected expense could present a crisis. Unlike parents, local authorities often seemed unable to react to appeals for help with any sense of urgency. For example, one young woman broke her only pair of glasses a few days before important exams. When she asked her social worker for help to pay for a replacement she was simply told, 'It's your responsibility – you should have had a spare pair.' Since student accommodation was often situated in crime-prone areas, having a computer stolen or damaged was another frequently reported problem. It could take several weeks or even months before the local authority would agree to replace it, during which time the student might have great difficulty in completing assignments and accessing the internet.

Here again, many foster carers provided invaluable support, and in addition, sometimes offered extra funds or loans to enable students to give up paid work during term time in their final year to allow them to concentrate on completing assignments and revising for exams.

## Good fortune or good planning?

Because this study did not include interviews with participants' social workers, other than for recruitment purposes or to re-establish contact with missing respondents, it is not possible to tell how far the successful foster placements occurred by chance or as the result of a well-considered plan. Most of the young people thought they had just been lucky. If they had been placed with carers who were thought especially likely to prioritise their educational needs, they had certainly not been told about it. There is no doubt that, for the 60 per cent of participants who were in foster placements, carers and their families played an important part in helping them to do well at school, encouraging their aspirations, prioritising school work and educational activities, smoothing their path to higher education, and providing often much needed support through their university courses. It is not clear, however, if the social worker had identified their potential and made the placement with that in mind, or if their academic ability only became apparent afterwards.

Several participants recognised in retrospect that they had given their carers and social workers a hard time and had been regarded as oppositional and over demanding. It is interesting to note that a study of young people in difficulties, including care leavers, found that some of those who were most self-directed and motivated to continue their education came into conflict with social workers or people in authority because they appeared unwilling to fall in with other people's plans or accept advice (Cameron *et al*, 2007). Some foster carers seemed better able to appreciate and value independent-mindedness and self-efficacy than professionals. There were remarkable stories of foster carers who had taken on young people of this kind, who seemed headed for disaster, and stuck with them through successive crises and incidents of unacceptable behaviour, from which they had finally emerged, contrary to all predictions, as happy and successful young adults. Engaging, or in many cases re-engaging, in learning always played a large part in this process.

## Foster care as an educational resource

"Support" for education is often discussed in rather simplistic terms, as if it were only a matter of helping with homework and attending the school concert. The detailed accounts of their foster care experience provided by the *By Degrees* participants made it clear that successfully promoting their educational attainment, as required by the Children Act 2004, was a delicate and sensitive task demanding a high level of skill and determination from foster carers. With young people who had entered care as asylum seekers they often had a head start, in the sense that most of those we interviewed had a clear sense that educational success was their best hope of integrating into British society. They were confident that if they worked hard enough higher education was within their grasp. For many, the importance of education had been emphasised by their parents from early childhood (Jackson *et al*, 2005). Children from British working-class homes, like the majority of those in care, had often absorbed a different message, that school had little to offer people like them and universities were remote and frightening places. Developing their confidence and motivation as learners might need years of patient encouragement and small experiences of success, and above all establishing a home environment that stimulated and supported education in the wider sense.

This is not something to which local authorities have given any priority in the past, and there are still major problems in the recruitment, training and support of foster carers. The Green Paper, *Care Matters*, proposes a tiered system of foster care, with enhanced payments for those who look after children with "complex needs", apparently meaning those with severe behavioural, health or learning difficulties. It does not seem to envisage specialist placements for unproblematic young people with particular talents or abilities who cannot live with their birth families. However, this could be an effective way of moving beyond the shrinking pool of foster carers of the traditional type, which is essential if children are to be offered a choice of placements suited to their individual needs. As yet we have made little progress in that direction. Ian Sinclair commented in his overview of fostering that the basic characteristics of foster carers are 'surprisingly similar' to those identified in the 1950s and 1980s (Sinclair, 2005, p 151).

We suggest a new form of fostering for young people who come into care around the age of 14, like many *By Degrees* participants, or who are not in a stable placement at that stage. "Education foster carers" could be recruited, contracted and paid to offer an educationally rich environment, to work closely with schools and to steer the child/young person through GCSEs, A-levels and higher education. There would be no expectation that either or both foster parents should give up work – indeed it would be a bonus if they had their own careers. Some people, including many professionals, could be attracted by foster care with an explicit educational remit, even if they had not previously thought of conventional fostering as something that they might do. For older adolescents, the arrangement might be closer to supported lodging, but whatever the starting point there is no reason why it should not develop into a warm, affectionate relationship, as for so many of those we interviewed.

## Conclusion

Going to university is rapidly becoming a normative experience for children living in their own families, but for most of those looked after by local authorities, like other children from severely disadvantaged backgrounds, it remains a remote dream. The difference is that local authorities have a special responsibility towards children and young people separated from their parents, a responsibility to ensure that being in care makes a positive difference to their life chances. The best way to do this is to enable as many as we can to continue their education to the highest possible level. Evidence from the *By Degrees* research project suggests that foster care can be a key resource for widening participation and opening up opportunities for this group of educationally and socially excluded young people. Foster care should be seen as an integral part of the education system, as important as the school, if not more so, in enabling children to fill the gaps caused by irregular attendance and lack of stimulation in their early years. Foster families can play a crucial role in raising aspirations, enabling young people to achieve the qualifications they need to access further and higher education and supporting them through their degree courses. A few local authorities have taken on that message and achieved large increases in the numbers of their care leavers who obtain useful qualifications and take up university places, but too many are stuck with an outdated model of foster care in which education is somebody else's business.

### *Acknowledgements*
The authors would like to thank Margaret Quigley for her substantial contribution to the research on which this article is based, and Hugo Perks, Gerri McAndrew, Karen Melton and Christine Stanton-Prior of the Frank Buttle Trust for their invaluable support and assistance over the five years of the *By Degrees* study.

# 14 Leaving care: looking ahead and aiming higher

*Sonia Jackson and Claire Cameron*

*People who have been in public care as children are at high risk of social exclusion as adults. Longitudinal research suggests that this is closely linked to their low level of educational attainment. This chapter, reprinted from* Children and Youth Services Review *(34:6, 2012), draws on evidence from a European Union funded project,* Young People in Public Care: Pathways to Education in Europe (YiPPEE) *which aimed to find out how more care leavers could be encouraged to remain in school longer and enabled to access further and higher education.*

## Introduction

The research on which this chapter is based was carried out over three years by a consortium of five countries: England, Denmark, Sweden, Spain and Hungary. Four principal methods were used: a thorough literature and policy review, secondary analysis of published and unpublished statistics, surveys of responsible public bodies in social care and education, including interviews with professionals and managers, and biographical narrative interviews with a sample of 170 young people aged 18–24. Individual country studies were consolidated at each stage into comparative reports.

In all the five European countries studied, remaining in formal education at least to age 18 or 19 has become the norm. However, this is not true for children in care and the gap in attainment is widening. Despite major differences in care and education systems between the five countries, the experiences of young people in transition from care to independence were found to be remarkably similar.

People who have been in public care as children are one of the groups in society at highest risk of social exclusion as adults. They are greatly over-represented on every measure of social pathology and disadvantage, such as unemployment, ill-health, premature parenthood, addictions and criminality (Mittler and Jackson, 2002; Simon and Owen, 2006). We know that the best guarantee of social inclusion is education. The history of immigrant communities in the 20th century tells us that those who invest their energies and resources in the education of their children are the ones who have done their best in their adopted countries (Winder, 2004). In many ways children in care are in a similar position to immigrants. They too have been uprooted, and placed in an unfamiliar and not always welcoming environment. Yet in the past policy-makers, service managers, social workers and carers, who in the UK are often referred to as their "corporate parents", have taken very little interest in their education (Jackson, 2010b, reprinted in this volume).

This is also true of academic research. Literature reviews in the USA and Canada all comment on the paucity of research in this area, in common with those in the UK and Europe (Borland *et al*, 1998; Goddard, 2000; Jackson and Sachdev, 2001; Vinnerljung *et al*, 2005; Höjer *et al*, 2008; Trout *et al*, 2008; Brodie, 2009).

### Rising educational expectations

Educational standards are constantly rising so that the gap in attainment between children in care and others is widening. Basic education is no longer enough. In most countries of Europe the official school-leaving age is still 16 but in practice almost all young people remain in full-time education until 18 or 19 (European Commission, 2009). At a time of rapidly increasing youth employment, those who leave at 16 with low-level educational qualifications or none find it harder and harder to get jobs. The official aim of the European Union is that 40 per cent of the population of member states should be educated to Bachelor degree level. Going to university has become part of the normative life path for middle-class children everywhere, and increasingly is a realistic aspiration even for young people from relatively low-income families with no experience of tertiary education (Ball, 2003, 2005). Family background and lack of "cultural capital" are still critical factors for all children but no longer insurmountable barriers for those who want to go to college or university (Finnie, 2011).

The situation for young people in public care is very different. An official UK government estimate in 2003 was that among those leaving care aged 19, no more than one in a hundred had succeeded in accessing higher education (SEU, 2003). There is only one European study to date focusing on university students with a background in care. This points out that the great majority of those in care never even reach the point where they could think of applying to university (Jackson *et al*, 2003). They have no chance to enter for the upper secondary examinations, usually taken at 18, because social workers and carers assume that they will leave school, and often care too, as soon as it is legally permitted at 16. That was the original impetus for the study which is the subject of this chapter. The questions we wanted to address were: How can we encourage and support young people in care to stay in education when it is no longer compulsory? How can we help them to develop a strong learning identity and to continue to the highest level of which they are capable?

## The *YiPPEE* Project

The opportunity arose to apply for funding under the European Union Framework 7 programme on Youth and Social Inclusion. We looked for partners among other European countries representing different types of welfare regime (Esping-Anderson, 1990) which would in turn, according to our hypothesis, influence their social care and education systems. All those we approached agreed to participate in the study. Denmark and Sweden are social democratic countries, although they differ quite markedly from each other in some respects. Spain and Hungary could both be seen as in transition, Spain from its previous conservative-familial regime towards a more egalitarian model (Casas *et al*, 2010), Hungary from Communism to capitalism with a reduced role for the state (Kennett, 2007). England is classified as neo-liberal although with some social democratic elements. During the final year of the project, and following the election of a Conservative-led coalition government in May 2010, England, although not other parts of the UK, moved further in a neo-liberal direction.

The five country research teams, co-ordinated from England, worked closely together throughout the project, meeting in each country in turn as well as in Brussels to plan data collection and analysis and to share and interpret findings. In accordance with EU practice, the project was given an acronym, *YiPPEE*, which stands for *Young People in Public Care: Pathways to Education in Europe*.

## Aims of the project

The overall aim of the project was to identify the reasons for the educational under-performance of young men and women who have been in care and find ways to increase their successful participation in post-compulsory education. This fitted well with the EU agenda and the framework for co-operation in the youth field towards reducing youth unemployment and enabling all young men and women to make the best of their potential.

More specific objectives were:

1. to find out what was already known about the education of children and youth in and leaving public care in the different partner states;
2. to establish a baseline of reliable statistical data to enable cross-country comparison and assessment of progress;
3. to compare education and care systems in the five countries to find out to what extent they facilitated or presented obstacles to participation and progression of young people with a care background;
4. to track the educational pathways of a sample of young men and women in public care after the end of compulsory schooling.

A multi-professional group of experts on foster care, meeting in California to discuss ways of reducing the gap in attainment between children in care and others, commented that they knew of no research that examined factors that contribute to resilience and high performance in school for children and youth in care (Berliner, 2010), although there are quite a few studies which discuss reasons for their poor performance (Heath *et al*, 1994; Berridge, 2007). We agree, as we show later, that there is a serious dearth of research on factors leading to school attainment for children in care, with only one series of studies in the UK focusing on more successful young people (Jackson and Martin, 1998; Jackson *et al*, 2003; Jackson *et al*, 2005; Jackson and Ajayi, 2007). The *YiPPEE* research aims to contribute to the evidence on this neglected subject.

## Methodology

### Research plan

The research fell into four phases, with parallel studies in each country. The findings were written up as individual country reports which were later combined to produce con-solidated comparative reports on each stage of the project.[16] The first stage, after setting up the project, was a state-of-the-art-literature review to find out what was already known. This was followed by secondary analysis of published and unpublished statistics comparing the attainment and participation of children in care with all young people of the same age in that country. The third phase consisted of case studies of selected local areas and interviews with social service managers and education professionals. The fourth stage consisted of in-depth face-to-face interviews with a sample of youth formerly in care in each country. Although this plan provided the methodological structure throughout the project, the different stages of the research could not be carried out in exactly the same sequence or time frame for different pragmatic reasons. Differences in education and social service systems in the different countries also necessitated some modifications to the research methods, as explained below.

### Availability of statistical data

Adjustments had to be made to this aspect of the project when it was found that England was the only country where national statistics combining care and education data were routinely collected and published (Hauari *et al*, 2010). Eventually, much later in the life of the project than originally intended, it was possible to purchase access to relevant databases in Sweden and Denmark but not in Spain or Hungary, so that the report on this phase only covers three of the five countries (Cameron *et al*, 2010).

### Local area studies

In each country between two and five areas or local authority districts were chosen for special study. These were selected to represent different conditions that might affect the opportunities and experiences of looked after children: large urban authorities and small rural ones, industrial or agricultural areas, disadvantaged and more prosperous places. These area profiles enabled us to explore the local educational environment for children and young people in the general population as well as more specifically for those in care.

---

16 All reports are available to read and download from the website: http://tcru.ioe.ac.uk/yippee where full details of research methods in each country are given.

## Interviews with professionals and carers

The object of these interviews was twofold. The first was to gather information on local educational provision and to explore the policies and attitudes of those with managerial responsibility for child protection, child welfare services and education. We also sought their views on factors that made it more likely that young people in care would continue into upper-secondary and tertiary education, and the obstacles that might stand in their way. The second objective was to use these contacts in recruiting the in-depth research sample. The number of these interviews varied between countries, and in Sweden it was possible to increase the numbers substantially by adding research questions to the telephone interview schedule of a study already in progress, as shown in Table 1 – 111 managers were interviewed in Sweden.

*Table 1*
**Interviews conducted in each country**

|  | *Denmark* | *England* | *Hungary* | *Spain* | *Sweden* | *Total* |
|---|---|---|---|---|---|---|
| Managers/ Professionals | 5 | 9 | 4 | 13 | 8 (111) | 39 |
| Telephone screening interviews | 75 | 74 | 133 | 132 | 53 | 467 |
| YP intensive sample first found | 35 | 32 | 35 | 35 | 33 | 170 |
| YP second round | 29 | 27 | 33 | 28 | 26 | 143 |
| Nominated adults | 14 | 18 | 34 | 20 | 25 | 111 |
| **Total** | **158** | **160** | **239** | **228** | **145** | **930** |

## Selection of participants for the in-depth sample

The core element of the research consisted of biographical studies of individual young people and detailed examination of their pathways through education, especially after the end of compulsory schooling. However, contacting suitable research participants and gaining their informed consent was by no means an easy task and the resulting samples cannot be considered strictly comparable due to the varying methods of recruitment.

The criteria for inclusion in the in-depth interview sample were the same in every country, namely for the young person to be aged 19–21, to have been in care at age 16 and to have spent at least a year in public care. The fourth criterion for selection was to have shown some indication of "educational promise" at the age of 16. This was set at having gained at least one qualification at that age or showing a commitment to progress into some kind of upper-secondary education. We wanted to find out if those who, if not in care, could reasonably have been expected to continue their education, did in fact do so.

For practical reasons, the means of identifying young people for the case studies differed considerably between countries and was much harder in some, notably England, where the problems of engaging looked after young people in research are well documented (Wigfall and Cameron, 2006). The general procedure was similar in all countries. A population of young people in or formerly in care was located by various methods, initially through agency records, and supplemented through nominations supplied by some of the key professionals referred to above. Those who agreed to participate were interviewed by telephone. The in-depth case study participants were drawn from those screening interviews (Jackson and Cameron, 2011).

The study design sought to include 35 young people from each country, purposively selected to reflect a range of identities in terms of class, gender, ethnicity and immigrant or asylum-seeking status. It proved much easier to identify potential interviewees in Hungary and Spain than in other countries. Those invited to participate in Hungary and Spain were also more likely to agree. By contrast, in Sweden, of 547 young people originally contacted, only 53 responded positively and 33 met the criteria for inclusion in the study.

The intention was to interview 35 young people in each of the five *YiPPEE* countries and this was almost achieved, amounting to 170 individual case studies in total. This is much the largest study undertaken to date of the education of young people with a care background in Europe. It is also the only one focusing on their progression from compulsory schooling to further and higher education. The age range of the final sample was 18–24, with most participants aged between 19 and 21 at first interview.

Two rounds of interviews were conducted, approximately a year apart. The first took the form of an informant-led life story interview in three sections: present, past and future. Specified topics were covered through prompts by the interviewer if they did not come up spontaneously. These were: family, housing, school/education, employment, caring responsibilities, relations with carers and post-care services, health, leisure activities and contact with official agencies such as courts or immigration authorities. Interviewees were also asked where they saw themselves in one and five years' time. The second interview was much more structured, designed to find out how far the young person's plans had been realised and how they hoped their life would unfold in the future. All interviews were recorded and transcribed for analysis using the N*Vivo qualitative software package.

At the first interview all respondents were asked to nominate an adult who had been important in supporting their educational progress. These nominated adults were later interviewed, either face to face or by telephone. They played a variety of roles in the young people's lives. Some were foster carers, others were teachers, pedagogues (in the European sense) or social educators (residential care workers). A few respondents named birth parents. There were 59 young people who could not think of a single person who had encouraged or supported them in their studies. Altogether 930 interviews were carried out in five countries, as shown in Table 1.

## Limitations of research methods

It cannot be claimed that the young people interviewed for the in-depth case studies constituted a representative sample because, as noted above, research participants had to be recruited using a variety of methods and in all countries we were dependent on the goodwill and co-operation of practitioners. One of the principal differences was in the proportion of the sample whose main placement was in foster family care (England and Sweden) compared with those who were mainly looked after in residential homes (Spain and Hungary), as shown in Table 2. About half of the Danish sample had also been mainly in residential care and some had attended boarding schools, a form of placement not found in the other national samples. These placement patterns were broadly similar to the distribution of placements in the care populations of their respective countries.

Post-care living arrangements also differed between countries. In Spain and Hungary a high proportion of young people at the time of the interview were living in extended residential provision, where they can stay up to the age of 25 if they are in full-time education. In Denmark and Sweden they were likely to be living independently, either alone or with partners, and in England it was more usual for them to have their own tenancies in social housing. One notably under-represented group in our research sample were those who had been in kinship care. This is the most common form of out-of-home placement in Spain, reflecting the cultural expectation that families will look after their

*Table 2*
**Proportion of age group in care and in different types of placement**

|  | % in care | % in foster care | % in residential care |
|---|---|---|---|
| Denmark | 1.3 | 47 | 41 (12) 4* |
| Hungary | 0.8 | 50 | 50 |
| Spain | 0.6 | 48 | 52 |
| Sweden | 1.0 | 75 | 25 |
| UK | 0.5 | 73 | 14 |

* 12% other forms of care including boarding school

own. The different traditions of placement in the five countries are further discussed later in this chapter.

The achieved sample of 170 young men and women did reasonably reflect the characteristics of the long-term care populations in all countries, with the exception that there were more females than males, especially in Sweden. The gender imbalance was partly accounted for by the inclusions criterion that the young person must have shown some "educational promise" at age 16, and in all countries girls perform better than boys in the general population as well as among those in care.

## Results

### The invisibility of young people in care

The most important finding from the early part of the study was how little is known about longer-term outcomes for children in care and an almost complete absence of information on their educational careers. The literature review carried out by the Sweden team (Höjer *et al*, 2008) found few items focusing on education or academic learning for this group, despite the very extensive literature on children and young people in out-of-home care. In no country other than England have they been identified as a group at particularly high risk of social exclusion due to low educational attainment, although this has been recognised by individual researchers in the USA and Canada (Flynn *et al*, 1998; Trout *et al*, 2008) and in Australia (Cashmore *et al*, 2007).

Because these young people make up such a small proportion of the school population they are rarely identified as needing special or enhanced provision. Yet there is clear evidence that without targeted additional support they are likely to fall behind their peers in the non-care population. Even in England, the only *YiPPEE* country which routinely publishes statistics on educational attainment, no detailed information is available on their post-compulsory education (Cameron *et al*, 2010). The result of this invisibility is that only in the UK has their under-achievement been recognised as a significant policy issue.

### How well are they doing?

In all the countries studied, those in care do much less well than other children, even compared with those from very disadvantaged backgrounds. At age 16, the differences between those in care and those not in care were least marked in Denmark and Sweden, where 70 per cent and 87 per cent respectively completed secondary education in 2006, compared to virtually all of young people in that age cohort (Cameron *et al*, 2010). In England, in the same year, only 12 per cent of young people in care gained sufficient qualifications to progress to the next stage of education, compared to 58 per cent of the age cohort. From the end of compulsory education onwards, cumulative delay in educational attainment becomes a highly significant factor. In Spain, two-thirds of those interviewed and on courses were delayed in acquiring qualifications against the normative expectations for their age (Casas *et al*, 2010). The risk is that they will become discouraged and give up the struggle, as did many of the able young people in our in-depth research sample.

## Family background

Because the first interview took the form of a chronological narrative of their lives, we learned a great deal about the birth families of those interviewed. The most striking finding was how similar they were across the five countries. In almost all cases the parents were separated or divorced, or had never lived together. Before coming into care, most of the research participants had lived with a single mother, a mother and step-father or a mother with a succession of male partners. One or both parents usually suffered from a mental disorder or was addicted to alcohol or drugs. Excluding those who arrived in the country seeking asylum, nearly all young people considered that they had suffered serious neglect as children and abuse of various kinds was the main reason for coming into care. All the families were highly volatile and chaotic, frequently changing their composition and living arrangements and moving house. Parents generally had low levels of education and unskilled occupations or were welfare-dependent.

Some of the interviewees maintained contact with birth parents, usually in order to see siblings still at home or under pressure from social workers or courts. It was more of an obligation for the young person rather than a need or longing for contact and relationship with birth parents. Many of them were quite clear that they wanted nothing to do with their birth families. Only a few reported that a parent had been interested in and supportive of their education, which we know from many decades of educational research is a major factor in academic success (MacBeth *et al*, 2001; Desforges and Abouchar, 2003).

## School experience

Growing up in the kind of family background described above, for most of the young people schooling had been severely disrupted. But rather unexpectedly, we found that young people in Sweden and Denmark were those most likely to have experienced long gaps in their education. In Sweden almost half of the in-depth interview sample (15/33) reported being out of compulsory school for at least one period of more than three months. Six of them had an absence lasting more than a year. They attributed this to a variety of reasons: parents being too incapacitated by alcohol or drugs to get them there in the morning; being kept out of school to look after younger siblings or do housework; or the family moving house and not enrolling them in school. On the other hand, some young people reported that, for them, school had been a haven from an abusive and disorganised home (Höjer *et al*, 2010).

Coming into care usually resulted in more regular attendance but not always. In one case in Denmark a residential institution proposed to set up an on-site school but failed to complete it in the planned time period. The young man concerned could have attended school in a neighbouring village but was not allowed to do so, and bitterly resented missing the whole of sixth grade as a result.

The *YiPPEE* young people had a higher than normal number of school changes, often associated with placement breakdown, and according to their own accounts, most social workers failed to give as much importance to school as to care placements, resulting in delays and gaps in attendance. In general, the young people who did best were those who had fewest changes of school. Many instances of bullying and stigmatisation were reported, especially by young people with a Roma background. Gaps in schooling and changes of school were associated with deficits in basic skills, which in turn prevented many young people in care from progressing to the next level commensurate with their ability. Kate (19), from Denmark, explained the effect of changing school from the student's perspective:

*When changing school you have to start from scratch with friends and everything. That is annoying because you just get adjusted to the classmates and teachers and get used to the books that are used and then you change school and it is all different. New friends, new teachers and new books. Totally different. There are different teaching systems and it is confusing and is bound to influence one's approach to learning.*

The damaging effects of instability on educational attainment were also acutely felt by José (19), a young man from Spain:

*I was doing the first year of upper-secondary education, I arrived at the residential home in the middle of the first year of upper-secondary education, they transferred me to a new school and I failed everything. I failed everything because you can't get into a rhythm, even less so in these situations where you have to go from one place to another, somewhere that isn't your home.*

As Table 3 shows, many of the *YiPPEE* young people had to cope with these difficulties repeatedly. Placements in Spain and Hungary were relatively stable but young people in England, as has been shown in previous research (Jackson and Thomas, 2001), were considerably more likely to have to move placement than those in the other countries.

*Table 3*
**Number of placements reported by 170 young people in five countries**

|  | *1 placement* | *2–3 placements* | *4–10 placements* | *10+ placements* | *Not reported* |
|---|---|---|---|---|---|
| Denmark | 14 | 16 | 5 | – | |
| England | 17 (1–3) | | 13 | 2 | |
| Hungary | 16 | 15 | 2 | – | 2 |
| Spain | 12 | 23 | – | – | |
| Sweden | 13 | 15 (2–4pl) | 5 (5–8) | – | |

## Care experience

The different traditions of care in the five countries are associated with varied experiences for the young people interviewed. Hungary and Spain are moving from the stage when large institutions were the usual form of care for children separated from their families, with, in the past, little prospect of restoration once admitted. There is now more emphasis on the rights and welfare of children and young people, and more attempt to choose the best placement for the individual child, together with an ethos of normalisation, the same progression as happened in the other three countries much earlier (Jackson, 2006). The legacy of the former system can be seen to have both positive and negative features. For example, it does seem to bring greater stability, as shown in Table 3, and a more controlled environment committed to promoting learning in its broader sense. Warm relationships were reported between staff and residents.

The respect for learning in residential settings both in Spain and Hungary shines through the young people's accounts. In Hungary, especially, several respondents emphasised the importance of learning being regarded as a basic value, together with the principle that everybody is studying for their own benefit. Both foster families and children's homes also promoted the idea that, in order to get further in life, school performance has to be good. Unfortunately this principle was sometimes in conflict with the imperative of becoming economically independent.

Extended residential provision in Spain and Hungary was helpful to many young people by easing the problems of everyday living, giving them more opportunity to concentrate on their studies. However, in Hungary especially, it went along with a degree of regimentation and control, even for those in their 20s, which would probably be unacceptable to their contemporaries in other countries. For instance, in some there were prescribed study times, known as *silentium*, when no other activities were allowed, and strict rules about time-keeping were enforced. Living conditions were sometimes Spartan – one young woman told how she had to sleep in the middle layer of a three-tier bunk bed (Casas *et al*, 2010).

Overall, foster care appeared to have a better record of promoting educational achievement, even in Denmark, where most residential workers are qualified pedagogues and which has a positive tradition of boarding education (Bryderup and Trentel, 2010). Whatever the placement type, there is clear evidence from this study that having well-educated carers, whether social educators, pedagogues or foster carers, makes a substantial contribution to engaging with education and progressing to higher levels.

## Attainment and participation across countries

Cross-country comparisons of achievement are difficult because the education systems and expectations in the five countries are so different. They are described in detail in the national reports which can be accessed on the *YiPPEE* website. They have in common a period of nine to 11 years of free compulsory education between the ages of five and 16 (18 in Hungary). In Denmark and Sweden education is comprehensive (non-selective) from three to 19. In the other countries pathways increasingly diverge with age, depending partly on personal choice. In Spain and Hungary diversification into specialist vocational routes occurs as early as 14. Students usually have to achieve a certain standard at age 16 to progress to upper-secondary education. This may either be academic, leading onto Bachelor's level courses in college or university, or vocational. Higher vocational courses may still leave open the possibility of accessing tertiary education, while lower level ones lead either to further training for skilled occupations or directly to employment (or unemployment).

### Typical pathways

In all countries, four or five typical pathways were identified:

1. progression through school in line with the age cohort on the academic route;
2. academic route with delay (i.e. repeating years, retaking courses of study, starting university later than normal);
3. vocational pathway leading either to study at college or university or work-based training (non-graduate);
4. specific short-cycle vocational training;
5. "yo-yo" pathways: enrolling and dropping out of courses, frequent changes of direction. This group also included some young people in every country whose progress was held back by ill-health, both physical and mental.

Bearing in mind that all young people interviewed had been selected for showing educational promise at 16, it was remarkable how few were able to follow Pathway 1. Direct comparison of the numbers entering university is difficult because of the custom for students in Denmark and Sweden to delay the start of their university studies, sometimes until their mid-20s. This meant that, because our target group was aged 19–21, some of those who might go to university later were not there at the time of the interview.

Table 4 shows the highest level attained by the time of the second interview, including the numbers enrolled on Bachelor-level courses at that point. The Danish team was initially optimistic that the low proportion of their young people in care accessing university (3% nationally) might change significantly with age. Examination of the national figures for a cohort of those in care at 16, born in 1976–79, shows that by age 30 the proportion only rises to six per cent, far below the figure for youth not in care (Bryderup *et al*, 2010). This proportion is similar to the findings for the other four countries, as shown in Table 4.

*Table 4*
**Educational qualifications attained and Bachelor qualifications being studied for**

|  | DK | EN | HU | SE | SP |
|---|---|---|---|---|---|
| Completed secondary-school qualification | 32 | 26 | 13 | 26 | 28 |
| **Highest qualification attained** | | | | | |
| Compulsory school-leaving qualification at age 16 | 15 | 1 | 25 | 7 | 1 |
| Academic qualification at age 18 | 10 | 5 | | 16 | 0 |
| Vocational qualification at age 18 | 9 | 6 | 8 | | 3 |
| Bachelor-level qualification | 0 | 1 | 0 | 0 | 1 |
| Enrolled on/attending Bachelor-level course | 10 | 12 | 11 | 7 | 5 |

### Academic versus vocational routes

In all countries there was a strong tendency for young people in or leaving care to be steered into vocational in preference to academic pathways. This may have been appropriate in some cases but often it seemed motivated by a desire by them to become self-supporting at the earliest possible opportunity, far sooner than their family-based peers. The tendency is well illustrated by the following quotations from a young woman from Spain and her social educator (residential care worker):

> Residential home social educator: *When she told us she wanted to do general (academic) upper-secondary education and go to university we told her to keep her feet on the ground. We told her, 'You're going to leave here soon, who's going to pay for your studies? How are you going to manage it?... If you don't want to go back to your family, you need to earn money to have a flat'... We talked to her and I saw the need for her to do some vocational training and work.*

Teresa (21): *I got really depressed then. Because I wanted to study general upper-secondary education, right . . . and I was very sure, I wanted to be a social educator, and I remember that at the residence . . . they told me, 'You can't,' because obviously, being at a residence I couldn't study general upper-secondary education, as it wouldn't give me a quick entry into the labour market . . . But I'm certain that my goal is university . . . I want to study business management and administration.*

Similar attitudes among professionals and residential carers were recorded in Hungary, where the young people were typically advised to undertake short-cycle vocational courses and sometimes piled up a series of low-level qualifications instead of building on their achievements and progressing to more advanced studies. These short training courses did not necessarily lead to employment: one young woman in Hungary recounted how she had successfully followed two different specialist cookery programmes but in the end was grateful to get a job as a cleaner on shift work.

The influence of different welfare regimes became increasingly evident at the post-secondary stage. In Denmark and Sweden, for instance, there are relatively generous educational grants and loans and a wide range of adult education opportunities available – 'One can never be locked out of education in Denmark' (Bryderup and Trentel, 2010). In Sweden there is a one-year "catch-up" programme for those who did not pass the basic secondary-school certificate first time round. However, things become more difficult after leaving care: of the eight young people in Sweden planning for university at the first interview, five had given up hope a year later. It is noteworthy that of the seven already enrolled on BA programmes, six were women. Educational pathways in Hungary and Spain were less flexible than in other countries, and once embarked on a non-academic vocational route, it was very difficult to switch back to one leading to university.

### The role of leaving care teams and advisers
In England there were signs that, as a result of the strong policy steer provided by the 1997–2010 Labour Government (DfES, 2006a), more leaving care workers were encouraging young people to stay in education longer and providing financial support for them to do so. This had enabled one authority which employed a qualified teacher as a member of its leaving care team to achieve a twentyfold increase over five years in the numbers of those going from care to university. However, in England too we observed a tendency for young people who lacked well-informed advice to enrol in a series of short courses not leading anywhere. Unfortunately the careers advisory service "Connexions" was severely cut back in 2011 as an economy measure and this is likely to leave many care leavers floundering in a maze of possible study options (Jackson and Cameron, 2011).

## The contribution of informal learning

European education policy strongly promotes informal learning – the kind of learning that goes on outside educational settings and in "free" time (Daly and Gilligan, 2005; European Commission, 2008). Participation in leisure activities varied considerably between countries and tended to fall off sharply when the young person left school. However, for children in care, such activities have a particular value in widening their social networks and bringing them into contact with adults well integrated into their communities, who can act as role models (often in contrast to their birth parents). On the whole those individuals who had been most successful in formal education settings were also those who engaged in the largest number and greatest variety of leisure and cultural activities, which is perhaps unsurprising. But there were also instances of people who had left school but were then drawn back into education through recreational pursuits. In England, volunteering was particularly popular and enabled some young people who had not flourished in the school environment to develop new skills and interests which eventually led to them to enrol on formal study courses (Hollingworth, 2012).

## Barriers and facilitators for continuing education

There was a wide measure of agreement among professionals and caregivers on the factors that enabled or prevented young people from doing well at school and continuing in education beyond the legally compulsory age. These factors fell into four groups: systemic, school-related, care-related and individual.

### Systemic factors

Many professionals cited as a major obstacle the division between social services and education and their failure to work together, sometimes leading to actual conflict, particularly over financial and disciplinary matters. England was the only country where these two aspects of children's care had been brought together (in 2004), both at central government and local levels, and this was thought to have made a big improvement, along with the appointment of senior teachers to take a strategic overview of education in care (Berridge *et al*, 2009).

### School-related factors

These can be summarised as: failure to recognise the numerous obstacles to attendance and learning faced by children before care; insufficient remedial help to catch up on missed schooling; unsympathetic responses to behavioural difficulties related to traumatic experiences; too little protection from bullying; allocation to schools (such as on-site schools in residential homes) only designed to prepare students for low-level occupations; and under-estimation of ability due to assumptions based on social class or ethnicity.

### Care-related factors

Factors in this group were: placement with carers who give little encouragement or support for educational achievement; changes of care placements, especially when they involve change of school; low expectations or lack of interest by social workers; lack of informed advice about routes to further or higher education; and promotion of early financial independence over investment in education.

### Individual factors

These were mainly: inadequate basic skills, lack of motivation; negative attitudes to education in birth family; depression and loss of hope due to repeated failure and lack of support from carers; financial pressures and exhaustion; and health problems, both physical and mental.

Young people themselves, especially in Hungary, were inclined to attribute success almost entirely to personal characteristics such as motivation, determination, persistence and hard work. It is important to note, however, that some recognised the role of teachers and carers who refused to give up on them. One example was the social educator who said:

> I and her teacher, we had to push her very hard. She wanted money, she wanted other things, but I just said, 'You've got to keep on with your education, that's what really matters,' and she did.

Two Spanish respondents illustrate the tendency of many able young people in care to drop out or lose motivation at the upper-secondary stage, sometimes because of lack of support and encouragement from carers and services but often owing to the stress of trying to find time to study while having to work to support themselves (Casas *et al*, 2010):

> ... it went very well, I got very good marks ... when I reached general upper-secondary education everything changed, of course ... I passed the first year, but in the second year I abandoned the course in the last two months. If I had tried, I could have done it ... I didn't manage my energy levels properly, because if I had, I would have finished that year, I know that. (Nuria, 21, SP)

> ... so I finished compulsory secondary education with top marks and everything. The beginning of upper-secondary education went well and then I started to have problems ... that's when I started to go downhill. (Nando, 21, SP)

## Discussion and conclusions

Identifying a social problem is the first step to addressing it. In the past the low educational attainment of children in care has been recognised by practitioners but simply accepted as the natural order of things or attributed to their family background (Berridge, 2007). Researchers began to challenge this perception in the 1980s (Jackson, 1987; Fletcher-Campbell and Hall, 1990; Jackson and Sachdev, 2001) but it was not until comparative statistics began to be routinely collected in the UK that policy-makers became aware of the enormous size of the gap between those in care and others, and the link was made with their stunted life chances (Feinstein and Brassett-Grundy, 2005; Jackson and Simon, 2006; DCSF, 2007; Jackson, 2007a). An important recommendation from the *YiPPEE* project, therefore, was that governments or agencies responsible for the out-of-home care of children should collect and publish annual statistics related to their educational participation and progress and compare them with those in the general population. Secondly, supporting educational attainment should be an explicit duty for social workers and caregivers and relevant training provided to foster carers and residential workers.

Some young people reported that teachers see promoting the social mobility of young people who show ability and motivation as an important aspect of their role. Our impression was that social workers in Europe rarely seem to share this perception. Children in care come overwhelmingly from the bottom of society; most of their parents could be considered socially excluded (Bebbington and Miles, 1989; Höjer *et al*, 2010; Cameron *et al*, 2012). Unless those who are looked after in public care can be enabled to reach educational levels substantially higher than their parents, leading to stable and rewarding employment, they are at great risk of slipping back as adults into the extremely disadvantaged social stratum from which they originated, undoing any beneficial effects of their care experience.

## Implications for practice

The young people we interviewed have no doubt that their social workers and carers need to be better informed about educational opportunities and to give far greater emphasis to educational achievement than they do at present, while on the other hand schools should show greater understanding of the effects of traumatic life experiences, bereavement and separation. Foster carers need to understand that providing support for education is one of their most important functions. There should be much more effort to place children with well-educated carers and to give them the financial and practical resources they need. Multi-professional teams responsible for supporting young people in their transition to adulthood should include well-qualified teachers and career advisers.

The findings from these five European countries are so consistent that it is likely that they would apply to the other developed countries. Clearly governments and agencies need to take a far more holistic view of children's lives in and after care. Even social educators or pedagogues in social democratic countries appear to operate within class-based systems that lead them to make assumptions about the type of education that is suitable for youth in care. There was a strong tendency to steer them down lower-level vocational rather than academic pathways irrespective of their cognitive ability or school performance. It is a mistake to think that because children in care come overwhelmingly from homes where parents are employed in manual or unskilled jobs (or none) that basic education is all they need. On the contrary, social mobility through education is even more important for them than for other young people if they are to achieve successful integration into adult society.

### *Acknowledgements*
This chapter is based on a project funded under the European Union Framework 7 Programme on Youth and Social Inclusion. The project was directed by Sonia Jackson and co-ordinated by Claire Cameron. It was carried out by a partnership of five EU countries:

Denmark: Inge M Bryderup, Marlene Quisgaard Trentel
Hungary: Marta Korintus, Andrea Racz, Robert Csak
Spain: Ferran Casas, Carme Monserrat Boada, Sara Malo
Sweden: Ingrid Höjer, Helena Johansson, Margreth Hill
England: Sonia Jackson, Claire Cameron, Hanan Hauari, Katie Hollingworth, Meli Glenn.

The contributions of the five country teams and the support of our EU scientific officer, Marc Goffart, are gratefully acknowledged. However, the views expressed are those of the authors and not necessarily those of the other researchers or of the European Union.

# 15 Education pathways for lone asylum-seeking and refugee young people

*Ala Sirriyeh and Jim Wade*

*This chapter draws on findings from a recent study on foster care for unaccompanied refugee and asylum-seeking young people to examine their educational pathways (see Wade et al, 2012). The study was funded by the Big Lottery and involved a partnership between BAAF and the universities of York and Bedfordshire. Its purpose was to:*

- *describe the fostering experiences of young people and foster carers;*
- *identify specific features of the fostering task in the context of the broad resettlement needs of young people;*
- *assess the support and services provided to young people and foster carers by local authorities and other agencies;*
- *identify factors that facilitated or constrained the making and support of placements.*

## Introduction

Unaccompanied refugee and asylum-seeking young people are under the age of 18, claiming asylum in their own right and with no parent/regular caregiver in the UK (Home Office, 2002). They are supported by children's services in the local authorities in which they present in a range of accommodation including residential care, but more commonly shared housing with floating support or foster care. They are likely to be placed in foster care if they are under 16 years old when they arrive or are deemed particularly vulnerable. In policy terms an "asylum seeker" is someone who has applied for asylum and is waiting for a decision on their claim. A "refugee" has been granted asylum and given leave to remain in the UK, initially for five years. Many unaccompanied asylum-seeking young people are granted Discretionary Leave to Remain until the age of 17.5 years (a temporary form of leave to remain).

The fieldwork for our study took place from 2009 to 2011 in four local authorities across England. The study incorporated: a census drawing on local authority information systems to provide a basic profile of all 2,113 unaccompanied minors looked after by the four local authorities; a postal survey of 133 foster carers who were caring for an unaccompanied young person on 31 December 2009; case-study interviews with 23 foster carers and 21 young people in their care;[17] three young people focus groups; four social

---

17 All names used in this chapter are fictitious.

worker focus groups; and interviews with children's asylum team managers (see Wade *et al*, 2012, for a complete description of the methods employed in this study).

Since most unaccompanied young people who access foster care do so before the age of 16, it was not surprising to find that most of the 133 young people in our survey of foster carers had entered the UK before this age, almost one-half before the age of 14, and most were still under 18 years of age at data collection (80% aged 15–17). The vast majority were male (88%), reflecting the distribution of countries of origin. Although these young people came from 17 different countries, the majority (69%) were from Afghanistan. At data collection, most had been in the UK for some time (median stay of 22 months) and had been living in these placements for one year or more (only 37% for a shorter period). All had been placed with unrelated foster carers, most transculturally with carers working in the independent sector (83%). The purpose of these placements was primarily for care and upbringing and to prepare young people for transition to adulthood. Despite their length of time in the UK, most of them (82%) were still awaiting a final decision on their asylum application at data collection.

This chapter explores the young people's educational backgrounds, their academic and social experiences in education in the UK and the support available from their foster carers, social workers and schools. Along with a secure home base, access to education and a positive educational experience are crucial aspects of resettlement. Access to education provision is essential for English language acquisition and for academic progress. However, it offers not only an opportunity to build for the future, but is also a pivotal site through which young people can re-establish the rhythms of ordinary living and begin to develop friendships and social networks in the UK (Kohli, 2007).

## Educational backgrounds

Research with refugee and asylum-seeking young people has highlighted the diversity of their educational backgrounds and experiences (Candappa and Egharevba, 2000; Wade *et al*, 2005; Rutter, 2006). These experiences were reflected in our sample, which included those who had no experience of education in their countries of origin but also young people who had been in school for several years, albeit often disrupted by conflict and/or their long migration journeys.

Education systems and access to education may vary between countries of origin. However, differences aligned to socio-economic backgrounds were also apparent within countries. Among the Afghan young people (the largest nationality represented in the sample) some had never attended school in Afghanistan while others had been in school on average for around five to six years.

Differences between schools in countries of origin and the UK were also outlined by young people. Although a few had studied English at school in their countries of origin, most had not. Young people highlighted key differences in approaches to teaching and access to some technology, including computers and science labs, which some had not used before. Those who had never attended school had to adjust to not only a new language, curriculum and educational approach, but also to the concept, routine and structure of school and to learning what it means to be a student.

## Experiences of education in the UK

### Access to education

Although refugee and asylum-seeking young people have a clear legal entitlement to places in mainstream education, there can be delays in accessing places and variations in the degree of co-operation between social care and education agencies in resolving these problems (Audit Commission, 2000; Candappa, 2000; Rutter, 2003; Hek, 2005a).

Around one-third (34%) of young people in the survey sample had experienced problems accessing education. Experiences varied according to their age at the time they arrived in the UK, the time of year they arrived, the degree to which local schools were oversubscribed and the extent to which foster carers and other professionals were active in mediating access. Young people experienced waiting times ranging from a few weeks to six months before gaining admission to school or college, which caused frustration for some:

> I keep asking my social worker . . . I know some boys, they live in a family, they went straightaway and I went after six, seven months and I said to my social worker, 'Why is that?' And they said, 'Because it's your age,' or something like that . . . I want to learn English. I don't care if I can't read and write it, but I want to learn to talk, how to talk to people. (Abbas)

Some young people had no access to education during this waiting period, while others attended short courses over the summer holidays or language lessons part-time at voluntary sector organisations. Although young people mostly enjoyed their time on these courses, they did not compare to full-time school or college, as Ermir explained:

> I was learning in the refugee centre, just a bit in English, like two hours a day. That was nothing like a school.

Young people who arrived part way through Year 11 or were age-disputed found it particularly difficult to get a school placement and often had a long wait before they could begin college (see also Wade et al, 2005). Those aged 16–17 were usually placed on English for Speakers of Other Languages (ESOL) courses at further education colleges rather than in school. Young people who arrived in the final term of a school year also experienced difficulties attaining a place as the school year was winding down.

Foster carers reported variations in the degree of co-operation and support between social work teams and Local Education Authorities (LEAs) in facilitating young people's access to education (Candappa, 2000; Children's Legal Centre, 2003; Wade *et al*, 2005). While some foster carers described young people's relatively smooth transition into local schools, often facilitated by joint action with social workers, the school and the LEA, others recounted being the sole advocates for young people. While some found this experience challenging, others simply "got on with it" either because they regarded this as properly being a part of their role or because it had to be done and no one else was doing it.

## Attitudes towards education

There is evidence that education is a high priority for many refugee and asylum-seeking young people in the UK (Jackson *et al*, 2005; Brownlees and Finch, 2010). They have been described by practitioners as often being highly motivated with regard to participation and progress in education (Wade *et al*, 2005; Kohli 2007; Jackson and Cameron, 2012, reprinted in this volume). This view was also prevalent among social workers in our study, who described young people's high aspirations and commitment to "making something of themselves". These were seen sometimes as unrealistic in the context of limited previous education experience and English-language skills and the short time available in which to accomplish these tasks (see Kohli, 2007; Watters, 2008). Social workers and foster carers admired young people's focus on education and the good progress they generally made. There were, however, also some echoes of questions asked by practitioners in an earlier study conducted by Wade and colleagues (2005) about the reasons behind this determination and the sometimes complex and multiple reasons for young people's journeys.

The survey asked foster carers to report on whether young people were enjoying their studies, whether they attended regularly and whether the courses they were pursuing were appropriate for their academic abilities as foster carers understood them.

*Table 1*
**Attendance, enjoyment and relevance of education – per cent**

|  | Not at all true | To some extent true | To a large extent true | Number |
|---|---|---|---|---|
| S/he enjoys education now | 2 | 33 | 65 | 129 |
| S/he attends regularly now | 3 | 9 | 88 | 124 |
| The courses s/he is doing are appropriate for his/her abilities | 3 | 26 | 71 | 124 |

Table 1 shows that very few young people had attendance problems and that, from the perspective of foster carers, most were enjoying and receiving an appropriate education. However, in these latter respects, some ambivalence was reported for around one-quarter to one-third of young people.

Some groups were rather more likely than others to be undertaking courses appropriate to their current abilities. This tended to be the case for those who were older, for young people without moderate to severe emotional, social or behavioural difficulties and for young people who had lived in the current placement for a longer period of time. Where they had experienced more placement moves in the past, there was also some association with a poorer current attendance pattern and for current courses to be less appropriate for their abilities.[18] Some caution is needed here, since none of these associations is particularly strong. Overall, however, the findings are consistent with the fragmented evidence that currently exists on the motivation and commitment of unaccompanied young people to the pursuit of education as one crucial means of finding constructive resettlement pathways (Hek, 2005b; Rutter, 2006).

Young interviewees expressed their determination to succeed and spoke of their intention to stay out of trouble, work hard and focus on their education. Omid's foster carer said:

> The only way I can put it is he has an agenda . . . wants to learn and didn't want to get into trouble.

Although most young people were strongly motivated to succeed in their education, this was not without exception. There were some reports from foster carers of poor attendance, a reluctance to attend school or college and a lack of motivation in completing homework. Aspirations to do well centred on a desire to make the most of their time in education and to achieve their potential. However, interests in educational progress were sometimes also tied into the recurring theme of future immigration pathways. Young people and foster carers hoped that educational progress would help young people with their asylum claim by demonstrating that they were making a successful life in the UK. Ban-hwa's carer was concerned about the effect his poor attendance and performance at school was likely to have on his application to extend his leave to remain. She had told him, 'If you carry on like this, it's not going to be good when you go in front of the immigration judge.'

---

18  Kendall's tau-b tests for courses appropriate for current abilities and older age ($p = 0.04$, t 0.167, N = 119); emotional, social or behavioural difficulties ($p = 0.019$, t 0.201, N = 120); time in placement ($p = 0.024$, t 0.178, N = 111). Past placement moves and appropriateness of current course ($p = 0.046$, t −0.174, N = 118); attendance ($p = 0.035$, t −0.185, N = 118).

## Education placement and language support

The vast majority of young people in our survey sample were attending mainstream schools (primary or secondary) or were in further education (see Table 2). None had yet progressed into higher education, although some were preparing to do so. Only five young people were aged 18 at the point of data collection and all of these were pursuing courses in further education or school. Two young people were reported by carers to have rejected education in favour of part-time employment.

*Table 2*
**Young people's education status (N = 130)**

|                                              | Number | Per cent |
|----------------------------------------------|--------|----------|
| Mainstream school                            | 88     | 67.5     |
| Special school                               | 4      | 3        |
| Further education                            | 31     | 24       |
| Higher education                             | 0      | 0        |
| English-language provision (not school based)| 4      | 3        |
| Pupil referral unit                          | 1      | 1        |
| Refuses education                            | 2      | 1.5      |

Many young people were in need of help to develop their English language skills. Some at college were attending ESOL courses, often in combination with other academic and/or vocational courses. A large minority who were attending mainstream school (43%) were receiving additional classroom-based language support. A smaller proportion of school students also received language support outside school (21%). This provision was organised through schools or children's services and tended to comprise private home tuition or tuition organised in community education centres. In many cases, it provided a valuable supplement to help young people catch up and take better advantage of subject-based teaching in the classroom.

Young people and foster carers agreed that acquiring and developing English-language skills was a crucial aspect of young people's resettlement needs (Candappa and Egharevba, 2000; Marriot, 2001; Stanley, 2001). First, it was important for future education progression. It enabled young people to participate and gain good qualifications, but also to move beyond ESOL courses to other academic and vocational subjects that would help them to pursue their chosen education and career paths. Second, learning English was also very important for enabling social interactions in school and beyond:

*Even if you want to try and make a friend you can't. When you don't know anything, how can you say something to them?* (Omid).

Language acquisition was therefore reinforced by foster carers helping young people to embed these skills through everyday routines within the home; initially, for example, by using dictionaries, flash cards and resources on the internet.

## Educational progress

Many unaccompanied young people are reported to progress well in education both academically and socially (Wade *et al*, 2005; Kohli, 2007; Cameron *et al*, 2012). It has been suggested that this level of engagement differs in comparison to many other looked after children who are more frequently reported as performing poorly in education (Berridge, 2007; Kohli, 2007; Berridge and Saunders, 2009).

However, young people's central focus on education and drive to succeed appeared to place some of them under considerable pressure. With insecure immigration status, the precariousness of plans for future residence in the UK and interruptions in earlier education experience, the time in which young people can achieve and progress in education is often compressed both by their experiences and by future possibilities. Many felt the pressure of the clock ticking as they sought to achieve their education goals. Samuel, aged 17, hoped to become a paramedic but after finding out from his teacher the qualifications he would need in order to do this, he was unsure if he could achieve this in time. He said:

*If it happened here when I was a kid, if I started here, so it could be all right, but now it's really, I think so, already my life's passed.*

Where a young person's age is disputed this can also create a compressed time period in which to achieve education goals. Rashid was initially placed in Year 9 before being age assessed and moved to Year 11 after his school suggested he might be older than the age he claimed, leaving him with insufficient time to prepare for his exams. Feelings of uncertainty about future education and employment prospects (and the timescales needed to achieve them) were only reinforced where asylum claims were unresolved and the risk of deportation continued to cloud the future.

Foster carers reported that most young people were doing "quite" (46%) or "very" well (25%) in their studies and that less than one-third (29%) were faring quite poorly. Most carers also reported that young people's educational circumstances had improved since they had first come to live with them "to a large extent" (75%) or at least "to some degree" (21%). There was an obvious association between young people being rated as doing well educationally and them enjoying their studies, attending regularly and participating in courses that were appropriate for their skills and abilities. It was in relation to the relevance of the educational programme for the young people, however, that the association with good educational progress was strongest.[19] Where this programme was considered strongly relevant, four-fifths of young people (81%) were thought to be making good educational progress compared to one-half (50%) where it was considered less relevant.

A number of other child and social work factors were also associated with educational progress. Young people were more likely to be rated as making good progress where:

- they were not considered to have emotional or behavioural difficulties (p<0.001);
- they had a range of hobbies and interests (p = 0.015);
- they had made fewer past placement moves (p = 0.034);[20]
- there was some evidence of positive social work planning (p = 0.01);[21]
- where contact with the young person's social worker was considered to be helpful for the young person (p = 0.002) and for the foster carer (p = 0.03).

The first three points relate to the young person, taking account of aspects of their characteristics, care careers and current interests. The second set refers to the framework of social work support that surrounded the young person and foster carer. Proactive social work support and planning for the child, combined with foster carers themselves feeling reasonably well supported and confident, presumably helped to provide an environment in which young people could harness their own motivation to succeed. However, this was less likely to be the case where young people presented significant emotional and behavioural challenges or, to some extent, where they had been unsettled by past placement moves.

To identify which of these factors were most closely associated with young people making good educational progress, the above list of variables was included in a stepwise linear regression. We also included the foster carers' assessment of whether the education the young person was receiving now was appropriate for their current abilities. As we have seen, this was closely associated with educational progress (p<0.001) while, *a priori*, retaining some independence from it.[22]

---

19 Kendall's tau-b tests for educational progress and enjoying education (p = 0.02, t 0.194, N = 123); attending regularly (p = 0.02, t 0.196, N = 120); appropriateness of courses for ability (p≤0.001, t 0.352, N = 120).

20 We also checked to make sure that past placement moves was not simply an effect of length of time in the UK (p=0.88) or of the young person's age (p = 0.16).

21 Our planning score provided a proxy measure of social work planning. It was based on responses to whether foster carers had received written copies of the child's care plan, personal education plan and health plan. These were combined to provide the 0–3 score. Possession of these provided an admittedly crude indication that social work planning was taking place.

22 Whether the young person enjoys education (p = 0.07) or attends regularly (p = 0.3) were excluded. The appropriateness of the course was much more strongly associated with educational progress (p<0.001) than either of these in multivariate analysis.

This analysis showed that good progress was more likely where:

- the young person was not considered to have emotional or behavioural difficulties (p = 0.001, Beta 0.305);
- the course s/he is doing now is appropriate for his/her current abilities (p<0.001, Beta 0.388).[23]

The first reinforces what is known about risks of poor educational attainment for young people with emotional and behavioural difficulties in adolescence (Farmer *et al*, 2008). In relation to looked after young people generally, studies have revealed relatively high levels of mental health, emotional and behavioural problems among young people in the care system (McCann *et al*, 1996; Meltzer, 2003). If these cannot be ameliorated there is also evidence of their lasting effects for young people leaving care (Dixon *et al*, 2006). Although there is some evidence that unaccompanied young people may fare rather better than their UK-born peers while they are looked after, and may be less likely to display challenging behaviours and emotional disturbance (Dixon *et al*, 2006; Sinclair *et al*, 2007), where they do have emotional or behavioural difficulties our evidence, unsurprisingly, suggests that they are more likely to struggle educationally.

The second brings the question of assessment and matching to the fore. Once young people arrive in the UK, the diversity of their social and educational backgrounds signals the need for careful assessment of their educational backgrounds, capabilities, interests and aspirations as a prelude to identifying appropriate education and training opportunities. Thorough assessment is important, not least because many education professionals feel they receive insufficient information about refugee children's educational histories and needs when they are referred to schools (Ofsted, 2003; Remsbury, 2003). Our evidence suggests that the educational progress young people are able to make may suffer where not enough attention is paid to finding an appropriate match. It would not be surprising to find that young people would find less enjoyment and motivation in education where they had been routinely allocated to courses that were not consistent with their interests and aspirations. Abbas, for example, was having difficulty staying motivated at college:

> They teach something like I done before. So it's a little bit boring for me because I've already done it.

The association between educational progress and social work support may therefore be mediated by the activities of social workers (in tandem with education professionals) directed at helping young people to access and manage courses that were reasonably well

---

23 This model explained 29 per cent of the variation in educational progress (R2 0.288).

matched to their abilities and interests and/or by facilitating foster carers to provide that day-to-day support. In these circumstances the prospects for educational success appeared to be propitious.

## Supporting education

Given the varied educational histories of unaccompanied young people and the challenges that are present during the broader resettlement process, placing them in well-supported educational placements as early as possible is likely to help their adjustment and well-being (Jones, 1998; Chase *et al*, 2008). The interest and encouragement of adults who are important to the young person (including teachers, foster carers and social workers) play a key role in supporting their educational progress (Gilligan, 2007b). When asked about who helped them with their education, most young people in our study focused on particular teachers or foster carers, but some described more of a 360-degrees base of support. Samir, for example, said he was "surrounded" by support from his foster family, friends and college.

Schools can provide a "safe and benevolent environment" where teachers have the potential to function as guides in a new society (Ruuk, 2002, cited in Watters, 2008). Most young people reported having positive relations with their teachers and felt encouraged and supported by them. Teachers and language support staff were often described as kind, helpful and encouraging, although occasionally there were more negative experiences.

Young people valued social workers' role in facilitating access to good schools, further education or material resources, such as laptops or bursaries. While a few spoke to their social workers about their progress at school, this day-to-day education support and nurturing outside school was generally provided by foster carers. In the words of one carer:

*Well, the social worker hasn't got time to do education with them, it's just social things, how things are improving and listen to their complaints.*

Unaccompanied minors in foster care and residential care have been found to be more likely to be continuously engaged in education than those living in semi-independent or independent accommodation (Wade *et al*, 2005). Stanley (2001) found that those living in semi-independent accommodation often had no one to show a day-to-day interest in their education progress. Gilligan (2007a) highlights the daily mentoring role that exists within many foster carers' and residential workers' relationships with young people and explains how this can promote educational performance (see also Jackson *et al*, 2005).

In the current study it was found that foster carers – and often their own birth children (see also Gilligan, 2007b) – frequently demonstrated this day-to-day support and interest in young people's education. They regarded education support as a key part of their role, most singled out educational progress as one of the main priorities they had for their foster children, and they tried to encourage and motivate young people to fulfill their potential. They liaised with school staff, attended parent evenings, helped with homework, supported their involvement in extra-curricular activities and helped to motivate young people to succeed:

> I've encouraged him to push himself, particularly intellectually, 'cos he's a bright boy... It's that thing you do with your children, you try to raise their aspirations. You just don't sort of settle. (Eleanor, Arian's foster carer)

Haaroon spoke to his foster carer every day about school during his first year in the UK:

> I used to come home, especially at the beginning, she used to talk to me every day after school: 'What happened? You all right? How was your day?' And we used to talk.

By maintaining regular communication with young people and their schools, foster carers were able to advocate and support young people early on if problems occurred and provide the support they needed through this intensive period of readjustment.

## Education and social relationships

School or college is a main site through which young people began building their social networks in the UK (Candappa and Egharevba, 2000; Wade *et al*, 2005; Beirens *et al*, 2007; Kohli, 2007). Young people who were initially placed in language support units at school described the supportive environment this provided at that stage:

> I could make some friends in that class as well because they all didn't know how to speak English so we had some funny conversations. It was all not even English but we had to talk to each other in English. It was really funny. (Ban-hwa)

Other young people attended schools which already had students from their countries of origin and spoke of the social and language support they provided. Although some had found it difficult starting at school when they were unable to communicate in English, most felt they had been welcomed by (at least some of) their peers. Studies have highlighted the importance of good welcome and induction procedures in schools and the development of a school ethos of inclusion and respect in order to enable refugee young people to settle in school (Richman, 1998; Rutter, 2001; Ofsted, 2003; Hek, 2005b). A number of young people mentioned the value of peer mentors. When Samuel started school he was assigned one who guided him towards a peer group that played football at break time and after school. Samuel had moved on to college, but was still in regular contact with these school friends. Others had themselves taken an active role in welcoming other newcomers into their schools.

The ethnicity and nationality of friends varied and unsurprisingly this was in part dependent on who young people came into contact with. Those studying ESOL were mainly friends with refugee and migrant young people from their or other countries (Refugee Action, 2003). Those who were in school were usually friends with young people from the ethnic backgrounds represented in their schools and neighbourhoods. Beirens and colleagues (2007) found that young people in their study who attended after-school clubs for refugees often felt a sense of belonging and security there, particularly in cases where they were subjected to racism and prejudice in mainstream school. Some in our study chose to focus their friendships around young people of their own nationality, perhaps because of the familiarity and security of shared language, cultural background and experiences, or because of experiences of racism and exclusion. However, in many cases these friendships were built alongside friendships with young people from other ethnic backgrounds.

While education is often a primary location for social integration, there have also been reports of young people having to contend with bullying and racism in the school environment (Hek, 2005b; Kohli, 2007). Many living in areas with a predominantly white population had experienced racism at school (Brownlees and Finch, 2010). It has been found that asylum seekers and refugees are most likely to experience racist harassment and violence in predominantly white, low-income neighbourhoods (Hemmerman *et al*, 2007; Spicer, 2008). In two schools there had been hostile responses to the presence of a small number of Afghan boys who started at the school around the same time.

Some young people experienced verbal bullying and name calling at school. Navid was being verbally bullied by young people at his school because he could not speak English and was an asylum seeker. Rafi shortened his Afghan name in response to bullying at school. Some of the Afghan boys had experienced violent physical assaults. Majeed had been set upon by a group of boys at the school he attended in his previous placement in a predominantly white area and had one of his teeth knocked out. He had been the only Afghan boy at that school. In contrast, at the school he moved on to there were other Afghan young people and Majeed had friends from a range of ethnic backgrounds. There were far fewer reports of racism in areas with multi-ethnic populations, although Navid (above) attended a school in a multi-ethnic neighbourhood and had experienced racist bullying there.

There was a mixed response from schools to racist behaviour and bullying. Some had strong anti-racism and anti-bullying policies and were swift to respond. Abraham's foster carers said:

*They have a zero tolerance of racism . . . The school phoned me up straight away and told me what had happened.*

In contrast, Navid's school informed his foster carer that the bullying was not serious, but rather just children making fun of other children and therefore "normal" playground behaviour.

Foster carers often advised young people to stay out of trouble, to walk away from the situation and not to retaliate. In addition to protecting young people from being harmed in violence and disorder, foster carers were also anxious about the effect any involvement could have on their application for asylum.

## Conclusion

Unaccompanied asylum-seeking young people come from diverse educational backgrounds, so education assessments play an important role in ensuring access to appropriate courses and support. Some young people had experienced delays in accessing school places. These were attributed to their arrival to the UK late in the school year, or when they were approaching 16 years of age. When their age was subject to uncertainty and/or their appearance was older than their official age, they may also be caught in the gap between school and college.

The development of English-language skills was crucial to young people's experience of successful resettlement. It was important for academic progression and also to enable social interactions in school and beyond. Education is a high priority for many refugee young people in the UK and unaccompanied minors have often been described as highly motivated with regard to participation and progress in education. Very few young people had attendance problems and most were enjoying and receiving an appropriate education. Most foster carers reported that young people's educational progress was on an upward curve. Good progress was less likely where young people had moderate to severe emotional, social and behavioural difficulties, where courses were considered inappropriate for their current needs and abilities and where the packages of support provided by social workers and foster carers were weaker.

Moreover, with an insecure immigration status and interruptions in earlier education experience, the time in which young people can achieve and progress in education is often compressed both by their past experiences and future possibilities. Education was a key area in which foster carers provided support to young people. Foster carers' advocacy and support for young people in education was crucial during a period in which young people had a short timeframe in which to achieve positive education outcomes.

Education was also an important arena within which young people could strengthen their network of social relationships, although experiences of marginality, racism and bullying were not uncommon. How these incidents were managed by foster carers and schools were influential for young people's experiences of cross-cultural relationships.

### *Acknowledgement*

This study was undertaken as a partnership between the University of York (Ala Sirriyeh and Jim Wade), BAAF (John Simmonds) and the University of Bedfordshire (Ravi Kohli). We gratefully acknowledge the vital contribution of all partners.

# 16  Education and self-reliance among care leavers

## Claire Cameron

*Recent English government policy has begun to rectify years of neglect of the education of children in public care. Since 2004 there has been a duty to promote the educational achievement of such children. This chapter, updated from an article in* Adoption & Fostering *(31:1, 2007), reports results from a study on the use of services by a group of young people who have left local authority care, where the proportion holding educational qualifications is above the average for care leavers. Using the concept of self-reliance, the chapter explores how care leavers managed and directed their educational participation and achievement against a background of a lack of financial, familial and inter-personal support. It is argued that self-reliance is a normative concept, but for care leavers, who have often developed self-reliance skills in highly disadvantaged circumstances, one that can be misinterpreted by professionals as being "difficult".*

## Introduction

The education of children in and leaving care has acquired a policy prominence within the UK after many years of neglect. In 2005, of those leaving care, 43 per cent of young people had at least one GCSE or GNVQ, but only six per cent had five GCSEs graded A*–C. This is about one-fifth of the proportion of all young people gaining five A*–C grades at GCSE. More than half (56%) of care leavers had no qualifications at all, which is seven times as many as other young people leaving with no qualifications (ONS, 2005). Information on higher levels of qualification, such as A-levels or university degrees, was not recorded for care leavers (DfES, 2005: Table 4).

Explanations for the low level of educational attainment include numerous adverse factors, such as that children who enter care are highly likely to have had disrupted and impoverished early childhoods; and once in care, they often experience numerous changes of placement and school. Major changes in their lives disrupt participation in examination courses, and historically, social services staff have placed insufficient emphasis on the importance of educational participation for children's future lives (Bebbington, 1998; Broad, 1998; Jackson *et al*, 2005). In recognition of this, the Children Act 2004 placed a new duty on local authorities to promote the educational achievement of children they look after.

While the educational outcomes for care leavers are documented, relatively little is known about how young people who have left care perceive educational participation and attainment and how those who do achieve educational success manage to complete their studies, although there is some evidence from retrospective studies (e.g. Jackson and Martin, 1998; Jackson *et al*, 2005; Mallon, 2007). This chapter examines these issues further, drawing on data from a larger study of care leavers and other young people "in difficulty" aged 17–24 years, and their use of health and other services.

It is argued that care leavers often have a considerable degree of interest in and commitment to education, and that central to their eventual success is their own motivation and initiative-taking, referred to here as "self-reliance". Self-reliance has two dimensions: having confidence in oneself to manage one's own affairs and preferring not to have help. These dimensions can operate either simultaneously or independently. Some people are happy to accept help and be independent – or are "interdependent"; others distrust offers of help following repeated experiences of being "let down".

The concept of self-reliance used here is close to Stein's (2005) discussion of "resilience" in care leavers, in terms of their capacity for overcoming the odds, and coping and recovering from adverse circumstances and debilitating relationships. On the basis of a review of studies of care leavers, Stein argued that they fell into three groups: those who were "moving on", those who were "surviving" and those who were "victims" of their care experience in their current lives. Those care leavers with most resilience were likely to be in the first and second group and less likely to be in the third.

However, in contrast to resilience as used by Stein, which sees care leavers as developing capacities to withstand structural, organisational and familial difficulties, the concept of self-reliance used here incorporates an active dimension. It refers to the young person's own sense of agency in decision-making and action-taking. Self-reliance is familiar to many care leavers, who have often had to take responsibility for family members beyond that expected of their age peers. It also has normative dimensions associated with independence in that it is widely expected of adults living away from others. Care leavers tend to live independently at a much younger age than their contemporaries (Dixon and Stein, 2005). But self-reliance can also have a negative dimension: being overly self-reliant can be interpreted either as rejecting help from professionals or as lacking the personal resources necessary to accept help. In using the concept of self-reliance, this chapter endeavours to locate the specific educational experiences of care leavers in terms of available resources within the context both of society's expectations of young people generally and of the emerging rights and participation agenda among service users of all kinds.

## The study

The data in this chapter are drawn from a larger study (Cameron *et al*, forthcoming), which had three main data sources: 1) literature review; 2) secondary analysis of large-scale data sets to situate care leavers on a continuum of all young people; and 3) an interview study of 80 care leavers, 59 young people "in difficulty" (but not previously looked after in public care) and 29 key service personnel. The aim of the study was to compare the experiences of young people who had been looked after by local authorities with those who had had difficulties but had not been in local authority care, focusing in particular on young people's access to and use of health, education, housing, employment and other services. A key objective was to identify features of young people's lives that facilitated service use.

The current chapter is based on data from 80 care leavers who participated in the third part of the study, and were interviewed between May 2004 and June 2005. Recruiting them was a protracted and difficult process (Wigfall and Cameron, 2006). The intention was to recruit a broadly based sample of care leavers through contacts with 13 local authority leaving care teams across England. Fifty-four care leavers interviewed were clustered primarily in four main areas (one each in the northwest, northeast, London and south of England), designated as "case studies", from which the other interview respondents were subsequently drawn. Twenty-six care leavers came from non-case study areas.

Staff in leaving care teams were asked to give care leavers information about the study, using the research team's materials, and to obtain permission for the researcher to contact them. A time gap of at least 12 months was needed between recruitment and interview to allow for care leavers to experience using services. Periodic questionnaires were sent in the interim, with completion rewarded by incentive vouchers. This process helped to build a relationship between the care leaver and the research team and thereby reduce the possibility of study participants losing interest. Over-sampling was used in the questionnaire phase of the study to allow for attrition, with a target set of 60 participants to be achieved in the final sample. In the event, very few of the original sample dropped away or failed to turn up for appointments, resulting in a final sample one-third larger than originally envisaged.

In-depth interviews covering family background, evaluations of local authority care experiences, informal sources of support, use of formal services and future prospects were completed face to face and recorded for later transcription.[24] Data about service use were coded and entered onto SPSS while NVivo "attributes" were assigned to data about the young people, enabling tables to be easily generated. Analysis was structured initially around the interview schedule questions, although not exclusively: transcripts were coded for data pertaining to questions that emerged in other sections of the interview. For example, questions about accommodation moves frequently generated data about the reasons for moves, such as difficulties with the neighbourhood or educational choices. Analysis then proceeded on a thematic basis, looking in all cases for evidence of the operationalisation of concepts identified from the wider literature on services of potential relevance for care leavers' experience. Self-reliance was one of these concepts.

---

24 All respondents were asked for a preferred pseudonym; these are used in this chapter.

## The sample of care leavers: some characteristics

The intention to achieve a broadly based sample was achieved. However, care leavers interviewed were more likely to be girls (69%), or from a minority ethnic background (31%) than would be expected in the populations of young people as a whole, or of young people in or leaving care in England.[25] The average age of study respondents was 19 years, with most respondents clustered between 18 and 20 years. Twenty-five per cent of study care leavers described themselves as having a disability of some kind, including learning and physical disabilities. Average age for entry into care was 14 years. Overall, respondents were more likely to have entered care between the ages of five and 15 than looked after children as a whole (DfES, 2005).

Study care leavers had experienced a range of placement types and length. The most common was long-term foster care (40%), followed by a mixture of foster care and residential care (25%). The remainder had been in and out of care during their childhood, or had had short-term episodes in residential or foster care or had been fostered by relatives. Just over one-third (39%) of study care leavers were living in a council or housing association social tenancy at the time of interview, and just over a fifth (23%) were living with others, with or without support. The remainder were living in a variety of housing projects, residential homes and lodgings, and nine per cent were in private tenancies. Half of care leavers were living in accommodation where they had some autonomy and could "shut their own front door". Of this group of 40 care leavers, 30 were living alone, nine were living with other people and only one had a formal support service connected to the housing provider.

The relationship between autonomy and having enough support can be problematic. Having autonomy in one's accommodation could be an indicator of self-reliant managing of daily life, or it could mean that the care leaver has insufficient support and feels isolated. Nearly two-thirds (61%) of care leavers thought they had enough support (from all sources including family, friends and formal services) for their daily life, but one-quarter (25%) thought they needed more.

Another indicator of being self-reliant could be the extent to which help from others is sought. When asked about their approach to sorting out problems, over half (58%) of care leavers said they would feel OK asking someone else for help, but a third (35%) said they preferred to sort out their own problems, as exemplified by Becca (20 years, white female), who said, 'I don't really like asking other people for help.' In terms of the two dimensions of self-reliance, the first response could be considered as having an inter-dependent orientation to help, and the second as preferring to act alone.

Furthermore, nearly half (49%) of the care leavers said they did not have any friends

---

25 The proportion of care leavers from minority ethnic backgrounds reflected the populations in the geographic areas selected for the study.

or family they could turn to for support. Among those who did identify such sources, almost three-quarters (71%) of care leavers mentioned a parent. These findings suggest that a sizeable minority are reliant on their own resources, whether by preference or habit, in addition to formal services. However, 61 per cent of the total of care leavers thought their life was easier at the time of interview than a year previously.

## Educational participation and achievement

Study care leavers were more likely to have educational qualifications than care leavers nationally (DfES, 2005). This may be due to more qualified care leavers being more likely to volunteer to take part in the study or it may be because study participants were reporting qualifications obtained after the end of compulsory schooling, which is when national data are collected. Barn *et al* (2005) used a similar age range for a study of care leavers and ethnicity and found that 27 per cent of care leavers aged 16–25 had no qualifications while 47 per cent had at least one GCSE graded A*–G. Table 1 shows that 66 per cent of study care leavers had some educational qualification on leaving school or attained prior to interview. Just over a quarter of the care leavers had attained target GCSEs of at least five A*–C grades. Just over one-third had no school leaving qualifications or had only special certificates for short-term courses which did not have the status of qualifications.

Many study care leavers were participating in education after the end of compulsory schooling. At the time of interview, half of the respondents were involved in some form of education or training or had taken practical steps towards achieving this, such as applying for places on courses. Twenty-eight per cent of care leavers were on a course, 14 per cent were on work-based training and a further 10 per cent were between courses, or waiting

*Table 1*
**Educational qualifications as reported by care leavers – numbers and percentages**

| Qualifications | Care leavers | |
|---|---|---|
| | N | % |
| 1–4 GCSEs (any grade) | 17 | 21 |
| 5+ GCSEs (any grade) | 21 | 26 |
| Target GCSEs (grades A*–C) | 15 | 19 |
| None* | 27 | 34 |
| **Total** | **80** | **100** |

*None includes three care leavers with severe disabilities, one with GCSE equivalent qualifications from Burundi, and awards below GCSE such as NVQ level 1 and special certificates.

*Table 2*
**Current educational engagement among care leavers**

|  | Care leavers | |
|---|---|---|
|  | N | % |
| Higher education | 2 | 3 |
| College-based qualification | 14 | 18 |
| A-levels | 3 | 4 |
| Short course qualification | 2 | 3 |
| Between courses | 18 | 10 |
| Work-based training | 11 | 14 |
| Short course, no qualification | 3 | 4 |
| Day centre | 1 | 1 |
| None | 36 | 45 |
| **Total** | **80** | **100** |

for courses to begin (see Table 2). However, this still left a sizeable proportion of care leavers (nearly half) who were not in education at a time in their lives when continuing education is, for most young people, a major activity. In 2003, among the general population in this age group, more than half (55%) of young people aged 17–19 were in full-time education, tapering to 22 per cent of all young people aged 20–25 (ONS, 2005). However, it is not possible to compare study care leavers with all 19-year-old care leavers. While local authority returns to the Department for Education and Skills (DfES) state that 59 per cent of this group are in employment, education or training, the figure for participation in education is not given separately (DfES, 2005).

## Assistance with education

Care leavers were asked what they were doing currently, whether attending college was part of their thinking and who, if anyone, had helped them gain entry to college. To ascertain what helped with education, two methods were used. First the NVivo attribute data on individual background, such as placement type, was cross-tabulated with having qualifications or not. Second, the discursive data were searched for evidence of assistance given with education from adults working in formal care and education support services. Two are examined here: foster carers and social workers; others may be relevant, such as teachers or birth parents. Although care leavers were not specifically questioned regarding support for educational attainment and participation, data on this emerged when they were requested to give examples of support from formal services. Care leavers holding qualifications and those currently participating in education were then compared with those without qualifications and not currently participating.

## Foster care and foster carers

Nearly all (90%) of the care leavers who held educational qualifications had had at least one placement with foster carers. Long-term foster care was to an extent important to acquiring educational qualifications. Forty per cent of care leavers overall had had a long-term foster care placement, but the proportion was larger, at 50 per cent, among those with educational qualifications. This is consistent with the well-established conclusion that a family base better supports educational achievement than an institutional one (Biehal *et al*, 1995; DH, 2001; Schofield, 2002). Too few respondents had had long-term residential care or schooling to make meaningful comparisons on placement type. Where care leavers had had a mixture of placements on a long-term basis, they were more likely not to have educational qualifications. Thirty-eight per cent of those with no educational qualifications had experienced this type of placement history, compared with 20 per cent of those with such qualifications.

While it is likely that those with long-term foster care experience are also those with fewer educational and other difficulties, the association of long-term foster care with higher educational attainment was striking when examining the highest achievers at GCSE. Table 3 shows that three-quarters of those who had lived in foster care on a long-term basis had five or more GCSES or target GCSEs of five or more A*–C grades.

A comparison of care leavers with educational qualifications with those without,

*Table 3*
**Type of care placement, care leavers with 5+ GCSEs and "target" GCSEs**

| Type of care | Eductional qualification | | | Total |
| | 5+ GCSEs (any grade) | Target GCSEs (grade A*–C) | N | |
|---|---|---|---|---|
| Fostered by relatives | 1 | 1 | 2 | |
| "In care" episode/s | 2 | 2 | 4 | |
| Long-term foster | 14 | 10 | 24 | |
| Long-term mixed | 1 | 1 | 2 | |
| Long-term residential | 1 | 1 | 2 | |
| Residential school | 1 | – | 1 | |
| Short-term foster | 2 | 2 | 4 | |
| Short-term residential | – | 1 | 1 | |
| **Total** | **22** | **18** | **40** | **100** |

focusing on their comments about foster carers, including whether they were still in touch at the time of interview, showed that the former group was more likely to have broadly positive views of their foster carers (61%) than the latter (48%).

However, during interviews very few spontaneous comments were made about foster carers' involvement in education. Only four respondents mentioned foster care as positively supporting educational achievement, for example, providing an environment in which educational participation and success were valued and resources made available for study. Ellie (18 years, white female) said:

> They [foster carers] made me go to school, came out with four As. If I hadn't gone to foster carers I don't know what would have happened.

Matthew (18 years, white male) had completed A-levels at the time of interview, despite disruptions in his home life, and was waiting to find out if he had obtained sufficiently high grades to take up a place in his preferred university. He had been supported through the final stages of schooling by his foster carers, both of whom were teachers, and he planned to stay with them during the university vacations as a private arrangement. Several young people referred to foster care as being part of a "normal" family. It may be that where foster care works well, and a child feels part of "normal family life", educational participation is supported because school attendance becomes an unremarkable and normative expectation.

However, 12 (out of 51 with educational qualifications and foster care experience) young people had had negative experiences of foster care, and in two cases this directly affected their education. In both examples, the foster carer reportedly questioned the young person's academic abilities, suggesting that he/she was "thick" or "stupid" and was not capable of going to college, despite having obtained GCSEs, but should instead go to work and pay rent. Other complaints concerned foster carers being overly strict, differentiating between birth children and foster children, and foster placements which were culturally inappropriate, such as a mixed-race young person being sent to Asian foster carers although herself unaccustomed to Asian cultural practices. Ekua (21 years, white female) explained that she attained her GCSEs despite lack of support from her foster carer 'because when I was at school I did work and I did pay attention'. Arguably Ekua was being self-reliant and also demonstrating resilience (Stein, 2005).

## Social workers

Respondents' references to help from social workers often confused social workers while in care with leaving care workers once they had left. For the most part, comments discussed here refer to social workers while in care. Few comments were made about social workers helping young people to remain in education or pursue educational goals. Overall, 17 of the 53 study care leavers with some educational qualifications said they could "talk to" their social workers (in general) compared to five of the 27 without qualifications. This may reflect a more confiding relationship with social workers established by care leavers who achieved educational success (already more likely to be in long-term foster care).

However, twice as many (18 out of 53) care leavers with educational qualifications said they "didn't like" their social workers relative to those without qualifications (4 out of 27). Many of the comments under this heading concerned not being able to confide in social workers, having trust betrayed, not being listened to and being coerced into specific action in the face of threats. For example, Chanu (20 years, Asian male) said, 'sometimes they frighten you with losing the flat or being sent somewhere else, so that you behave yourself'. The fact that some care leavers still attained their educational qualifications, despite failings in this type of support service, suggests that for some young people, having a trusting and confiding relationship with a social worker is not critical to educational success.

In some cases, social workers had actively supported educational plans, such as the worker who helped to argue Lulu's (18 years, white female) cause when the local authority planned to withdraw financial support for her college course. Jonathan (20 years, white male) cited his local director of social services as a source of support when he gained a university place after doing voluntary work within the department. But in other cases lack of conviction in a young person's goals was evident. Ryan (18 years, white male) was pressured by his social worker to go to a college she maintained was more suitable than the one he had favoured since the age of 10. Ignoring her advice, Ryan was proud to have come out with 'all-right grades' contrary to her predictions: 'She said I wouldn't last two months there.'

## Self-reliance

Among those currently attending college (which included further education, university, sixth-form college or other vocational college), the predominant themes in response to questions about how they arranged entry and managed participation were self-reliance and taking the initiative. Fourteen of those in college recounted examples where they had been the principal agent of their educational direction and success.

Among these 14, examples given of self-reliance included getting "myself through school"; exhorting all care leavers to "have a reality check and get on with it", following up information and going unaccompanied to enrolment days, ringing up universities and applying through UCAS, and realising that:

> I needed to be in education, or in a job where I could get a career out of it. I want to do something with me life because I have seen how bad it can be with other people.

Some mothers with young children were attending college and this group was especially self-reliant. As Sarah A (22 years, white female) explained:

*It is a lot of homework . . . 'cos you come home and you have to cook. And then after you've put them to bed you just want to sit down, but then you've got loads of homework. Yes, it does keep you busy.*

Self-reliance also took the form of self-development. One young woman, DG (18 years, white), said she had 'seen a great improvement in myself since attending college'. Another young man had demonstrated self-reliance in serving both his own interests and those of his younger brother: Ian (24 years, black African male) and his brother had arrived in the UK as unaccompanied asylum seekers. Ian wanted to set a good educational example for his brother. He received no help from carers to negotiate entry to college or university; he did not tell his university tutor about his background and he found claiming housing and other benefits so traumatic he took out expensive personal loans to pay rent and living expenses while at university.

Among those young people not currently attending college, the study revealed 11 examples of self-reliance related to planning for education or skill development. This was a group interested in self-improvement. As Tee (22 years, black African) with two young children said: 'Achievement comes from you. I'm just waiting for the right time to get back into college.'

Many of the young people in this group had started college and then either changed subjects or institutions or stopped going altogether. Negotiating change was something that was largely self-organised. John A (18 years, white male) found out about a training scheme through a friend and changed from a subject about which he was unenthusiastic to one he was confident he would enjoy. Simon (20 years, white male) had never previously contemplated becoming a student, but was:

*. . . thinking about enrolling in college again to complete me painting and decorating courses . . . Just so I've got a little bit more experience because that's basically what I want to do . . . [I've been] asked . . . to start up a business . . . [and] I like to do things that challenge us.*

Similarly, Sam (24 years, white female) said:

*I don't want to go to college [to train to become a social worker, but] if I have to go to training, then I'll do it . . . I think I need to do something about it. And then when I choose what I want to do then I think the services . . . will help me.*

Other young people anticipated college as something in the future after they had sorted out other difficulties and could "move on", or, as Darren (18 years, white male) said, had 'saved sufficient money just to keep me going when I'm up there'. The image of the care leaver as self-reliant principal agent vividly emerges through these accounts.

## Lack of support

Self-reliance needs to be considered within a context. The care leavers in this study were often self-reliant and managing with limited support for education from formal services. Fourteen of those currently participating in education and 17 of those not currently in education reported one or more incidents of lack of support, either for their current education or for their plans for education in the future.

Among those in education, a major difficulty was inadequate and fragmented financial support, particularly for those in further education who also bore sole responsibility for housing costs. For example, Angel (18 years, black African female), was 'not getting the support I need at the moment', even though she was at college studying for A-levels. She was entitled to neither income support, nor Educational Maintenance Allowance (EMA)[26] because she was also working part-time to gain relevant work experience in social services before going to university. Lulu (18 years, white female) claimed that she would be pressured to work full-time to pay her rent and bills, thereby jeopardising both her college course, and subsequently the opportunity of a university place, if social services forced her to go on Job Seekers Allowance rather than supported her financially.

Lack of support from foster carers and social workers has been noted above. Other examples where support appeared lacking included the Connexions service, reported to be unhelpful when approached; difficulties with accommodation which got in the way of completing college commitments; and shortage of affordable child care that had temporarily halted four young mothers in their pursuit of further education plans.

However, the most basic lack of support was an inadequate school education while in care. Sev (18 years, white male) was on work-based training. He echoed the perspectives of many care leavers with few or no qualifications when he said:

> I haven't actually come out of care with any kind of education. I went to college but it didn't work out. I didn't finish my course. I couldn't actually deal with the situation.

Care leavers not currently in education reported even more instances when support had been lacking. Nine of this group recounted dropping out of college, due to a variety of problems: funding, housing, family difficulties, homelessness, lack of incentive from workplaces, inadequate preparation for the course, or recognition that the course was not the right one for them.

---

26 The EMA was a benefit payable to young people from poorer backgrounds and designed to support participation in further education. It was abolished by the Coalition Government in 2011.

Becca's experience (20 years, white female) illustrates what can happen when financial support evaporates. She had been studying for a diploma, with no financial support, when her application for a £30-a-week grant to help with travel costs was refused. To meet her rent obligations she 'had to pack in college to be able to keep the flat on'. Dropping out of college for her was a 'dream being taken away'. In the same way, Victoria (19 years, white female) had been caught between educational ambition and independent living. She said:

> There was problems . . . I was living as an independent in that flat and going to college, which was hard. It was really difficult. And I couldn't cope with it.

When interviewed, she said she had not 'really got time to study'.

Financial problems also stopped Anita (18 years, white female) from going to college because she 'hadn't been able to crack the funding'. She had begun a course but left to take on a job because the subject was not what she wanted to do. If she now walked out of her job, she predicted she would face six months without benefits and nothing to live on before she could contemplate a return to education. The prospect of future debt incurred through studying was also off-putting. Cheyenne (20 years, African-Caribbean female) described herself as motivated by money. She wanted to become a social worker but doubted her ability to cope with:

> . . . university, three years of studying and unnecessary debt and [I] might not have a job at the end of it. If someone could tell me I'd get no university debts I'd be more inspired to go.

Some care leavers reported a perceived lack of support from college authorities themselves. Mel (19 years, white female) was frustrated to be kept on menial tasks rather than permitted to take on the full range of required activities for her hairdressing course, and Nikita (18 years, Asian female) lost her college place following her absence for an urgent family trip to Bangladesh, despite having notified the college in advance. Naomi (21 years, black African female) reported being denied a place on an access to social work course until she had "proved" herself to the tutor by first attending English, maths and IT courses, even though she already held GCSEs in these subjects. With two young children, Naomi had had no choice but to apply to the local college; she commented that she was 'really struggling in getting into [the course] . . . it's really getting me down'.

Three other care leavers had secured college places but failed to take them up. Billie (18 years, white female) blamed her lack of schooling, claiming she 'needed teaching first, because I didn't know very much' while Frankie (19 years, white female) was let down by her social worker who had not registered her in time. The third was Ekua (21 years, white female), whose foster carers told her she should work in McDonalds rather than follow through her original plan to attend college.

It is possible that during interviews, care leavers were highlighting their own contributions rather than those of others when considering their use of services and their evaluation of support. Nevertheless, the consistency of these examples shows how care leavers were strongly influenced either to take up education, or not to do so, by the degree of support from formal and informal sources, as well as from financial and organisational sources. Those young people currently not in education were by no means uninterested in self-development, as evidenced by the sizeable minority who had tried attending college courses in the past or intended to do so in the future.

## Possible changes: lessons from care leavers

The group of care leavers interviewed for this study was better educationally qualified at GCSE level than care leavers as a whole. The findings therefore give valuable insights into the levels of support needed to achieve such educational outcomes. In contrast to the policy rhetoric about this group, which emphasises their problems (cf. DfES, 2006a), a significant number of study care leavers held an "education ethic" that underpinned their desire to study and to achieve educational success. In many cases, the key to success was reliance on their own resources, taking the initiative, rather than depending on any external sources of formal support, regardless of availability.

In practice, support for educational participation was often substantially lacking. The obstacles were both structural, particularly for those attending further education colleges, who struggled to achieve their educational goals while trying to balance access to welfare benefits and independent living, and also interpersonal, from professionals responsible for providing opportunities and support in colleges, and from social workers.

By exploring care leavers' views of and experiences in education, the evidence from this study suggests that there are valuable lessons to be learned for the policy agenda of widening participation in education. The first step might be to recognise the value of interrogating current policies on housing, financial support and educational participation from the perspective of care leavers who, without family support, have had first-hand experience of trying to negotiate further education in the face of earlier poor school experience. A second step might be to acknowledge that for care leavers, like other young people, pathways through major institutions and service areas may not be linear. Their progress may advance and recede in waves, over time building knowledge and skills on some fronts while facing new problems on others.

## Conclusion

In many areas of their lives – access to support, sorting out difficulties, dealing with living arrangements, resolving health problems – study care leavers were largely reliant on themselves. In this context, it is perhaps not surprising that care leavers expressed their educational participation in self-reliant terms as well. However, as noted in the introduction, increasing educational attainment for care leavers is now a policy target. Ensuring children's educational participation while in local authority care is a condition of being a "corporate parent". One might expect therefore, that formal services such as foster care and social services would be highly proactive in working with young people to ensure educational participation and success. That this was not often reported by care leavers may reflect a time lag between policy and practice; it may reflect poor professional practice; or it may reflect care leavers' construction of themselves as principal agents rather than partners in their management of present and future service use. If the latter applies, this may suggest that professionals need to adjust their ways of working to ensure that self-reliance is valued as a normative, contextualised approach to addressing care leavers' orientations towards formal service use, without also implying that support is not needed. Furthermore, they need to guard against interpreting self-reliance and self-advocacy, which are functional in the longer term, as difficult behaviour. Endorsing this view, care leavers in the study praised their leaving care workers where they both "understood" the young person's self-reliant approach and also provided practical and emotional support when required.

### *Acknowledgements*

This chapter draws on a study of care leavers and access to health and other services carried out between 2003 and 2005, at Thomas Coram Research Unit at the Institute of Education, University of London, and funded by the Department for Education and Skills (DfES). The research team was Kristina Bennert, Claire Cameron, Antonia Simon and Valerie Wigfall. The views expressed in this publication are those of the author and not necessarily those of the Department.

Without the active and expressive participation by the young people and professionals in local authority areas, the study could not have been completed: to them special thanks. The author would also like to thank Valerie Wigfall, Antonia Simon, Marjorie Smith and Peter Moss, who provided helpful comments and discussions in the preparation of this chapter.

## 17  Making up lost ground: supporting the education of looked after children beyond Key Stage 4[27]

*Jenny Driscoll*

*Looked after children continue to perform poorly at school compared to their peers and care leavers are at increased risk of unemployment and poverty. Although there is a growing body of research on their education and recent studies have identified the factors associated with successful educational outcomes, less attention has been paid to whether, and if so how, the majority of children finishing Key Stage 4 with disappointing qualifications may be supported to make up any educational deficit beyond compulsory school-leaving age (see Jackson footnote, p 24). Care leavers can exhibit remarkable resilience and leaving care may be an opportunity for positive change. This chapter reports on a small pilot study which explored young people's own accounts and explanations in relation to their educational experiences and attainment, together with their attitudes to and engagement with education, particularly with regard to their aspirations and motivation to persevere with it. The challenges for schools in providing support to young people, who are notoriously self-reliant and resistant to accepting help, are considered in the context of current tensions in educational policy.*

*The chapter is updated from an article first published in* Adoption & Fostering *(35:2, 2011).*

## Introduction

Global youth unemployment reached record levels as a consequence of the economic crisis, and is not expected to improve significantly in the medium term (ILO, 2012). Job-seekers with poor secondary educational qualifications are particularly vulnerable in such conditions and the decline in the employment rate in the UK for those with limited GCSE or equivalent qualifications exceeds the OECD average (Chung, 2012). Care leavers remain an especially vulnerable group in this regard, with 32 per cent of those in England not in education, employment or training (NEET) at the age of 19 for reasons other than illness or disability, an increase of eight per cent since 2008 (DfE/National Statistics, 2012a). Poor performance at Key Stage 4[28] compared with their peers (DfE/National

---

27 Compulsory secondary education in the UK comprises Key Stage 3 (students aged 11–14) and Key Stage 4 (students aged 14–16). After the age of 16, students may enter further education at school or college, followed by higher education (degree level), from the age of 18.

28 Measured by General Certificate of Secondary Education (GCSE) attainment at age 16.

Statistics, 2012c), coupled with typically 'accelerated and compressed' transitions to adulthood (Stein, 2006a, p 274), create barriers to further and higher education and skilled work for care leavers and consequentially a high risk of social exclusion in adulthood (Stein, 2006b; Jackson, 2007).

Although there is now a significant body of research on the education of looked after children, the majority of this focuses on children up to the current school-leaving age of 16, although researchers (Jackson *et al*, 2003; Jackson *et al*, 2005; Ajayi and Quigley, 2006) have followed some of the small proportion of care leavers entering higher education through their degree courses. Less attention has been paid to whether, and if so how, looked after young people finishing Key Stage 4 with disappointing qualifications can be supported to make up any educational deficit. Challenging economic circumstances, together with the forthcoming requirement for young people in England to remain in education and/or training until 18 (Education and Skills Act 2008, Part 1 and Education Act 2011, section 74), increase the importance of attention to the most appropriate ways by which older children in state care can be encouraged and supported to participate in further and higher education and training.

This chapter considers the findings of a pilot study for a qualitative longitudinal research project designed to explore some of the factors that influence care leavers' decisions in relation to their future education and training, and the support which they themselves identify as beneficial. It focuses on three related issues arising from participants' accounts of their experiences. First, it explores young people's accounts and explanations in relation to their educational experiences and attainment. Second, it considers their aspirations and motivation. Finally, it reflects on the challenges in providing support to young people who are notoriously self-reliant and resistant to accepting help, and considers ways forward for supporting this vulnerable group beyond Key Stage 4.

## The educational attainment of looked after children

The low educational attainment of "looked after" children[29] in relation to their peers has been a matter of concern internationally for some years (Stein, 2008b). In the UK, the New Labour Government tackled the issue as part of its social inclusion agenda, introducing a target to narrow substantially the gap between the educational attainment and participation of looked after children and that of their peers (SEU, 2003). The Children Act 2004 amended the Children Act 1989 through the insertion of section 22(3A), which states that the local authority's duty to safeguard and promote the welfare of children in their care includes a particular duty to promote the child's educational

---

29 Defined in the Children Act 1989 (section 22(1)) to include children who are voluntarily accommodated as well as those in the care of their local authority.

achievement. Fulfilment of this duty is expected to be 'monitored rigorously by a senior manager in the local authority (eg a virtual school head)' (DCSF, 2010c, 17.5). Looked after children have preferential access to their choice of school (School Admissions (Admission Arrangements) (England) Regulations 2008), and statutory guidance stipulates that placement moves in Years 10 and 11 (age 15–16) should be avoided save in exceptional circumstances (DCSF, 2010c). Further support has been introduced through the Children and Young Persons Act 2008, section 20 of which places the status of the designated teacher for looked after children on a statutory footing.

Notwithstanding these initiatives, the differential between the educational achievement of looked after children and others at Key Stage 4 has widened in the last decade (DfE/ National Statistics, 2012c; DH, 2003) although the most recent statistics show a welcome narrowing of the gap in 2011–12 (DfE/National Statistics, 2012c). A range of factors has been identified as contributing to looked after children's poor attainment. These include: teachers' low expectations; failure by social workers or carers to prioritise children's education; instability in care placements; missed schooling; insufficient help to make up educational deficits; inadequate responses to children's emotional, mental and physical health needs; inadequacies in social work management and resources; and deficiences in multi-agency working (Ofsted/SSI, 1995; SEU, 2003; Jackson and Simon, 2006; Berridge, 2007; Jackson, 2010b, reproduced in this volume). In 2006, the government acknowledged that 'the care system seems all too often to reinforce early disadvantage, rather than helping children to successfully overcome it' (DfES, 2006a, p 3).

Some commentators, however, advocate caution in attributing blame to the care system (Berridge et al, 2008; Hannon et al, 2010). There is growing evidence that care improves the life chances of most children (Hannon et al, 2010; Wade et al, 2010), and a high proportion consider entering care to have been beneficial to their education (C4EO, 2010). Research has demonstrated that educational outcomes for looked after children can be improved, with key factors including stability of placement and education, high expectations, individually tailored learning, encouragement from birth parents, help with schooling from foster carers and being in care longer (Aldgate et al, 1992; Ajayi and Quigley, 2006; Connelly et al, 2008; Stein, 2008b). However, in attempting to address outcomes for this group of children, it is notoriously difficult to disentangle the harm suffered by children which led to their being placed in the care of the state from their experiences while there. Many move in and out of care: during the year ending 31 March 2012, 28,220 children came into care in England (21% more than in 2008) and 27,350 left (DfE/National Statistics, 2012a). In the same period, 42 per cent of care entrants were over the age of 10 (DfE/National Statistics, 2012a), leaving limited opportunity to address educational deficits before public examinations. Furthermore, the challenges faced by this group are formidable. Around 45 per cent of looked after children in Britain are assessed as having a mental health disorder – four to five times higher than for children living in private households (Meltzer *et al*, 2003; Meltzer *et al*, 2004a; Meltzer *et al*, 2004b). The incidence of statements for special educational needs is also over 10 times higher for looked after children than for children in the general school population (DfE/National Statistics, 2012b; DfE/National Statistics, 2012c).

These difficulties are unsurprising given the reasons children enter care. Over three-quarters of looked after children in England are in care as a result of abuse, neglect or family dysfunction (DfE/National Statistics, 2012a). Consideration of their educational outcomes must therefore be made within the context of their vulnerability and wider needs. Young people in Year 11 are often preoccupied with planning for leaving care, aggravating the stress of preparing for GCSEs (Fletcher-Campbell and Archer, 2003; Driscoll, 2013). Berridge *et al* (2008, p 183) conclude that it is unlikely that the GCSE attainment gap will narrow significantly. It is imperative, therefore, that attention be paid to opportunities for young people to enhance their academic qualifications beyond Key Stage 4.

## Leaving care

As a group, care leavers remain 'among the most excluded groups of young people in society' (Stein, 2006b, p 423) and 'generally experience deplorable life outcomes' (Lonne *et al*, 2008, p 173). These are well documented and include a greater likelihood of involvement in the criminal justice system and higher rates of depression and anxiety, as well as a higher risk of poverty and homelessness when compared with their peers (Utting, 1997; Wade and Dixon, 2006; Berridge, 2007). In recent years there has been an increased focus on the vulnerability of children leaving state care and the lack of support accorded them by their corporate parent, in comparison with that generally expected by young people cared for by their parents. In England and Wales, the Children (Leaving Care) Act 2000 amended the Children Act 1989 and imposed a number of duties upon local authorities to support children leaving their care. These include keeping in touch with the child, appointing a personal adviser, preparing a pathway plan and, in some circumstances, maintaining the child and providing him or her with suitable accommodation (Children Act 1989, sections 23B-23E).[30]

The Children and Young Persons Act 2008 has strengthened further the duties owed by local authorities to young adults leaving their care in relation to educational support, including through extending the time during which young people continuing in education and training are entitled to assistance from their former corporate parent. Some progress is demonstrated by a rise from five per cent of care leavers aged 19 in higher education in 2004 in England (DCSF, 2008) to seven per cent in 2012 (DfE/National Statistics, 2012a),

---

30 The situation in Scotland is rather different, being governed primarily by the Children (Scotland) Act 1995 and the Regulation of Care (Scotland) Act 2001.

and an increase in the number in education other than higher education from 18 per cent to 28 per cent over the same period. Academic achievement has been identified as a key factor in determining adult success and well-being in relation to fostered children in the US (Pecora *et al*, 2006) and children growing up in care in the UK (Jackson and Martin, 1998). Care leavers can be remarkably resilient and studies suggest that leaving care can provide a turning point for positive change (Dixon *et al*, 2006; Wade and Munro, 2008), so there may be a window of opportunity at this stage in their lives for care leavers to redress educational deficits.

## Research methods

The study reported here focused exclusively on young people's accounts of their educational trajectories. The justification for this approach is fourfold. First, the participants were of an age (16–20) at which they were increasingly autonomous. While the fact that children and adults often have different perspectives does not imply that either view is "right" or "wrong" (Holland, 2009, p 232), the perspectives of young people are the driving force behind their decisions and, therefore, it is argued, of primary significance. Winter (2006, p 58) asserts that the research literature reflects an approach which 'does not easily accommodate a view of looked after children as active, skilled and competent agents in social processes', but tends to be founded on a view of children as recipients of a service, the outcomes of which are defined by adult values. Although some ground has been covered since Winter concluded that 'the detailed accounts of looked after children themselves' are missing from the literature (Winter, 2006, p 55), this study attempts to contribute to these accounts. Arguably, this approach is particularly pertinent in respect of the children of corporate parents, who are not only expected to achieve independence earlier than their peers (Stein, 2006a) but are also often on the receiving end of decisions over which they have no influence (Leeson, 2007). Second, research involving young people is an important means by which to engage their participation rights under the United Nations Convention on the Rights of the Child (Winter, 2006), a consideration of particular significance in relation to marginalised groups (Wigfall and Cameron, 2006). Third, Wigfall and Cameron (2006) argue that the recent focus on performance management and value for money may result in local authority data that are not as reliable or comparable as they might be and that it must be counter-balanced by research which reflects the views of service users. Finally, as Samuels and Pryce (2008) attest in relation to fostered children, care leavers have a particular sense of identity arising from their fractured experience of family life, which renders research into their own perspectives of particular value.

Since the focus of the study was the young people's perspectives, a qualitative methodology was employed. There are specific methodological challenges in carrying out research involving care leavers, arising from the vulnerability of the participants, the size, mobility and geographical spread of the population, and their tendency to be socially excluded and stigmatised (Wigfall and Cameron, 2006). All of these were encountered in this study. In order to ensure that participants were not too vulnerable to participate and that a support network was at hand should it be needed, they were approached through an invitation extended to members over the age of 16 at a Local Authority Children in Care Council meeting. Since Care Councils are the means through which looked after children contribute to decisions made by children's services authorities, the sample may have comprised young people who are more readily engaged by service providers.

The research was conducted in accordance with the National Children's Bureau (NCB) Guidelines for Research (NCB, 2009), which have since been superseded (Shaw *et al*, 2011). Approval was granted both by King's College London and by the local authority. Data were collected by means of in-depth semi-structured interviews with seven care leavers aged 16 to 20. A flexible approach was adopted to allow participants to focus on aspects of their experiences which they perceived to be most significant. Data were analysed using a grounded theory approach (Corbin and Strauss, 2008) in light of the power of this method to promote conceptualisation from participants' experiences (Shepherd *et al*, 2010). To foreground young people's voices, in vivo codes were preferred where appropriate during the initial phase. Descriptive categories were generated prior to the development of conceptual categories. The themes considered here – focusing on motivational issues, the desire to be a "normal" teenager and feelings of being over-whelmed by their personal circumstances – derive from in vivo codes.

## The sample

The sample is a small one and the local authority in which the research was carried out was a "home counties" county council in England. Therefore, the participants do not reflect the diverse ethnicities that would be expected in most London boroughs (all were white British), nor do they all adhere to the stereotype of children in care as emanating from deprived backgrounds: one had previously attended an independent school. Nonetheless, in many ways they reflect the diversity of the care population (Rutter, 2000; Fletcher-Campbell, 2008) and are remarkably varied in their family backgrounds and histories. There are many well-rehearsed limitations to the use of small samples. However, as Wade and Munro (2008, p 219) point out, at the present time:

> We know much more about the problems or risks faced by young people leaving care [about what does not work] than we do about the forms of support that may be effective in helping them to negotiate a successful transition to adulthood.

This study endeavoured to contribute to such understanding in relation to educational transitions.

The participants comprised four young men and three young women. Table 1 summarises some of their key characteristics. "Time in care" denotes the length of time since the participant last lived with his or her birth family. However, a number of the participants had previously lived at home under a care order or experienced social work intervention throughout their childhood before finally being placed in care as older children or adolescents. Where this is the case, a + sign is used to indicate a lengthier history of moving in and out of care or having remained at home under a care order.

*Table 1*
**Research participants**

| Name* | Age at interview | Time in care | Living arrangements | Current education/career |
|-------|------------------|--------------|---------------------|--------------------------|
| Anabel | 16 | 2 years+ | Foster care | A-levels at school |
| Bob | 7 | 2½ years | Foster care | BTEC level 2 at College |
| Charlotte | 19 | 7 years | With boyfriend | PT work & NVQ level 2 |
| Dean | 20 | 6 years + | Foster care | Unemployed |
| John | 17 | 12 years | Own flat | PT work: awaiting sentence |
| Sally | 18 | 2 years + | Foster care | Unemployed/Sat job: planning foundation degree |
| Scott | 20 | 14 years | Supported lodgings | PT work: about to start College (BTEC level 3) |

*pseudonyms have been used to ensure anonymity

## Research findings

All the participants considered that they had not achieved educational qualifications commensurate with their own expectations. So although Berridge *et al* (2008) may well be right that objectively, given their life histories, care leavers generally should not be regarded as having under-achieved educationally, all the young people taking part in this research, while philosophical about their experiences, were clear that by their own standards they had not achieved as well as they could – or should – have.

## Educational disruption and attainment

Undoubtedly disruption to their education – a common finding of studies with looked after children (Dixon *et al*, 2006) and experienced by all participants – played a large part in their lower than expected attainment. Charlotte was the only one for whom entering care had stabilised her education: her mentally ill mother had frequent changes of mind about Charlotte's schooling: 'Mum was like, "let's try this for a change".' None questioned the need to be in care, and perhaps the late entrants would have benefited from earlier removal from home, as suggested by studies such as Hannon *et al* (2010), but all the participants had encountered problems either as a result of their initial placement on entry into care or through barriers encountered there. Bob entered care in Year 10 and was placed a considerable distance away from home and school, as a result of which he missed school for around six months of his GCSE programme. Anabel also attributed her poorer than expected GCSE grades to moving school midway through Key Stage 4 to access a school closer to her foster placement. However, the transfer had been her choice and she felt that her new school was an improvement educationally and socially. Three of the seven participants attributed their disappointing academic results directly to their relationships with their carers. John and Scott each blamed the breakdown of the relationship between their foster parents for triggering a downward spiral of problems at home and school, resulting for Scott in expulsion from six primary schools and placement in a series of children's homes where his education was intermittent and inconsistent, and for John in a criminal record, which had led to rejection of his college application for a course for which his GCSEs and practical experience made him highly eligible. Sally, who had achieved well at GCSE notwithstanding severe abuse including starvation at home, considered her unhappiness in her placement to be at the root of her disappointing A-level results. Only Dean attributed his difficulties in focusing at college to his complex relationship with his birth family.

## Aspiration and motivation

A small-scale survey published by the UK Department for Education (DfE, 2010b) concluded that, as a cohort, looked after children have the same aspirations as others, although the 32 young people in the English case study from the European *YiPPEE* project (Cameron *et al*, 2011) were found to have somewhat modest and general career ambitions. For the young people in this study, the specific circumstances of their care history could have a major impact on their ambitions. Charlotte's birth family expected her to go to university, as had her sister, who was significantly older and had never been in care. Charlotte's carer did her best to persuade Charlotte to meet her family's expectations, but Charlotte, who was training to be a barber, explained that her experiences had taught her the value of family life and her measure of success would lie in providing a stable and happy family for her children. Money was not important to her: 'I just want to be . . . likeable and just have a nice . . . family and friends around me.' Bob explained his determination to join the army as rooted in a desire to spite his mother, whereas Scott, who belonged to the third generation of his family to have been brought up in care, expressed a need for material success (identified as being able to support his family) in order to 'make his family name right'.

While Allen (2003) found that care leavers came to value education and training through the bitter experience of the job market, all the participants were acutely aware of the perceived significance of qualifications in the modern world, in keeping with studies such as Ball *et al* (2000). Only John, who ironically would probably have benefited most from such a requirement, opposed the idea of extending compulsory participation in education to the age of 18. Scott and Charlotte both considered it would have prevented them from dropping out of college, and Sally and Anabel appeared to take for granted the expectation of continuing to university. Sally had taken A-levels rather than more vocational qualifications because she 'thought it was more of a proper education'. She believed that remaining in education would enhance young people's life chances, although at the time of the interview her disappointing A-level results had meant that she had not gained a university place to read Art and she was working part-time as a shop assistant. Anabel, who had just started the sixth form, felt that few people are 'ready to go into the adult world' at 16.

The attainment of qualifications was a strong motivating factor for these young people, but setbacks and disappointments undermined their motivation, as illustrated by Bob's account. Bob had wanted to join the army as a trainee officer but had lost motivation when missed school forced him to take foundation instead of higher level GCSEs and he 'just didn't really bother'. At the time of the interview, he was studying for a BTEC First (a level 2 vocational qualification) in Public Services, with a view to training as an engineer and joining the army at 18. He had not gone to college that day because he 'couldn't be bothered'. He said his attendance had lapsed 'a few times', explaining that it was 'just the same thing every time . . . I was fed up with it . . . and I just can't concentrate.' Cognitive evaluation theory suggests that to achieve high levels of intrinsic motivation a person must feel highly competent yet challenged by an activity and perceive that activity as self-determined (Hallam, 2002). Like others in the study, Bob's sense of competence had been undermined by disappointing qualifications and he had been forced to engage in a less challenging course than he wished. Nonetheless, Bob was clear that he would not drop out entirely because he knew he needed the qualification and was determined to rise through the ranks to officer status.

For Scott and Charlotte, attaining qualifications was also about proving something to themselves. Charlotte wanted to succeed as a tribute to the memory of her foster carer who had died earlier in the year, explaining: 'I'm going to stick something out now, and gonna, sort of, make her proud.' Scott explained 'I want to do it as a test to myself, to prove that I can learn, that I am normal.' He felt that lack of support in his children's homes had left him without the necessary skills to study effectively, but expressed determination to succeed in what he regarded as his 'last chance'. However, Dean, who was also 20, had concluded that it was too late for him to return to education: he craved the self-respect he felt would come with financial self-sufficiency, although he had recently drifted from a few poorly remunerated jobs into unemployment.

## Supporting looked after children in school

School plays an important normalising role in the lives of looked after children and young people are generally reluctant to be singled out in any way in the school environment: 'It makes you feel really different. I absolutely hate it' (Anabel). With the exception of John, who was comfortable with his status as a looked after child and valued the fact that there was someone in school who 'understood what was going on' in his life, the young people in this study were unenthusiastic about the concept of a designated teacher. To some extent, this appeared to be because designated teachers were not always sensitive to young people's care status in front of other pupils, who may not have known that they were "in care". Scott referred to not wanting to 'get that label again' and, more generally, participants expressed a preference to use the same sources of advice for learning support and career planning as everyone else. Moreover, in common with other studies (Cameron, 2007, reproduced in this volume; Samuels and Pryce, 2008), participants conveyed a strong sense of self-reliance. Having been let down, as they saw it, both by their birth families and professionals, self-reliance was regarded as a positive attribute, recounted with some pride and emphasised particularly by the boys.

Cameron (2007) has suggested that refusal of professional support may be indicative of excessive self-reliance and that professionals should beware of regarding it as "difficult" behaviour. Although Scott was able to acknowledge that he needed to learn to ask for help, and that self-reliance could become a limiting quality, participants explained their rejection of professional help in terms of the need for such relationships to be built on mutual respect and trust, and identified the need for personal advice from a consistent and trusted source. "Too many people" was a recurring refrain in relation to their dealings with social care professionals, and in this regard the continuity that a designated teacher can provide can only be an advantage. Furthermore, while relationships with social care professionals were widely characterised as transient and frustrating, relationships with teachers appeared to be far less problematic. In a number of cases, young people remembered with enormous respect and gratitude teachers who had helped them beyond the boundaries of their professional role. However, recent initiatives to enhance professional communication and information-sharing within the care system, as well as to improve attainment, have spawned a system of multiple reviews and planning processes, including the personal education plan and the pathway plan. Young people were cynical about these and described becoming disengaged, so that they were compliant with the form-filling but ceased to engage meaningfully with making realistic plans because they had no expectation that this would lead to any change.

## Support for care leavers beyond school

The importance of continued support for care leavers into young adulthood was highlighted by Scott, Charlotte and John. Scott and Charlotte had both dropped out of college when living independently at 18 because of overwhelming financial and personal pressures: Scott described 'working from 11pm until six in the morning and going to college at nine'. However, both had been determined to return to education once these pressures were resolved and Charlotte had re-enrolled part-time at college for a National Vocational Qualification (NVQ) level 2, while Scott was about to start a level 3 BTEC course, subject to local authority funding. The factor enabling each of them to return to education had been giving up their local authority tenancies to live, in Scott's case, in supported lodgings, and in Charlotte's, with her boyfriend. John was awaiting sentence for breach of a community service order at the time of the interview and could face imprisonment, but he lived independently and appeared to lack the financial means and personal skills to ensure his attendance in accordance with the order.

Dean, at 20, was still living with his foster carer, a situation with which he felt uncomfortable since, now he was older, she was being paid less. He wished he could contribute financially but was unemployed and at a loss as to what to do with his life. He claimed that the local authority had refused to fund a carpentry course he wished to take after he had not achieved as well as he had hoped in a BTEC qualification; perhaps he would have benefited from the increased support now available through the Children and Young Persons Act 2008. He had left his previous two poorly paid jobs after difficulties with the culture at work. Although he wanted to work, there was 'no work around' and he felt overwhelmed by the problems in his personal life. Dean seemed to feel responsible for providing emotional support to his birth family and described himself as 'just surviving . . . managing, coping', unconsciously but accurately categorising himself in the second of Stein's classification of care leavers as "moving on", "survivors" or "victims" (Stein 2006a).

These young people's experiences are in keeping with the findings of Allen (2003, p 27) and Wade and Dixon (2006) that financial circumstances lead to some care leavers dropping out of education. Research suggests that looked after children may also be at higher risk of "dropping out" of college as a result of reduced support, greater social demands and increased independence compared with school (Driscoll, 2013). The potential contribution of supportive foster carers (Lipscombe and Farmer, 2007) in this regard is highlighted particularly by the experiences of Dean, who did not think he would have been able to accomplish the BTEC National Diploma without his foster carer's help. However, while the provisions of the Children and Young Persons Act 2008 are very welcome with regard to support for care leavers who continue in education or training, this research supports the view of the House of Commons Children, Schools and Families Committee (HC CSFC, 2009, p 88) that 'the terms on which this provision has been extended risk excluding some of the most vulnerable young people from continuing support'. Research has highlighted the value of higher education in facilitating a gradual transition to independent living (Stein, 2008b) and young people who do not continue in further or higher education are likely to be more vulnerable in a range of ways than those who do, and may be less well-equipped for independence.

## Discussion

Schools and colleges face a difficult balancing act in supporting older looked after children. This research highlights two key tensions. First, while the troubled histories of this cohort are such that their education cannot be viewed in isolation from their wider care needs (Berridge, 2007; Jackson, 2010b), the importance of school in providing a normalising environment in which children can detach themselves from their looked after status should not be underestimated, but may be undermined by an overemphasis on children's social care status within school. Nonetheless, young people identify a need for consistent and trusted sources of support and continue to report that these are rarely accessed through social services. Designated teachers may provide looked after children with a consistent professional to advise and support them in their educational career, although to date, there is little research on their role. There is considerable potential for virtual schools to promote effective communication between education and social care, including through enhancing the capacity of social workers to challenge schools and in relation to transition planning at 16 (Ofsted, 2012a; Driscoll, 2013).

The second tension concerns the conflict between the imperative for schools to perform well in league tables and the needs of young people with disrupted educational histories. Commentators have argued that the *Every Child Matters* agenda (a policy initiative of the UK Labour Government of 1997–2010 intended to improve the life chances of vulnerable children), while demonstrating an admirable desire to bring together services for children, was nonetheless concerned primarily with investment in children as the future workforce (Piper, 2008; Wade and Munro, 2008), whereas the function of education is the creation of responsible future citizens (Williams, 2004). These aims were framed within an "outcomes" driven agenda, in which the success of the care "system" was measured in terms such as educational attainment and avoidance of the criminal justice system. However, the Wolf report concluded that such an agenda creates 'perverse incentives which currently encourage schools and colleges to steer young people into easy options, rather than ones which will help them progress' (Wolf, 2011, p 11). This is of particular concern in the case of young people whose full academic potential may not as yet be evident. Many schools have defined entry criteria into their sixth forms (age 16–

19), making it more likely that such young people progress into more vocational courses at further education colleges. Targets for the educational attainment of looked after children post-16 have been recommended by researchers such as O'Sullivan and Westerman (2007, reproduced in this volume). Their continued omission appears to support Scott's view that care leavers are often not given sufficient encouragement to continue their education, and Jackson's assertion that there is a tendency to assume that care leavers 'are more suited to vocational than academic routes' (2010b, p 56). Research suggests that with appropriate support young people may be able to make up considerable ground at Key Stage 5 (Driscoll, 2013), but enabling them to do so requires a reversal of the tendency of professionals to prioritise the immediate self-sufficiency of care leavers over longer-term educational and career goals (Jackson and Cameron, 2012).

## Conclusion

In keeping with the previous findings (e.g. Allen, 2003; Cameron, 2007), the participants in this study displayed an admirable level of motivation and resilience in pursuing their education and career plans in the face of significant practical and emotional challenges. None were content to remain unemployed. Interviews took place in the summer and early autumn, and all but Dean were in college or some kind of work, however limited or menial. The perhaps unexpected finding of a high degree of support among those interviewed for requiring young people to continue in education or training to the age of 18 is testament to their capacity for self-development and ambition, notwithstanding significant personal obstacles. However, the strong motivation demonstrated by all the young people in the face of considerable challenges appeared for a number to have been eroded over time by severe financial pressures or continued disruption in their personal lives, including the influence of their birth families.

Understanding the way in which care leavers' lives develop in young adulthood is complicated by the complex interplay of many factors (Allen, 2003), coupled with an often deep-seated resistance to professional help. Support for some of the most vulnerable members of society to fulfil their educational potential requires a sensitive and flexible response to the needs of young people whose personal histories have prevented them from progressing in their education in line with the expectations of the school system. There has been slow but significant progress in the educational attainment of looked after children since implementation of the Children Act 1989, but the variability of performance between local authorities suggests that much more could be done Jackson (2010b). For care leavers, educational transitions at 16–18 coincide with disruption in other areas of their lives, including transition to the leaving care team and for many, moving to live independently. In line with the conclusions of Cameron et al (2011), the experience of this small cohort of young people demonstrates the atypical and often prolonged paths that care leavers may have to take in order to make up lost ground in their education.

Further consideration needs to be given to enhancing the support available post-16, through initiatives such as the Buttle UK Quality Mark for Higher and Further Education, and introduction of a designated professional role, as recommended by the All Party Parliamentary Group for Looked After Children and Care Leavers (APPG, 2012). Giving statutory status to virtual school heads (also recommended by the APPG) and extending the remit of virtual schools to graduation would enable continuity of support to be offered to young people throughout their educational career. Allowing young people to remain in foster care during this period to ensure stability and continuity of supportive relationships also offers significant benefits (Munro *et al*, 2012). The recent requirement for local authorities to have a "staying put" policy is welcome, although the guidance (DfE *et al*, 2013) may be regarded as weak.[31] Care leavers should be entitled to the kind of seamless support that is typically available to their peers growing up within their own families.

---

31 See also the Planning Transition to Adulthood for Care Leavers Regulations and Guidance 2010 and the Fostering Regulations and Guidance 2011 (Children Act 1989).

# Afterword

The message of this book is in many ways a hopeful one. Compared with other countries, we have a good policy and legislative framework for improving educational outcomes. We have enough high-quality research to tell us what enables children and young people in public care to make the most of educational opportunities and what gets in their way. We know that, given a stable placement with a foster parent or carer who loves and believes in them, together with intensive help to compensate for the effects of earlier neglect and adversity, they can do as well as any other children. We know that many looked after children desperately want to succeed in education and go on to college and university like so many of their contemporaries. They just need more time, well-informed advice and adequate personal and financial support.

But we also know that for too many the future holds disappointment, fading hopes and diminished aspirations. The promising initiatives described in this book are mostly localised, short-term and time limited. We will not see real improvement until they become part of mainstream provision, available to all children in care.

# References

A National Voice (2011) *CiCCs across England: Mapping performance and function*, London: Department for Education

Ajayi S. and Quigley M. (2006) 'By degrees: care leavers in higher education', in Chase E., Simon A. and Jackson S. (eds) *In Care and After: A positive perspective*, London: Routledge

Akister J., Owens M. and Goodyear I. (2010) 'Leaving care and mental health: outcomes for children in out-of-home care during the transition to adulthood', *Health Research Policy and Systems*, 8, pp 1–7

Aldgate J., Colton M. J., Ghate D. and Heath A. (1992) 'Educational attainment and stability in long-term foster care', *Children & Society*, 6:2, pp 91–103

Aldgate J., Heath A., Colton M. and Simm M. (1999) 'Social work and the education of children in foster care', in Hill M. (ed), *Signposts in Fostering: Policy, practice and research issues*, London: BAAF

Allardice B. and Ginsburg H. (1983) 'Children's psychological difficulties in mathematics', in Ginsburg H. (ed) *The Development of Mathematical Thinking*, London: Academic Press

Allen M. (2003) *Into the Mainstream: Care leavers entering work, education and training*, York: Joseph Rowntree Foundation

Almquist Y., Modin B. and Östberg V. (2010) 'Childhood status in society and school: implications for the transition to higher levels of education', *British Journal of Sociology of Education*, 31:1, pp 31–45

Antonovsky A. (1988) *Unravelling the Mystery of Health*, London: Jossey-Bass Publishers

APA (1994) *Diagnostic and Statistical Manual of Mental Disorders*, Washington, DC: American Psychiatric Association

APPG (2012) *Education Matters in Care: A report by the independent cross-party inquiry into the educational attainment of looked after children in England*, London: University and College Union; www.thewhocarestrust.org.uk/data/files/Education_Matters_in_Care_September_2012.pdf

Archer M. (1999) 'Careless treatment', *Special Children*, 120, pp 8–9

Ashcroft B. (2013) *Fifty-one Moves*, Hook, Hants: Waterside Press

Audit Commission (2000) *Another Country: Implementing dispersal under the Immigration and Asylum Act 1999*, London: The Audit Commission

Audit Scotland (2010) *Getting it right for children in residential care*, Edinburgh: Audit Scotland; www.audit-scotland.gov.uk

Badia X., Montserrat S., Roset M. and Herdman M. (1999) 'Feasibility, validity and test-retest reliability of scaling methods for health status: the visual analogue scale and the time trade-off', *Quality Life Research*, 8, pp 303–10

Ball S. (2003) 'The risk of social reproduction', *London Review of Education*, 1:3, pp 163–175

Ball S. (2005) *Education Policy and Social Class: The selected works of Stephen Ball*, London: World Library of Educationalists

Ball S., Maguire M. and Macrae S. (2000) *Choice, Pathways and Transitions Post-16: New youth, new economies in the global city*, London: Routledge/Falmer

Barber B., Stone M., Hunt J. and Eccles J. (2005) 'Benefits of activity participation: the roles of identity affirmation and peer group norm sharing', in Mahoney J., Larson R. and Eccles J. (eds), *Organised Activities as Contexts of Development: Extracurricular activities, after-school and community programs*, Mahwah, NJ: Lawrence Erlbaum Associates

Barber M. and Mourshed M. (2007) *How the World's Best Performing School Systems Come out on Top*, London: McKinsey & Co

Barn R., Andrew L. and Mantovani N. (2005) *Life After Care: A study of the experiences of young people from different ethnic groups*, York/Bristol: Joseph Rowntree Foundation/The Policy Press

Barnardo's (2006) *Failed by the System*, Ilford: Barnardo's

Barth R. (1990) 'On their own: the experiences of young people after foster care', *Child and Adolescent Social Work*, 7, pp 419–40

Bebbington A. and Miles J. (1989) 'The background of children who enter local authority care', *British Journal of Social Work*, 19, pp 349–368

Bebbington E. (2005) *Stop Wasting My Time! Case Studies of Pupils with Attachment Issues in Schools, with Special Reference to Looked After and Adopted Children*, Stirling: PACS

Bebbington P. (1998) *The Educational Attainment of Care Leavers*, Cardiff: Department of Social Sciences, University of Cardiff

Beck J.S., Beck A.T. and Jolly J. B. (2004) *Beck Young People Inventories*, Manual, Swedish version, Stockholm: Psykologiforlaget, 2004

Beckett C. and McKeigue B. (2009) 'Objects of concern: caring for children during care proceedings', *British Journal of Social Work*; doi: 10.1093/bjsw/bcp118

Beery K.E. and Beery N.A. (2004) *The Beery-Buctenica Developmental Test of Visual-motor Integration*, Manual, Minneapolis, MN: NCS Pearson Inc.

Beirens H., Hughes N., Hek R. and Spicer N. (2007) 'Preventing social exclusion of refugee and asylum seeking children: building new networks', *Social Policy and Society*, 6:2, pp 219–229

Benson C. (1996) 'Resisting the trend to exclude', in Blyth E and Milner J (eds), *Exclusion from School: Inter-professional issues for policy and practice*, London: Routledge

Bercow J. (2008) *The Bercow Review of Services for Children and Young People (0–19) who have Speech, Language and Communication Needs*, London: DCSF

Berger L., Bruch S., Johnson E., James S. and Rubin D. (2009) 'Estimating the "impact" of out-of-home placement on child well-being: approaching the problem of selection bias', *Child Development*, 80, pp 1856–76

Berliner B. (2010) *Grappling with the Gaps: Towards a research agenda to meet the educational needs of children and youth in foster care*, Santa Cruz, CA: Centre for the Future of Teaching and Learning

Berridge D. (1985) *Children's Homes*, Oxford: Blackwell, 1985

Berridge D. (1994) 'Foster and residential care reassessed: a research perspective', *Children & Society*, 8:2, pp 132–50

Berridge D. (1997) *Foster Care: A research review*, London: The Stationery Office

Berridge D. (2007) 'Theory and explanation in child welfare: education and looked after children', *Child & Family Social Work*, 12:1, pp 1–10

Berridge D. and Brodie I. (1998) *Children's Homes Revisited*, London: Jessica Kingsley Publishers

Berridge D. and Saunders H. (2009) 'The education of fostered and adopted children', in Schofield G. and Simmonds J. (eds), *The Child Placement Handbook*, London: BAAF

Berridge D., Dance C., Beecham J. and Field S. (2008) *Educating Difficult Adolescents: Effective education for children in public care of with emotional and behavioural difficulties*, London: Jessica Kingsley Publishers

Berridge D., Henry L., Jackson S. and Turney D. (2009) *Looked After and Learning: Evaluation of the Virtual School Head Pilot*; www.education.gov.uk/publications/standard/publicationDetail/Page1/DCSF-RR144

Berzin S.C. (2008) 'Difficulties in the transition to adulthood: using propensity scoring to understand what makes foster young people vulnerable', *Social Service Review*, 82, pp 171–96

Bidart C. and Lavenu D. (2005) 'Evolution of personal networks and life events', *Social Networks*, 27:4, pp 359–76

Biehal N., Clayden J., Stein M. and Wade J. (1995) *Moving on: Young people and leaving care schemes*, London: HMSO

Blome W.W. (1997) 'What happens to foster kids: educational experiences of a random sample of foster care young people, and a matched group of non-foster care young people', *Child and Adolescent Social Work Journal*, 14, pp 41–53

Blower A., Addo A., Hodgson J., Lamington L. and Towlson K. (2004) 'Mental health needs of looked after children: a needs assessment', *Clinical Child Psychology and Psychiatry*, 9, pp 117–29

Blyth E. and Milner J. (1996) *Exclusion from School: Interprofessional issues for policy and practice*, London: Routledge

Boden J., Horwood J. and Ferguson D. (2007) 'Exposure to childhood sexual and physical abuse and subsequent educational achievement outcomes', *Child Abuse and Neglect*, 31, pp 1104–14

Bohman M. and Sigvardsson S. (1980a) 'A prospective, longitudinal study of children registered for adoption: a 15-year follow-up', *Acta Psychiatrica Scandinavia*, 61, pp 339–55

Bohman M. and Sigvardsson S. (1980b) 'Negative social heritage', *Adoption & Fostering*, 3, pp 25–31

Bookbinder G.E., revised by Vincent D. and Crumpler M., (2002) Salford Sentence Reading Test (3rd edition), London: Hodder Education

Borland M., Pearson C., Hill M., Tisdall K. and Bloomfield I. (1998) *Education and Care Away from Home*, Edinburgh: Scottish Council for Research in Education

Broad B. (1998) *Young People Leaving Care: Life after the Children Act 1989*, London: Jessica Kingsley Publishers

Brodie I. (2001) *Children's Homes and School Exclusion: Redefining the problem*, London: Jessica Kingsley Publishers

Brodie I. (2009) *Improving Educational Outcomes for Looked After Children and Young People*, C4EO Review; http://www.c4eo.org.uk/themes/vulnerablechildren/educationaloutcomes/default.aspx?themeid=7

Brodie I. (2010) *Improving Educational Outcomes for Looked After Children and Young People: C4EO vulnerable children knowledge review*, 1, London: Centre for Excellence and Outcomes in Children and Young People's Services (C4EO)

Brodie I. and Norris M. (2009) *Improving Educational Outcomes for Looked after Children and Young People*, London: C4EO

Broh B. (2002) 'Linking extracurricular programming to academic achievement: who benefits and why', *Sociology of Education*, 75:1, pp 69–91

Brooks G. (2007) *What Works for Children with Literacy Difficulties? The effectiveness of intervention schemes* (3rd edition), London: DCSF

Brown D., Scheflin A.W. and Hammond D.C. (1998) *Memory, Trauma Treatment and the Law*, New York: WW Norton

Brown G. and Moran P. (1997) 'Single mothers, poverty and depression', *Psychological Medicine*, 27, pp 21–33

Brownlees L. and Finch N. (2010) *Levelling the Playing Field*, London: UNICEF

Bryderup I. and Trentel M (2010) 'Young people in public care: background pathways to education in Denmark', (WP 6); http://tcru.ioe.ac.uk/yippee

Bryderup I., Trentel M. and Kring T. (2010) *Young People in Public Care: Analysis of quantitative data from Denmark*, Copenhagen: University of Aarhus

Buchanan A. and Flouri E. (2001) '"Recovery" after age 7 from "externalizing" behaviour problems: the role of risk and protective clusters', *Children and Youth Services Review*, 23:12, pp 899–914

Buttle UK (undated); www.buttleuk.org/pages/quality-mark-for-care-leavers.html

Cairns K. (2002) *Attachment, Trauma and Resilience: Therapeutic caring for children*, London: BAAF

Cairns K. (2010) *Circles of Harm: Surviving paedophilia and network abuse*, London: Lonely Scribe

Cairns K. and Stanway C. (2013) *Learn the Child: Helping looked after children to learn*, London: BAAF

Cameron C. (2007) 'Education and self-reliance among care leavers', *Adoption & Fostering*, 31:1, pp 39–49

Cameron C. and Jackson S. (2012) 'Leaving care: looking ahead and aiming higher', *Children and Youth Services Review*, 34, pp 1107–114

Cameron C., Hollingworth K. and Jackson S. (eds) (2010) *Young People from a Public Care Background: Secondary analysis of national statistics on educational participation*, London: Thomas Coram Research Unit, Institute of Education

Cameron C., Bennert K., Simon A. and Wigfall V. (2007) *Using Health, Education, Housing and Other Services: A study of care leavers and other young people in difficulty*, London: Thomas Coram Research Unit; http://webarchive.nationalarchives.gov.uk/20130401151715/https://www.education.gov.uk/publications/eOrderingDownload/TCRU-01-07.pdf

Cameron C., Jackson, Hauari H. and Hollingworth K. (2011) *Young people from a Public Care Background: Pathways to further and higher education in England: a case study, YIPPEE WP5 UK Report*, London: Thomas Coram Research Institute

Cameron C., Jackson S., Hauari H. and Hollingworth K. (2012) 'Continuing educational participation among children in care in five countries: some issues of social class', *Journal of Education Policy*, 27:3, pp 387–399

Candappa M. (2000) 'The right to education and an adequate standard of living: refugee children in the UK', *International Journal of Children's Rights*, 8:3, pp 261–270

Candappa M. and Egharevba I. (2000) *Extraordinary Childhoods: The social lives of refugee children*, Hull: ESRC Children 5-16 research programme

Caplan G. and Capland R. (1993) *Mental Health Consultation and Collaboration*, San Francisco, CA: Jossey-Bass Publishers

Carr W. and Kemmis S. (1986) *Becoming Critical: Education, knowledge and action research*, London: Routledge

Casas F., Montserrat C. and Malo S. (2010) 'The case study report for Spain'; http://tcru.ioe.ac.uk/yippee

Casey Family Programs (2003) *Higher Education Reform: Incorporating the needs of foster care youth*, Seattle, WA: Casey Foundation

Cashmore J. and Paxman M. (1996) *Wards Leaving Care: A longitudinal study*, Sydney: NSW Department of Community Services

Cashmore J. and Paxman M. (2006) 'Predicting after-care outcomes: the importance of "felt" security"', *Child & Family Social Work*, 11, pp 232–41

Cashmore J., Paxman M. and Townsend M. (2007) 'The educational outcomes of young people 4–5 years after leaving care: an Australian perspective', *Adoption & Fostering*, 3:1, pp 50–61

Cassen R., Feinstein L. and Graham P. (2008) 'Educational outcomes: adversity and resilience', *Social Policy and Society*, 81, pp 73–85

Celeste Y.S.C. (2011) 'Perspectives of looked after children on school experience: a study conducted among primary school children in a children's home in Singapore', *Children & Society*, 25:2, pp 139–150

Ceredigion County Council (2010) *Wales Children in Need Census*; www.ceredigion.gov.uk/index. cfm?articleid ¼ 14550

C4EO (2009) *Improving Educational Outcomes for Looked After Children and Young People*; www. c4eo.org.uk/vulnerablechildren

C4EO (2010) *Vulnerable (Looked After) Children: final summary and recommendations*; www.c4eo. org.uk/themes/vulnerablechildren/files/vulnerable_children_final_summary.pdf

Chance P. (2008) *The Teacher's Craft: The ten essentials skills of effective teaching*, Long Grove, IL: Waveland Press Inc.

Chase E., Knight A. and Statham J. (2008) *The Emotional Well-being of Unaccompanied Young People Seeking Asylum in the UK*, London: BAAF

Cheung S.Y. and Heath A. (1994) 'After care: education and occupation of adults who have been in care', *Oxford Review of Education*, 20, pp 361–74

Christoffersen M.N. (1993) *Anbragte börns livsförlöp* [The life course of children in care] Copenhagen: SFI, Rapport 93:11, 1993

Christoffersen M.N. (2010) *Child Maltreatment, Bullying in School and Social Support*, Copenhagen: SFI, Working Paper 02:2010

Chung J. (2012) *Education at a Glance: OECD Indicators 2012*, Country Note: UK: Organisation for Economic Co-operation and Development

Clarke M. (1998) *Lives in Care: Issues for policy and practice in children's homes*, Dublin: Children's Research Centre

Clausen S.-E. and Kristofersen L. (2008) *Barnevernsklienter I Norge 1990–2005: En longitudinell studie* [Child welfare clients in Norway 1990–2005: a longitudinal study] Oslo: NOVA, Rapport 3/08

Comfort R. (2004) *Meeting the Educational Needs of Looked After and Adopted Children*, Bristol: Our Place

Comfort R. (2007) 'For the love of learning: promoting educational achievement for looked after children', *Adoption & Fostering*, 31:1, pp 28–34

Commission on School Reform (2013) *By Diverse Means: Improving Scottish education*, final report, Edinburgh; http://reformscotland.com/public/publications/bydiversemeans1.pdf

Connelly G. and Chakrabarti M. (2008) 'Improving the educational experience of young people in care: a Scottish perspective', *International Journal of Inclusive Education*, 12, pp 347–61

Connelly G. and Furnivall J. (2013) 'Addressing low attainment of children in public care: the Scottish experience', *European Journal of Social Work*, 16:1, pp 88–104; doi: 10.1080/13691457. 2012.722986

Connelly G. and Matheson I. (2012) 'The education of looked after children in Scotland: some comparisons with Scandinavian countries and Finland', Research Briefing 1; www.celcis.org/media/resources/publications/CELCISResearchBriefing1Web.pdf

Connelly G., Siebelt L. and Furnivall J. (2008) *Supporting Looked after Children and Young People at School: A Scottish case study*; http://personal.strath.ac.uk/g.connelly/public.html

Connelly G., Forrest J., Furnivall J., Siebelt L., Smith I. and Seagraves L. (2008) *The Educational Attainment of Looked After Children – Local Authority Pilot Projects: Final Research Report*, Scottish Government; www.scotland.gov.uk/Resource/Doc/238207/0065397.pdf

Cook R. (1994) 'Are we helping foster care young people prepare for their future?', *Children and Youth Services Review*, 16, pp 213–29

Corbin J. and Strauss A. (2008) *Basics of Qualitative Research: Techniques and procedures for developing Grounded Theory*, Los Angeles, CA: Sage

Coulling N. (2000) 'Definitions of successful education for the "looked after" child: a multi-agency perspective', *Support for Learning*, 15, pp 30–35

Courtney M., Piliavin I., Grogan-Kaylor A. and Nesmith A. (2001) 'Foster young people transitions to adulthood: a longitudinal view of young people leaving care', *Child Welfare*, 80, pp 685–717

Currie J. (2000) *Early Childhood Intervention Programs: What do we know?*, JCPR Working Paper No. 169, Chicago, IL: Northwestern University/University of Chicago Joint Center for Poverty Research

Curtis M. (1946) *Report of the Care of Children Committee*, cmnd 6922, London: HMSO

CWIG (2009) *Understanding the Effects of Maltreatment on Brain Development*, Child Welfare Information Gateway; www.childwelfare.gov

Daly F. and Gilligan R. (2005) *Lives in Foster Care: The educational and social support experiences of young people aged 13–14 years in long-term foster care*, Dublin: Children's Research Centre

Darling N. (2005) 'Participation in extracurricular activities and adolescent adjustment: cross-sectional and longitudinal findings', *Journal of Youth and Adolescence*, 34:5, pp 493–505

Davey D. and Pithouse A. (2008) 'Schooling and looked after children: exploring contexts and outcomes in Standard Attainment Tests (SATS)', *Adoption & Fostering*, 32:3, pp 60–72

DCSF (2007) *Care Matters: Time for change*, White Paper, London: Department for Children, Schools and Families

DCSF (2008) *Children Looked After in England (including adoption and care leavers) – Year ending 31 March 2008*, SFR 23/2008

DCSF (2008a) *Care Matters: Time to deliver for children in care*, Nottingham: DCSF

DCSF (2008b) (2010) *Outcome Indicators for Children Looked After: Twelve months to 30 September 2007, England*; www.dcsf.gov.uk/rsgateway/DB/SFR/s000785/SFR082008v2.pdf

DCSF (2008c) *Personal Education Allowances for LAC: Statutory Guidance for local authorities*, DCSF-00416-2008; www.teachernet.gov.uk/publications

DCSF (2009a) *Children Looked After in England (Including Adoption and Care Leavers) Year Ending 31 March 2009*; www.dcsf.gov.uk/rsgateway/DB/SFR/s000878/index.shtml

DCSF (2009b) *Guidance for Local Authorities and Schools on Setting Education Performance Targets for 2011: LA statutory targets for Key Stages 2, 4, Early Years outcomes, children in care, underperforming groups and attendance*, London: DCSF

DCSF (2009c) *Improving the Attainment of Looked After Children in Primary Schools: Guidance for schools*; http://publications.teachernet.gov.uk/eOrderingDownload/01047-2009.pdf

DCSF (2009d) *Improving the Educational Attainment of Children in Care (Looked After Children)*; http://publications.everychildmatters.gov.uk/eOrderingDownload/DCSF-00523-2009.pdf

DCSF (2010a) *Statistics of Education First Release*, London: DCSF

DCFS (2010b) *Virtual School Head Toolkit*, March 2010; http://media.education.gov.uk/assets/files/pdf/v/virtual%20school%20head%20toolkit.pdf

DCFS (2010c) *Promoting the Educational Achievement of Looked After Children: Statutory Guidance for local authorities*, DCSF-00342-2010

de Ruuk N. (2002) *The Pharos School Prevention Programme Manual*, Canterbury: University of Kent

Desforges C. and Abouchar A. (2003) *The Impact of Parental Involvement, Parental Support and Family Education on Pupil Achievement and Adjustment*, DfES Research Report 433, London: DfES

DfE (2010a) *Outcomes for Children Looked After by Local Authorities in England, as at 31st March 2010*; http://www.education.gov.uk/rsgateway/DB/SFR/s000978/index.shtml

DfE (2010b) *Customer Voice – Wave 9: Aspirations of children in care*, Research Brief DFE-RBX-10-03, London: DfE

DfE (2011a) *Support and Aspiration: A new approach to Special Educational Needs and disability: A consultation*; http://webarchive.nationalarchives.gov.uk/20130401151715/https://www.education.gov.uk/publications/eOrderingDownload/Green-Paper-SEN.pdf

DfE (2011b) *2011–12 Children in Need Census Technical Specification*; www.education.gov.uk/researchandstatistics/statisticalreturns/cincencus/a0063842/cin-for-2011-12

DfE (2011) *Statistical First Release*, 2010–2011 (SFR21/2011) London: DfE

DfE (2012) *The Virtual School Head for Looked After Children*; www.education.gov.uk/childrenandyoungpeople/families/childrenincare/education/a00208592/virtual-school-head)

DfE/National Statistics (2011) *Outcomes for Children Looked After by Local Authorities in England, as at 31 March 2011*, Statistical First Release (SFR) 30/2011, DfE/National Statistics; www.education.gov.uk/rsgateway/DB/SFR/s001046/sfr30-2011V2.pdf

DfE/National Statistics (2012a) *Children Looked After in England (Including Adoption and Care Leavers) – Year Ending 31 March 2012*, Statistical First Release SFR 20/2012, London: DfE

DfE/National Statistics (2012b) *Special Educational Needs in England: January 2012*, Statistical First Release (SFR) 14/2012, DfE/National Statistics; www.education.gov.uk/rsgateway/DB/SFR/s001075/sfr14-2012v2.pdf

DfE/National Statistics (2012c) *Outcomes for Children Looked After by Local Authorities in England, as at 31 March 2012*, Statistical First Release (SFR) 32/2012, DfE/National Statistics; www.education.gov.uk/rsgateway/DB/SFR/s001046/sfr30-2011at.pdf

DfE, HM Revenue and Customs and Department for Work and Pensions (2013) *Staying Put: Arrangements for care leavers aged 18 and above*, DFE-000-61-2013

DfEE/DH (1994) *The Education of Children Looked After by Local Authorities*, Circular 13/94 LAC(94)11, London: DfEE/DH

DfEE/DH (2000), *Education of Children in Public Care: Guidance*, London: DfEE Publications

DfES (2003a) *Education Protects: The role of the school in supporting the education of children in public care*, London: DfES

DfES (2003a) *Every Child Matters*, London: DfES

DfES (2003b) *The National Literacy Strategy: Targeting support, choosing and implementing interventions for children with significant literacy difficulties* (Ref: 0201), London: DfES

DfES (2005) *Children Looked After in England (including Adoptions and Care Leavers) 2004–05*; www.education.gov.uk/rsgateway/DB/SFR/s000615/sfr51-2005.pdf

DfES (2006a) *Care Matters: Transforming the lives of children and young people in care*, Green Paper; www.education.gov.uk/consultations/downloadableDocs/6781-DfES-CM%20Summary.pdf

DfES (2006b) *Outcome Indicators for Looked After Children to Year ending September 30, 2005*, London: DfES

DfES/DH (2000) *Guidance on the Education of Children and Young People in Public Care*, London: DfES/DH

DfES/DH (2002) *Education Protects: Collecting and using data to improve educational outcomes for children in public care*, London: DfES/DH

DH (1990) *The Care of Children: Principles and practice in Regulations and Guidance*, London: DH

DH (1991a) *The Children Act 1989 – Guidance and Regulations, Volume 6, Children with Disabilities*, London: HMSO

DH (1991b) *The Children Act 1989 – Guidance and Regulations, Volume 3, Family Placements*, London: HMSO

DH (1991c) *The Children Act 1989 – Guidance and Regulations, Volume 4, Residential Care*, London: HMSO

DH (1998) *Quality Protects*, London: DH

DH (2001) *Educational Qualifications and Care Histories of Care Leavers in England*; www.education.gov.uk/rsgateway/DB/SBU/b000519/cl2000eq.pdf

DH (2002) *Children Looked After by Local Authorities – Year ending 31 March 2001*, Government Statistical Service

DH (2003) *Outcome Indicators for Looked After Children: Twelve months to 30 September 2002*, England, London: Office for National Statistics

DH (2004) *Children Looked After by Local Authorities – Year ending 31 March 2003*, Government Statistical Service

Dixon J. and Stein M. (2005) *Still a Bairn? Throughcare and aftercare services in Scotland*, Final Report to the Scottish Executive; www.york.ac.uk/inst/swrdu/Publications/stillabairn.pdf

Dixon J., Wade J., Byford S., Weatherly H. and Lee J. (2006) *Young People Leaving Care: A study of costs and outcomes – Final Report to the Department for Education and Skills*, York: University of York

Doyle J. (2007) 'Child protection and child outcomes: measuring the effects of foster care', *The American Economic Review*, 97, pp 1583–610

Driscoll J. (2013) 'Supporting the educational transitions of looked after children at Key Stage 4: the role of virtual schools and designated teachers', *Journal of Children's Services*, 8:2, pp 110–122

DuBois D. and Silverthorn N. (2005) 'Natural mentoring relationships and adolescent health: evidence from a national study', *American Journal of Public Health*, 95:3, pp 518–24

Dumaret A (1985) 'IQ, scholastic performance and behavior in sibs raised in contrasting environments', *Journal of Child Psychology and Psychiatry*, 26, pp 553–80

Duncan G., Dowsett C., Claessens A., Magnuson K., Huston A., Klebanov P., Pagani L., Feinstein L., Engel M., Brooks-Gunn J., Sexton H. and Duckworth K. (2008) 'School readiness and later achievement', *Developmental Psychology*, 43, pp 1428–446

Durlak J.A. (1997) *Successful Prevention Programs for Children and Adolescents*, New York: Plenum

Dworsky A. (2005) 'The economic self-sufficiency of Wisconsin's former foster youth', *Children and Youth Services Review*, 27:10, pp 1085–118

Dymoke S. and Griffiths R. (2010) 'The Letterbox Club: the impact on looked after children and their carers of a national project aimed at raising achievements in literacy for children aged 7 to 11 in foster care', *Journal of Research in Special Educational Needs*, 10, pp 52–60

Education and Culture Committee of the Scottish Parliament (2012) *Inquiry into the Educational Attainment of Looked After Children*; www.scottish.parliament.uk

Egelund T. and Hestbæk A.-D. (2007) '*Sma° børn anbragt udenfor hjemmet* [Young children in out of home care]', *Nordisk Sosial Arbeid*, 127, pp 120–33

Egelund T., Andersen D., Hestbaek A.-D., Lausten M., Knudsen L., Olsen R. F. and Gerstoft F. (2008) *Anbragted börns udvikling og vilkår* [Development and living conditions of looked after children], Copenhagen: SFI, Rapport 08:23

Elze D.E., Auslander W.F., Stiffman A. and McMillen C. (2005) 'Educational needs of youth in foster care', in Mallon G.P. and McCartt Hess P. (eds) *Child Welfare for the 21st Century: A handbook of practices, policies and programs*, New York: Columbia University Press

Engström A. and Magne O. (2003) *Medelsta, Math Diagnostic Test*, Örebro: Örebro Universitet

Essen J., Lambert L. and Head J. (1976) 'School attainment of children who have been in care', *Child Care, Health and Development*, 2, pp 339–51, 1976

Esping-Anderson F. (1990) *The Three Worlds of Welfare Capitalism*, Cambridge: Polity Press.

European Commission (2008) 'Valuing learning outside formal education and training'; http://ec. europa.eu/education/lifelong-learning-policy/doc52_en.htm

European Commission (2009) *EU Youth Report, 2009*, Brussels: European Commission Directorate-General for Education and Culture

Evans R. (2003) 'Equality and the education of children looked after by the state', *International Journal of Human Rights*, 7, pp 58–86

Fahlberg V. (1994) *A Child's Journey through Placement*, London: BAAF

Fanshel D. and Shinn E. (1978) *Children in Foster Care: A longitudinal investigation*, New York: Columbia University Press

Farmer E. (1998) *Sexually Abused and Abusing children in Substitute Care*, Chichester: Wiley

Farmer T.W., Estell D.B., Hall C.M., Pearl R., Van Acker R. and Rodkin P.C. (2008) 'Interpersonal competence configurations, behaviour problems and social adjustment in preadolescence', *Journal of Emotional and Behavioural Disorders*, 16, pp 195–212

Feinstein L. and Brassett-Grundy A. (2005) *The Life Course Outcomes for Looked After Children: Evidence from the British cohort study 1970*, London: Institute of Education

Feinstein L. and Bynner J. (2004) 'The importance of cognitive development in middle childhood for adulthood socioeconomic status, mental health, and problem behaviour', *Child Development*, 75, pp 1329–39

Fernandez E. (2008) 'Unravelling emotional, behavioural and educational outcomes in a longitudinal study of children in foster care', *British Journal of Social Work*, 38, pp 1283–301

Ferrer-Wreder L., Stattin H., Lorente C.C., Tubman J. and Adamson L. (2004) *Successful Prevention and Young People Development Programs: Across borders*, New York: Kluwer Academic

Festinger T. (1983) *No One Asked us . . . A postscript to foster care*, New York: Columbia University Press

Finn M. (2008) *Evaluation of the Reading Rich Programme*, Edinburgh: The Scottish Government; www.scotland.gov.uk/Publications/2008/07/14103033/0

Finney D. (2009) 'The road to self-efficacy: a discussion of generic training in mental health competences for educational professionals', *Pastoral Care in Education*, 27:1, pp 21–28

Finnie R. (2011) 'Who goes to college or university: the importance of "culture",' *Presentation at the PART conference, Improving educational outcomes of children and youth in care*, Ottawa, ON: University of Ottawa

Firth H. and Fletcher B. (2001) 'Developing equal chances: a whole authority approach', in Jackson S. (ed) *Nobody Ever Told Us School Mattered: Raising the educational attainment of children in care*, London: BAAF

Firth H. and Horrocks C. (1996) 'No home, no school, no future: exclusions and children who are "looked after"', in Blyth E. and Milner J. (eds) *Exclusion from School: Inter-professional issues for policy and practice*, London: Routledge

Fletcher B. (1996) *Who Cares? about Education: The education of children who are looked after by local authorities – a guide for school governors*, London: Who Cares? Trust

Fletcher B. (1998) *Who Cares? about education: The education of children who are looked after by local authorities – a guide for elected members*, London: Who Cares? Trust & Local Government Association

Fletcher-Campbell F. (1997) *The Education of Children Who Are Looked After*, Slough: NFER

Fletcher-Campbell F. (2008) 'Pupils who are "in care": What can schools do?', in Baginsky M. (ed) *Safeguarding Children and Schools*, London: Jessica Kingsley Publishers

Fletcher-Campbell F. and Archer T. (2003a) *Achievement at Key Stage 4 of Young People in Care*, Slough: NFER

Fletcher-Campbell F. and Archer T. (2003b) 'Reasons for Non-attainment of GCSE/GNVQ by Key Stage 4 Students in Public Care', in Fletcher-Campbell F. and Archer T., *Achievement at Key Stage 4 of Young People in Care*, DfES Research Report 434, London: DfES

Fletcher-Campbell F. and Hall C. (1990) *Changing Schools, Changing Lives: The education of children in care*, Slough: NFER

Fletcher-Campbell F., Archer T. and Tomlinson K. (2003) *The Role of the School in Supporting the Education of Children in Public Care*, DfES Research Report 498, London: DfES

Flynn R.J., Dudding P.M. and Barber J.G. (eds) (1998) *Promoting Resilience in Child Welfare*, Ottawa, ON: University of Ottawa Press

Flynn R., Paquet M.-P. and Marquis R. (2010) 'Can tutoring by foster parents improve foster children's basic academic skills?', in Fernandez E. and Barth R. (eds) *How Does Foster Care Work? International evidence on outcomes*, London: Jessica Kingsley Publishers

Flynn R., Ghazal H., Legault L., Vandermeulen G. and Petrick S. (2004) 'Use of population measures and norms to identify resilient outcomes in young people in care: an exploratory study', *Child & Family Social Work*, 9:1, pp 65–79

Fong R., Schwab J. and Armour M. (2006) 'Continuity of activities and child well-being for foster care youth', *Children and Youth Services Review*, 28:11, pp 1359–374

Ford T., Vostanis P., Meltzer H. and Goodman R. (2007) 'Psychiatric disorder among British children looked after by local authorities: comparison with children living in private households', *British Journal of Psychiatry*, 190, pp 319–25

Forrester D. (2008) 'Is the care system failing children?', *The Political Quarterly*, 79, pp 206–11

Forrester D., Goodman K., Cocker C., Binnie C. and Jensch G. (2009) 'What is the impact of public care on children's welfare? A review of research findings from England and Wales and their policy implications', *Journal of Social Policy*, 38, pp 439–56

Fostering Network (2007) *Can't Afford to Foster: A survey of fee payments to foster carers in the UK*, London: Fostering Network

Francis J. (2000) 'Investing in children's futures: enhancing the educational outcomes of "looked after" children', *Child & Family Social Work*, 5:1, pp 241–60

Fredricks J. and Eccles J. (2006) 'Is extracurricular participation associated with beneficial outcomes? Concurrent and longitudinal relations', *Developmental Psychology*, 42:4, pp 698–713

Furnivall J. (2011) 'Attachment-informed practice with looked after children and young people'; http://www.iriss.org.uk/resources/attachment-informed-practice-looked-after-children-and-young-people

Garnett L. (1994) 'Education of Children Looked After', Humberside Social Services Department, Unpublished paper, cited in Evans R (2003) 'Equality and the education of children looked after by the state', *International Journal of Human Rights*, 7:1, pp 58–86

Galton M., Gray J. and Ruddock J. (2003) *Transfer and Transitions in the Middle Years of Schooling Continuities and Discontinuities in Learning (7–14)*, Research Report RR44; http://www.dcsf.gov.uk/research/programmeofresearch/projectinformation.cfm?projectid=13346&resultspage=1

Gaskell C. (2010) ' "If the social worker had called at least it would show they cared": young care leavers' perspectives on the importance of care', *Children & Society*, 24, pp 136–47

Ghate D. and Hazel N. (2002) *Parenting in Poor Environments: Stress, support and caring*, London: Jessica Kingsley Publishers

Gilligan R. (1999) 'Enhancing the resilience of children and young people in public care by encouraging their talents and interests' , *Child & Family Social Work*, 4:3, pp 87–96

Gilligan R. (2000) 'Adversity, resilience and young people: the protective value of positive school and spare time experiences', *Children & Society*, 14:1, pp 37–47

Gilligan R. (2007a) 'Spare time activities for young people in care: what can they contribute to educational progress?', *Adoption & Fostering*, 31:1, pp 92–99

Gilligan R. (2007b) 'Adversity, resilience and the educational progress of young people in public care', *Emotional and Behavioural Difficulties*, 12:2, pp 135–145

Glaser D. (2003) 'Child abuse and neglect and the brain – a review', *Journal of Child Psychology and Psychiatry*, 41, pp 97–116

Goddard J. (2000) 'The education of looked after children: a research review', *Child & Family Social Work*, 5:1, pp 79–86

Goldschmied E. and Jackson S. (2004) (2nd edition) *People Under Three: Young children in day care*, London: Routledge

Goldsworthy H. (2011) *Moving On: A guide for care leavers and those who support them*, Bath: Aimhigher West Area Partnership

Goleman D. (1996) *Emotional Intelligence*, London: Bloomsbury

Good T.L. (1987) 'Two decades of research on teacher expectations: findings and future directions', *Journal of Teacher Education*, 38:4, pp 32–47

Goodman R. (1997) 'The Strengths and Difficulties Questionnaire: a research note', *Journal of Child Psychology and Psychiatry*, 38, pp 581–86

Gregory E., Long S. and Volk D. (eds) (2004) *Many Pathways to Literacy: Young children learning with siblings, grandparents, peers and communities*, London: Routledge

Griffiths R. (2009) 'Evaluating the Letterbox Club: developing assessment items to examine the progress in number of children aged 7 to 11 in public care', in Novotna J. and Moraova H. (eds), *Proceedings of SEMT '09: International Symposium Elementary Mathematics Teaching*, August 23–28, Prague: Charles University

Griffiths R. (2012) 'The Letterbox Club: an account of a postal club to raise the achievement of children aged 7 to 13 in foster care', *Children and Youth Services Review*, 34:6, pp 1101–1106

Griffiths R., Comber C. and Dymoke S. (2010) *The Letterbox Club 2007 to 2009: Final Evaluation Report*, London: Booktrust

Griffiths R., Dymoke S. and Comber C. (2008) *The Letterbox Club: Evaluation report Part One*, London: Booktrust

Grossman J. and Bulle M. (2006) 'Review of what youth programs do to increase the connectedness of youth with adults', *Journal of Adolescent Health*, 39, pp 788–99

Grossman J. and Rhodes J. (2002) 'The test of time: predictors and effects of duration in youth mentoring relationships', *American Journal of Community Psychology*, 30:2, pp 199–219

Hallam S. (2002) 'Musical motivation; towards a model synthesising the research', *Music Education Research*, 4:2, pp 225–44

Hannon C., Bazalgette L. and Wood C. (2010) *In Loco Parentis*, London: Demos; http://www.barnardos.org.uk/in_loco_parentis_-_web.pdf

*Hansard*, 9 February 2005, Column 849

Hare A. and Bullock R. (2006) 'Dispelling misconceptions about looked after children', *Adoption & Fostering*, 30:4, pp 26–35

Harker R., Dober-Ober D., Berridge D. and Sinclair R. (2004a) *Taking Care of Education: An evaluation of the education of looked after children*, London: National Children's Bureau

Harker R., Dobel-Ober D., Berridge D. and Sinclair R. (2004b) 'More than the sum of its parts? Inter-professional working in the education of looked after children', *Children & Society*, 18, pp 179–93

Harker M., Dobel-Ober D., Lawrence J., Berridge D. and Sinclair R. (2003) 'Who takes care of education? Looked after children's perceptions of support for educational progress', *Child & Family Social Work*, 8:2, pp 89–100

Harker R., Dobel-Ober D., Akhurst S., Berridge D. and Sinclair R. (2004b), 'Who takes care of education 18 months on? A follow-up study of looked after children's' perceptions of support for educational progress', *Child & Family Social Work*, 9:2, pp 273–84

Hart S., Dixon A., Drummond M.J. and McIntyre D. (2004) *Learning without Limits*, Maidenhead: Open University Press

Hattie J. (2009) *Visible Learning: A synthesis of over 800 meta-analyses relating to achievement*, Oxon: Routledge

Hauari H., Hollingworth K., Glenn M., Cameron C. and Jackson S. (2010) *The Educational Pathways of Young People from a Public Care background in Five EU Countries: Analysis of national statistics and survey of local agencies to establish a baseline of post-compulsory educational participation*, London: Thomas Coram Research Unit, Institute of Education; http:/tcru.ioe.ac.uk/ yippee

Hay D., Asten P., Mills A., Kumar R., Pawlby S. and Sharp D. (2001) 'Intellectual problems shown by 11-year-old children whose mothers had postnatal depression', *Journal of Child Psychology and Psychiatry*, 42, pp 871–89

Hay D., Pawlby S., Cerith S., Waters C., Perra O. and Sharp D. (2010), 'Mothers' antenatal depression and their children's antisocial outcomes', *Child Development*, 81, pp 149–65

Hayden C. (2005) 'More than a piece of paper? Personal education plans and "looked after" children in England', *Child & Family Social Work*, 10:4, pp 343–52

HC CSFC (House of Commons Children, Schools and Families Committee) (2009) *Looked after Children: Third Report of Session 2008–09, Volume I Report, together with formal minutes*, HC111-I, London: The Stationery Office

Heath A., Aldgate J. and Colton M. (1989) 'The education of children in and out of care', *British Journal of Social Work*, 19:6, pp 447–60

Heath A., Colton M. and Aldgate J. (1994) 'Failure to escape: a longitudinal study of foster children's educational attainment', *British Journal of Social Work*, 24:3, pp 241–60

Heath A., Colton M. and Jackson S. (1994) *Oxford Review of Education: Special Issue on the Education of Children in Care*, 20:3

Hek R. (2005a) 'The experiences and needs of refugees and asylum seeking children in the UK: a literature review', London: Department for Work and Pensions

Hek R. (2005b) 'The role of education in the settlement of young refugees in the UK: the experiences of young refugees', *Practice*, 17:3, pp 157–171

Hemmerman L., Law I., Simms J. and Sirriyeh A. (2007) 'Situating racist hostility and understanding the impact of racist victimisation in Leeds', Leeds: Centre for Ethnicity and Racism Studies

Henderson G. and Whitehead I. (2013) *How Much is Education Included in the Plans of Children on Supervision Requirements?, SCRA Research Report*, Stirling: Scottish Children's Reporter Administration (SCRA)

Her Majesty's Inspectors of Schools and Social Work Services Inspectorate (2001) *Learning with Care: The education of children looked after away from home by local authorities*, Edinburgh: HMI and SWSI; www.scotland.gov.uk/library3/education/lacr-00.asp

Hobcraft J. and Kiernan K. (2001) 'Childhood poverty, early motherhood and adult social exclusion', *British Journal of Sociology*, 52, pp 495–17

Höjer I., Johannson H. and Hill M. (2010) *A long and winding road: The Swedish national report of the YiPPEE project* (WP9) University of Gothenburg

Höjer I., Johannson H., Hill M., Cameron C. and Jackson S. (2008) *State of the Art Literature Review: The educational pathways of young people from a public care background in five EU countries* (WP2) London: Thomas Coram Research Unit, Institute of Education

Holland S. (2009) 'Listening to children in care: a review of methodological and theoretical approaches to understanding looked after children's perspectives', *Children & Society*, 23:3, pp 226–35

Hollingworth K.E. (2012) 'Participation in social, leisure and informal learning activities among care leavers in England: positive outcomes for educational participation', *Child & Family Social Work*, 17:4, pp 438–447

Home Office (2002) *Unaccompanied Asylum Seeking Children Information Note*, London: Home Office

Howell S. (2011) *Pupil Referral Units and the Mental Health Needs of their Students*, National Children's Bureau Highlight no. 264, London: NCB

Hauari H., Hollingworth K., Glenn M., Cameron C. and Jackson S. (2010) *The Educational Pathways of Young People from a Public Care background in Five EU Countries: Analysis of national statistics and survey of local agencies to establish a baseline of post-compulsory educational participation*, London: Thomas Coram Research Unit, Institute of Education. Available at http:/tcru.ioe.ac.uk/yippee

ILO (International Labour Office) (2012) *Global Employment Trends for Youth 2012*, Geneva; http://www.ilo.org/global/research/global-reports/global-employment-trends/youth/2012/WCMS_180976/lang--en/index.htm

In Care, In School (2012) *Teachers' Pack: A learning resource helping school communities understand what it means to be in care and in school*, Bath: Bath Spa University

Iwaniec D., Larkin E. and Higgins S. (2006) 'Research review: risk and resilience in cases of emotional abuse', *Child & Family Social Work*, 11:1, pp 73–82

Jablonska B., Lindberg L., Lindblad F., Rasmussen F., Östberg V. and Hjern A. (2009) 'School performance and hospital admissions due to self-inflicted injury: a Swedish national cohort study', *International Journal of Epidemiology*, 38:5, pp 1334–41

Jacklin A., Robinson C. and Torrance H. (2006), 'When a lack of data is data: do we really know who our looked-after children are?', *European Journal of Special Needs Education*, 21, pp 1–20

Jackson B. and Marsden D. (1962) *Education and the Working Class*, London: Routledge & Kegan Paul

Jackson S (1987) 'The education of children in care', *Bristol Papers in Applied Social Studies*, 1, Bristol: University of Bristol

Jackson S. (1988) *Evaluation of Southlands Children's Home*, Consultancy for National Children's Homes

Jackson S. (1994) 'Educating children in residential and foster care', *Oxford Review of Education*, 20:3, pp 267–279

Jackson S. (1998a) *High Achievers: A study of young people who have been in residential or foster care*, Final report to the Leverhulme Trust, Swansea: University of Wales

Jackson S. (1998b) 'Educational success for looked after children: the social worker's responsibility', *Practice: Social Work in Action*, 10:4, pp 47–56

Jackson S. (2000) 'Promoting the educational achievement of looked after children', in Cox T (ed) *Combating Educational Disadvantage*, London: Falmer Press

Jackson S. (ed) (2001a) *Nobody Told us School Mattered: Raising the educational attainments of children in care*, London: BAAF

Jackson S. (2001b) 'The Education of Children in Care', in Jackson S. (ed) *Nobody Ever Told Us School Mattered: Raising the educational attainments of children in care*, London: BAAF

Jackson S. (2006) 'Looking after children away from home: past and present', in Chase E., Simon A. and Jackson S. (eds), *In Care and After: A positive perspective*, London: Routledge

Jackson S. (2007a) 'Care leavers, exclusion and access to higher education', in Christian J., Abrams D. and Gordon D. (eds), *Multidisciplinary Handbook of Social Exclusion Research*, Hoboken: John Wiley & Sons

Jackson S. (2007b) 'Progress at last?', Editorial, *Adoption & Fostering*, 31:1, pp 3–5

Jackson S. (2008) 'Care leavers, exclusion and access to higher education', in Christian J. and Abrams D. (eds) *Multidisciplinary Handbook of Social Exclusion Research*, London: Sage

Jackson S. (2010a) *Education for Social Inclusion: Can we change the future for Children in Care?* Professorial Lecture, April 27, London: Institute of Education

Jackson S. (2010b) 'Reconnecting care and education: from the Children Act 1989 to Care Matters', *Journal of Children's Services*, 5:3, pp 48–59

Jackson S. and Ajayi S. (2007) 'Foster care and higher education', *Adoption & Fostering*, 31:1, pp 62–72

Jackson S. and Cameron C. (2009) *Unemployment, Education and Social Exclusion: The case of young people from public care*, Brussels: European Commission

Jackson S. and Cameron C. (eds) (2011) *Young People From a Public Care Background: Pathways to further and higher education in five European countries*, Final Report of the YiPPEE Project, WP12, London: Thomas Coram Research Unit, Institute of Education

Jackson S. and Cameron C. (2012) 'Leaving care: looking ahead and aiming higher', *Children and Youth Services Review*, 34, pp 1107–1114

Jackson S. and Höjer I. (2013) 'Prioritising education for children looked after away from home', Editorial, *European Journal of Social Work*, 16:1, pp 1–5

Jackson S. and McParlin P. (2006) 'The education of children in care', *The Psychologist*, 19, pp 90–3

Jackson B. and Marsden D. (1962) *Education and the Working Class*, London: Routledge & Kegan Paul

Jackson S. and Martin P.Y. (1998) 'Surviving the care system: education and resilience', *Journal of Adolescence*, 21:5, pp 569–83

Jackson S. and Preston-Shoot M. (1996) *Educating Social Workers in a Changing Policy Context*, London: Whiting & Birch

Jackson S. and Roberts S. (2000) *A Feasibility Study on the Needs of Care Leavers in Higher Education*, Report to the Gulbenkian Foundation UK, Swansea: University of Swansea School of Social Sciences and International Development

Jackson S. and Sachdev D. (2001) *Better Education, Better Futures: Research, practice and the views of young people in public care*, Ilford: Barnardo's

Jackson S. and Simon A. (2006) 'The costs and benefits of educating children in care', in Chase E., Simon S. and Jackson S. (eds) *In Care and After: A positive perspective*, London: Routledge

Jackson S. and Thomas N. (1999) *On the Move Again? What works in creating stability for looked after children?* Ilford: Barnardo's

Jackson S. and Thomas N. (2001) *What Works in Creating Stability for Looked After Children?*, Ilford: Barnardo's

Jackson S., Ajayi S. and Quigley M. (2003) *By Degrees: The first year – from care to university*, London: National Children's Bureau/Frank Buttle Trust

Jackson S., Ajayi S. and Quigley M. (2005) *Going to University from Care*, Final report of the *By Degrees* project, London: Institute of Education

Jacobson C. (2004) *Letter-Word Chains*, Manual, Stockholm: Psykologiförlaget

Janoff-Bulman R. (1992) *Shattered Assumptions: Towards a new psychology of trauma*, New York: Free Press

Jarpsten B. (1999) *DLS Spelling Ability*, Manual, Stockholm: Psykologiförlaget

Jarpsten B. and Taube K. (1997) *DLS Reading Speed and Spelling Ability*, Manual, Stockholm: Psykologiförlaget

Jones C. (1998) 'The education needs of refugee children', in Rutter J. and Jones C. (eds), *Refugee Education: Mapping the field*, Stoke on Trent: Trentham Books

Joseph S. (2012) *What Doesn't Kill Us: The new psychology of post-traumatic growth*, London: Piatkus

Joseph S., Williams R. and Yule W. (1997) *Understanding Post-traumatic stress: A psychological perspective on PSTD and treatment*, Chichester: Wiley

Kennett P. (2007) *Comparative Social Policy*, Maidenhead: Open University Press

Kilpatrick J., Swafford J. and Findell B. (eds) (2001) *Adding it Up: Helping children learn mathematics*, Washington, DC: National Academy Press

Kinchin D. (2004) *Post-traumatic Stress Disorder: The invisible injury*, Didcot: Success Unlimited

Kohli R.K.S. (2007) *Social Work with Unaccompanied Asylum-seeking Children*, Basingstoke: Palgrave Macmillan

Lansford J., Dodge K., Pettit G., Crozier J. and Kaplow P.A. (2002) 'A 12-year prospective study of the long-term effects of early child physical maltreatment on psychological, behavioural and academic problems in adolescence', *Archives of Pediatric and Adolescent Medicine*, 13, pp 824–30

Laursen E.K. and Birmingham S.M. (2003) 'Caring relationships as a protective factor for at-risk youth: an ethnographic study', *Families in Society*, 84:2, pp 240–46

Leeson C. (2007) 'My life in care: experiences of non-participation in decision-making processes', *Child & Family Social Work*, 12:3, pp 268–77

Leeson C. (2009) *The Involvement of Looked after Children in Making Decisions about their Present and Future Care Needs*, Unpublished PhD thesis, University of Plymouth

Lipscombe J. and Farmer E. (2007) 'What matters in fostering adolescents?', *Social Work & Social Sciences Review*, 13:1, pp 41–58

Lonne B., Parton N., Thomson J. and Harries M. (2008) *Reforming Child Protection*, London: Routledge

Lucey H. and Walkerdine V. (2000) 'Boys' under-achievement: social class and changing masculinities', in Cox T. (ed) *Combating Educational Disadvantage: Meeting the needs of vulnerable children*, London: Falmer Press

MacBeth J., Kirwan T., Myers K. *et al* (2001) *The Impact of Study Support: A report of a longitudinal study into the impact of participation in out-of school hours learning on the academic attainment, attitudes and school attendance of secondary school students*, DfES Research Report 273; www.Dfes.gov.uk/research/data/ upload files/RR273.PDF

MacLullich A. (2012) *The Perceptions of Adoptive and Foster Parents in their Engagement with the Educational System: Building bridges in managing attachment difficulties – training notes*, Edinburgh: St Andrew's Children's Society Limited

McAuley C. and Young C. (2006) 'The mental health needs of looked after children: challenges for CAMHS provision', *Journal of Social Work Practice*, 20, pp 91–103

McCann J., James A., Wilson S. and Dunn G. (1996) 'Prevalence of psychiatric disorders in young people in the care system', *British Medical Journal*, 313, pp 1529-1530

McClung M. and Gayle V. (2010) 'Exploring the care effects of multiple factors on the educational achievement of children looked after at home and away from home: an investigation of two Scottish local authorities', *Child & Family Social Work*, 15:4, pp 409-31

McCool S. (2008) 'Communication impairments in children in residential care: an overlooked aspect of their education and well-being?', *Scottish Journal of Residential Child Care*, 7:2, pp 1478–840

McGee R., Williams S., Howden-Chapman P., Martin J. and Kawachi I. (2000) 'Participation in clubs and groups from childhood to adolescence and its effects on attachment and self-esteem', *Journal of Adolescence*, 29, pp 1–17

McKechnie J., Hobbs S., Lindsay S. and Lynch M. (1998) 'Working children: the health and safety issue', *Children & Society*, 12:1, pp 38–47

McMurray I., Connolly H., Preston-Shoot M. and Wigley V. (2008) 'Constructing resilience: social workers' understandings and practice', *Health and Social Care in the Community*, 16:3, pp 299–09

Mahoney J., Cairns B. and Farmer T. (2003) 'Promoting interpersonal competence and educational success through extracurricular activity participation', *Journal of Educational Psychology*, 95:2, pp 409–18

Mahoney J., Larson R., Eccles J. and Lord H. (2005) 'Organised activities as developmental contexts for children and adolescents', in Mahoney J., Larson R. and Eccles J. (eds) *Organised Activities as Contexts of Development: Extracurricular activities, after-school and community programs*, Mahwah, NJ: Lawrence Erlbaum Associates

Mallon J. (2007) 'Returning to education after care: protective factors in the development of resilience', *Adoption & Fostering*, 31:1, pp 106–117

Manning M., Homel R. and Smith C. (2010) 'A meta-analysis of the effects of early developmental prevention programs in at-risk populations on non-health outcomes in adolescence', *Children and Youth Services Review*, 32, pp 506–19

Martin P. and Jackson S. (2002) 'Educational success for children in public care: advice from a group of high achievers', *Child & Family Social Work*, 7:2, pp 121–30

Marriot K. (2001) *Living in Limbo: Young separated refugees in the West Midlands*, West Midlands: Save the Children

Matthews D. (1997) *Time in Foster Care and Children's Developmental Status*, PhD thesis, New York: Fordham University

Maxwell C., Statham J. and Jackson S. (2009) *Boarding School Provision for Vulnerable Children*, DCSF Report RR070

Meltzer H. (2003) *The Mental Health of Young People Looked After by Local Authorities in England*, London: The Stationery Office

Meltzer H., Gatward R., Goodman R. and Ford F. (2000) *The Mental Health of Children and Adolescents in Great Britain*, London: The Stationery Office

Meltzer H., Gatward R., Corbin T., Goodwin R. and Ford T. (2003) *The Mental Health of Young People Looked After by Local Authorities in England*, London: Office for National Statistics

Meltzer H., Lader D., Corbin T., Goodwin R. and Ford T. (2004a) *The Mental Health of Young People Looked After by Local Authorities in Scotland*, London: Office for National Statistics

Meltzer H., Lader D., Corbin T., Goodwin R. and Ford T. (2004b) *The Mental Health of Young People Looked After by Local Authorities in Wales*, London: Office for National Statistics

Menmuir R. (1994) 'Involving residential social workers and foster carers in reading with young people in their care: the PRAISE reading project', *Oxford Review of Education*, 20:3, pp 329–38

Millham S., Bullock R. and Hosie K. (1980) *Learning to Care: The training of staff for residential social work with young people*, Farnborough: Gower

Mittler P. (2000) *Working towards Inclusive Education: Social contexts*, London: David Fulton Publishers

Mittler P. and Jackson S. (2002) 'Social exclusion and education', *MCC – Building Knowledge for Integrated Care*, 10:3, pp 5–13

Montgomery P., Donkoh C. and Underhill K. (2006) 'Independent living programs for young people leaving the care system: the state of the evidence', *Children and Youth Services Review*, 28, pp 1435–48

Mooney A., Statham J. and Monck E. (2009) *Promoting the Health of Looked after Children: A study to guide the implementation of the 2002 Guidance*, DCSF Research Report 125, Nottingham: The Stationery Office

Morgan R.T. (1976) 'Paired reading tuition: a preliminary report on a technique for cases of reading deficit', *Child Care Health Development*, 2:1, pp 13–28

Munro R.E., Lushey C., National Care Advisory Service, Maskell-Graham D. and Ward H. with Holmes L. (2011) *Evaluation of the Staying Put: 18+ Family Placement Programme Pilot: Final Report*, London: Department for Education

Munro E., Lushey C., National Care Advisory Service, Maskell-Graham D. and Ward H. (2012) *Evaluation of the Staying Put: 18+ Family Placement Pilot Programme: Final Report DfE* RR-191, Loughborough University

Muschamp Y., Wikely F., Ridge T. and Balarin M. (2007) *Parenting, Caring and Educating*, Primary Review Research Survey 7/1, Cambridge: University of Cambridge Faculty of Education

NCB (2009) *Guidelines for Research with Children and Young People*, London: National Children's Bureau

Neale M. (1997) *Neale Analysis of Reading Ability* (2nd revised British edition), London: NFER/Nelson

Newman T. (2004) *What Works in Building Resilience?*, Ilford: Barnardo's

NICE (2010) *Promoting the Quality of Life of Looked after Children and Young People*, NICE Public Health Guidance 28, London: National Institute for Health and Clinical Excellence

Nutbrown K. and Clough P. with Atherton F. (2013 – 2nd edition) *Inclusion in the Early Years*, London: Sage

O'Connor M. and Russell A. (2004) *Identifying the Incidence of Psychological Trauma and Post-trauma Symptoms in Children: A survey of three Clackmannanshire schools*, Clackmannanshire Council Psychological Service; www.clacksleisure.co.uk/document/2031.pdf

Ofsted (2003) *Ofsted: Education of asylum seeker pupils*, Norwich: Ofsted Publications Centre

Ofsted (2008) *Looked After Children: Good practice in schools*, London: Ofsted

Ofsted (2009) *Family Learning: An evaluation of the benefits of family learning for participants, their families and the wider community*, London: Ofsted

Ofsted (2010) *Promoting the Educational Achievement of Looked after Children*, March 2010

Ofsted (2012a) *The Impact of Virtual Schools on the Educational Progress of Looked After Children*, Ofsted; www.ofsted.gov.uk/resources/impact-of-virtual-schools-educational-progress-of-looked-after-children

Ofsted (2012b) *Inspection of Safeguarding and Looked After Children Services*, Bath and North East Somerset, February 2012:

Ofsted (2012c) *After Care: Young people's views on leaving care*, reported by the Children's Rights Director for England; www.rights4me.org

Ofsted (2012d) *Inspection of Safeguarding and Looked After Children Services*, Bath and North East Somerset, February 2012

Ofsted/SSI (1995) *The Education of Children who are Looked After by Local Authorities*, London: Department of Health

Oldfield S (2008) *Jeanie, an 'Army of One': Mrs Nassau Senior 1828–1877, The First Woman in Whitehall*, Eastbourne: Sussex Academic Press

Olisa J., Stuart M., Hill V., Male D. and Radford J. (undated) *Intervention to Promote Good Literacy in Looked After Children*, Report, London: Institute of Education, Project 2001–02S30

ONS (2005) Social Survey Division and Northern Ireland Statistics and Research Agency, Central Survey Unit, *Quarterly Labour Force Survey, March May, 2003* [computer file] (3rd edition), Colchester: UK data archive [distributor] June, SN:4712

Osborn A., Delfabbro P. and Barber J. (2008) 'The psychosocial functioning and family background of children experiencing significant placement instability in Australian out-of-home care', *Child and Youth Services Review*, 30, pp 847–60

O'Sullivan A. and Millward J. (2008) 'The outcomes of the "Way Ahead" project in Leicestershire', Paper presented at the *Care Matters: Transforming Lives – Improving Outcomes Conference*, incorporating the *8th International Looking After Children Conference*, 7–9 July 2008, Keble College, Oxford; http://www.lboro.ac.uk/research/ccfr/Transforminglivesconference/Digest%20 of%20papers.pdf

O'Sullivan A. and Westerman R. (2007) 'Closing the gap: investigating the barriers to educational achievement for looked after children', *Adoption & Fostering*, 3:1, pp 13–20

Pallett C., Simmonds J. and Warman A. (2010) *Supporting Children's Learning: A training programme for foster carers*, London: BAAF

Parker R. (1990) *Away from Home: A history of child care*, Ilford: Barnardo's

Parker R., Ward H., Jackson S., Aldgate J. and Wedge P. (1991) *Looking After Children: Assessing outcomes in child care*, London: HMSO

Pawlby S., Sharp D., Hay D. and O'Keane V. (2008) 'Postnatal depression and child outcome at 11 years: the importance of accurate diagnosis', *Journal of Affective Disorders*, 107, pp 241–5

Pecora P., Williams J., Kessler R., Hiripi E., O'Brien K., Emerson J., Herrick M. and Torres D. (2006) 'Assessing the educational achievements of adults who were formerly placed in family foster care', *Child & Family Social Work*, 11:3, pp 220–31

Pecora P., Kessler R., O'Brien K., White C. R., Williams J., Hiripi E., English D., White J. and Herrick M.A. (2006) 'Educational and employment outcomes of adults formerly placed in foster care: results from the Northwest Foster Care Alumni Study', *Children and Youth Services Review*, 28, pp 1459–81

Perry B. (2001) 'The neurodevelopmental impact of violence in childhood', in Schetky D. and Benedek E. (eds), *Textbook of Child and Adolescent Forensic Psychiatry*, Washington, DC: American Psychiatric Press

Perry B. (2002) 'Childhood experience and the expression of genetic potential: what childhood neglect tells us about nature and nurture', *Brain and Mind*, 3, pp 79–100

Petrie P. and Simon A. (2006) 'Residential care: lessons from Europe', in Chase E., Simon A. and Jackson S. (eds) *In Care and After: A positive perspective*, London: Routledge

Petterson S. and Albers A. (2001) 'Effects of poverty and maternal depression on early child development', *Child Development*, 72, pp 1974–813

Phillips R. (2007) 'The need for information on how the attachment difficulties of adopted and looked after children affects their schooling', *Adoption & Fostering*, 11, pp 28–38

Piper C. (2008) *Investing in Children: Policy, law and practice in context*, Cullompton: Willan Publishing

Pittman G. and Morley J. (2009) 'When words are not enough . . .', Research Commission; www.bristol.ac.uk/norahfry/teachinglearning/dedpsy/commissions/words1.pdf

Poverty (2010) 'United Kingdom – Educational attainment at age 16'; www.poverty.org. uk/26/index.shtml

Pringle M.L.K. (1965) *Deprivation and Education*, London: Longman

Qualifications and Curriculum Authority (1999) *The National Curriculum: Handbook for primary teachers in England Key Stages 1 and 2*, Norwich: HMSO

Rees J. (2001) 'Making residential care educational care', in Jackson S. (ed) *Nobody Ever Told Us School Mattered: Raising the educational attainments of children in care*, London: BAAF

Reimer D. (2010) ' "Everything was strange and different": young adults' recollections of the transition into foster care', *Adoption & Fostering*, 34:2, pp 14–22

Remsbury N. (2003) *The Education of Refugee Children*, London: National Children's Bureau

Rhodes J., Grossman J. and Resch N. (2000) 'Agents of change: pathways through which mentoring relationships influence adolescents' academic adjustment', *Child Development*, 71:6, pp 1662–71

Rhodes J., Spencer R., Keller T., Liang B. and Noam G. (2006) 'A model for the influence of mentoring relationships on youth development', *Journal of Community Psychology*, 34:6, pp 691–707

Richardson J. and Lelliott P. (2003) 'Mental health of looked after children', *Advances in Psychiatric Treatment*, 9, pp 249–56

Richman N. (1998) *In the Midst of the Whirlwind: A manual for helping refugee children*, London: Save the Children

Ripley K. and Yuill N. (2005) 'Patterns of language impairment and behaviour in boys excluded from school', *British Journal of Educational Psychology*, 75, pp 37–50

Rosenthal R. and Jacobson L. (1992) *Pygmalion in the Classroom: Teacher expectation and pupils' intellectual development*, New York: Irvington

Roth J. and Brooks-Gunn J. (2003) 'What exactly is a youth development program? Answers from research and practice', *Applied Developmental Science*, 7:2, pp 94–111

Runyan D. and Gould C. (1985) 'Foster care for child maltreatment II: impact on school performance', *Pediatrics*, 76, pp 841–47

Rutter J. (2001) *Supporting Refugee Children in 21st Century Britain: A compendium of essential information*, Stoke-on-Trent: Trentham Books

Rutter J. (2003) *Working with Refugee Children*, York: Joseph Rowntree Foundation

Rutter J. (2006) *Refugee Children in the UK*, Maidenhead: Open University Press

Rutter M. (2000) 'Children in substitute care: some conceptual considerations and research implications', *Children and Youth Services Review*, 22:9–10, pp 685–703

Samuels G. and Pryce J. (2008) ' "What doesn't kill you makes you stronger": survivalist self-reliance as resilience and risk among young adults aging out of foster care', *Children and Youth Services Review*, 30, pp 1198–210

Scannapieco M. (2008) 'Developmental outcomes of child neglect', *The APSAC Adviser*, American Professional Society on the Abuse of Children

Schofield G. (2002) 'The significance of a secure base: a psychosocial model of long-term foster care', *Child & Family Social Work*, 7:4, pp 259–72

Schofield G., Beek M. and Sargent K. with Thoburn J. (2000) *Growing Up in Foster Care*, London: BAAF

Schofield G., Thoburn J., Howell D. and Dickens J. (2007) 'The search for stability and permanence: modeling the pathways of long-stay looked after children', *British Journal of Social Work*, 37, pp 619–42

Scotland's Commissioner for Children and Young People (2008) *Sweet 16? The age of leaving care in Scotland*; www.sccyp.org.uk/webpages/Leaving_Care_Report_for_Web_20080325.pdf

Scottish Executive (2007) *Looked After Children and Young People: We can and must do better*, Edinburgh: The Scottish Executive; www.scotland.gov.uk/Publications/2007/01/15084446/0

Scottish Government (2008) 'Getting it right for every child: an overview of the getting it right approach', Scottish Government; http://www.scotland.gov.uk/gettingitright

Sergeant H. (2006) *Handle with Care: An investigation into the care system*, London: Centre for Policy Studies

SEU (2003) *A Better Education for Children in Care*, London: Social Exclusion Unit

Shaw C. (1998) *Remember my Messages: The experiences and views of 2000 children in public care in the UK*, London: Who Cares? Trust

Shaw C., Brady L.-M. and Davey C. (2011) *Guidelines for Research with Children and Young People*, London: National Children's Bureau

Shepherd C., Reynolds F. and Moran J. (2010) ' "They're battle scars, I wear them well": a phenomenological exploration of young women's experiences of building resilience following adversity in adolescence', *Journal of Youth Studies*, 13:3, pp 273–90

Sheppard M. (1997) 'Double jeopardy: the link between child abuse and maternal depression in child and family social work', *Child & Family Social Work*, 2, pp 91–107

Shotter J. (1984) *Social Accountability and Selfhood*, Oxford: Basil Blackwell

Siegel D. (2011) *Mindsight: Transform your brain with the new science of kindness*, London: Oneworld Publications

Simon A. and Owen C. (2006) 'Outcomes for children in care: what do we know?', in Chase E., Simon A. and Jackson S. (eds), *In Care and After: A positive perspective*, London: Routledge

Sinclair R. (1998) *The Education of Children in Need*, Dartington: Research in Practice, 1998

Sinclair I. (2005) *Fostering Now: Messages from research*, London: Department for Education and Skills

Sinclair I. and Gibbs I. (1996) *Quality of Care in Children's Homes*, York: University of York

Sinclair I., Baker C., Lee J. and Gibbs .I (2007) *The Pursuit of Permanence: A study of the English care system*, London: Jessica Kingsley Publishers

Smedje H., Broman J.E., Hetta J. and von Knorring A.L. (1999) 'Psychometric properties of a Swedish version of the Strengths and Difficulties Questionnaire', *Journal of European Children and Adolescent Psychiatry*, 8, pp 63–70

Social Work Task Force (2009) *Building a Safe, Confident Future*, London: DCSF

Solomon Y., Warin J. and Lewis C. (2002) 'Helping with homework? Homework as a site of tension for parents and teenagers', *British Educational Research Journal*, 28:4, pp 603–622

Spicer N. (2008) 'Places of exclusion and inclusion: asylum-seeker and refugee experiences of neighbourhoods in the UK', *Journal of Ethnic and Migration Studies*, 34:3, pp 491–510

SSI/DH (1993) *Corporate Parents: Inspection of residential child care services in 11 local authorities*, London: Social Services Inspectorate

SSI/Ofsted (1995) *The Education of Children who are Looked After by Local Authorities*, London: HMSO

Stahmer A., Jurlburt M., Horwitz S. M., Landsverk J., Zhang J. and Leslie L. (2009) 'Associations between intensity of child welfare involvement and child development among young children in child welfare', *Child Abuse & Neglect*, 33, pp 598–611

Stanley K. (2001) *Cold Comfort: Young separated refugees in England*, London: Save the Children

Steckley L. (2005) 'Just a game? The therapeutic potential of football', in Crimmens D. and Milligan I. (eds) *Facing Forward: Residential child care in the 21st century*, Lyme Regis: Russell House Publishing

Stein M. (1997) *What Works in Leaving Care?*, Ilford: Barnardo's

Stein M. (2005) *Resilience and Young people Leaving Care: Overcoming the odds*, York: Joseph Rowntree Foundation

Stein M. (2006a) 'Research review: young people leaving care', *Child & Family Social Work*, 11:3, pp 273–274

Stein M. (2006b) 'Young people aging out of care: the poverty of theory', *Children and Youth Services Review*, 28:4, pp 422–434

Stein M. (2008a) 'Resilience and young people leaving care', *Child Care in Practice*, 141, pp 35–44

Stein M. (2008b) 'Transitions from care to adulthood: messages from research for policy and practice', in Stein M. and Munro E. (eds), *Young People's Transitions from Care to Adulthood: International research and practice*, London: Jessica Kingsley Publishers

Stein M. and Carey K. (1987) *Leaving Care*, Oxford: Basil Blackwell

Stone S. (2007) 'Child maltreatment, out-of-home placement and academic vulnerability: a fifteen-year review of evidence and future directions', *Children and Youth Services Review*, 29, pp 139–61

Streeter A. (2012) *A study into the effectiveness of the In Care, In School resources in de-stigmatising looked after children, and raising the awareness of their real situation amongst their peers*, PGCE Assessment Assignment, Bath Spa University: Centre for Education Policy in Practice

The Children's Legal Centre (2003) *Mapping the Provision of Education and Social Services for Refugee and Asylum Seeker Children: Lessons from the Eastern region*, University of Essex: The Children's Legal Centre

Thumbirajah M., Grandison K. and De-Hayes L. (2008) *Understanding School Refusal: A handbook for professionals in education, health and social care*, London: Jessica Kingsley Publishers

Tomlinson S. (1982) *A Sociology of Special Education*, London: Routledge

Topping K.J. (1985) 'Parental involvement in reading: theoretical and empirical background', in Topping K.J. and Wolfendale S. (eds), *Parental Involvement in Children's Reading Ability*, Worcester: Billings & Son Ltd

Topping K.J. (1992) 'Short- and long-term follow-up of parental involvement in reading projects', *British Educational Research Journal*, 18:4, pp 369–79

Topping K.J. (1997) 'Process and outcome in Paired Reading: a reply to Winter', *Educational Psychology in Practice*, 13:2, pp 75–86

Topping K.J. (2001) *Thinking, Reading, Writing: A practical guide to paired learning with peers, parents and volunteers*, New York/London: Continuum International

Topping K.J. and Lindsay G.A. (1992) 'Paired reading: a review of the literature', *Research Papers in Education*, 7, pp 199–246

Triseliotis J., Borland M. and Hill M. (2000) *Delivering Foster Care*, London: BAAF

Trout A.L., Hagaman J., Casey K., Reid R. and Epstein M.H. (2008) 'The academic status of children and youth in out-of-home care: a review of the literature', *Children and Youth Services Review*, 30, pp 979–994

Utting Sir W. (1991) *Children in the Public Care: A review of residential child care*, London: HMSO

Utting W. (1997) *People Like Us: The report of the review of safeguards for children living away from home*, DH/TheWelsh Office: HMSO

van der Kolk B.A., McFarlane A.C. and Weisaeth L. (eds) (1996) *Traumatic Stress: The effects of overwhelming experience on mind, body and society*, New York: Guilford Press.

Veland J. (1993) *Hvordan gikk det med barnevernets barn? Resultater fra barnevernsarbeid i 5 kommuner i Rogaland* [How did the child welfare children fare? Results from child welfare work in 5 local authorities in Rogaland] Stavanger: Fylkeshelsechefen i Rogaland

Viner R. and Taylor B. (2005) 'Health outcomes at 30 years after being in public care in childhood: a population study', *Pediatrics*, 115, pp 894–9

Vinnerljung B. (1996) *Fosterbarn som vuxna* [Foster children as adults] Lund: Arkiv Förlag

Vinnerljung B., Berlin M. and Hjern A. (2010) 'Skolbetyg, utbildning och risker för ogynnsam utveckling hos barn' [School performance, education, and risks for unfavourable development among children] in *Social Rapport*, pp 228–66, Stockholm: Socialstyrelsen

Vinnerljung B., Öman M. and Gunnarson T. (2005) 'Educational attainments of former child welfare clients: a Swedish national cohort study', *International Journal of Social Welfare*, 14:4, pp 265–76

Vinnerljung B., Hjern A., Ringbäck Weitoft G., Franzén E. and Estrada F. (2007) 'Children and young people at risk', *International Journal of Social Welfare*, 16, Supplement 1 (Social Report 2006), pp S163-S202

Wade J. and Dixon J. (2006) 'Making a home, finding a job: investigating early housing and employment outcomes for young people leaving care', *Child & Family Social Work*, 11:3, pp 199–2008

Wade J. and Munro E. (2008) 'UK', in Stein M and Munro E (eds), *Young People's Transitions from Care to Adulthood: International research and practice*, London: Jessica Kingsley Publishers

Wade J., Mitchell F. and Baylis G. (2005) *Unaccompanied Asylum-seeking Children: The response of social work services*, London: BAAF

Wade J., Biehal N., Farrelly N. and Sinclair I. (2010) *Maltreated Children in the Looked After System: A comparison of outcomes for those who go home and those who do not*, DFE-RBX-10-06, University of York: Social Policy Research Unit; www.education.gov.uk/publications/eOrdering Download/DFE-RBX-10-06.pdf

Wade J., Sirriyeh A., Kohli R. and Simmonds J. (2012) *Fostering Unaccompanied Asylum-seeking Young People: Creating a family life across a 'world of difference'*, London: BAAF

Walker T. (2002) *Caring for the Education of Looked After Children*, Manchester: National Teaching and Advisory Service

Walker J., Wilson G., Laing K. and Pennington M. (2010) *Care Matters: Budget Holding Lead Professionals (BHLPs) with looked after children in England*, DCSF Research Report 225

Walker-Gleaves A. and Walker C. (2008) 'Imagining a different life in school: educating student teachers about "looked after" children and young people', *Teachers and Teaching*, 14, pp 465–79

Ward H. (ed) (1995) *Looking After Children: Research into action*, London: HMSO

Warnock M. (2005) *Special Educational Needs: A new look*, London: Philosophy of Education Society of Great Britain

Watters C. (2008) *Refugee Children: Towards the next horizon*, London: Routledge

Wechsler D. (1999) *The Wechsler Intelligence Scale for Children* (3rd edition) Manual, Swedish version, Stockholm: Psykologiförlaget

Weiner A. and Weiner E. (1990) *Expanding the Options in Child Placement: Israel's dependent children in care from infancy to adulthood*, Lamham, MD: University Press of America

Welsh Assembly Government (2010) *Wales Children in Need Census 2010*; http://wales.gov.uk/docs/statistics/2011/110224sdr191920en.pdf

Welsh Assembly Government (2011) *Wales Children in Need Census 2010*; http://wales.gov.uk./docs/statistics/2011/110224sdr192011en.pdf

Wetz J (2009) *Urban Village Schools: Putting relationships at the heart of secondary school organisation and design*, London: Calouste Gulbenkian Foundation

Weyts A (2004) 'The educational achievements of looked after children: do welfare systems make a difference to outcomes?', *Adoption & Fostering*, 28:3, pp 7–19

Who Cares? Trust (undated) 'Virtual head teachers'; www.thewhocarestrust.org.uk/pages/virtual-headteachers.html

Who Cares? Trust (1994/2010) *Who Cares? About Education*, London: Who Cares? Trust

Wigfall V. and Cameron C. (2006) 'Promoting young people's participation in research', in Chase E., Simon A. and Jackson S. (eds), *In Care and After: A positive perspective*, London: Routledge

Williams F. (2004) 'What matters is who works: why every child matters to New Labour', *Critical Social Policy*, 24:3 pp 406–27

Winder R. (2004; updated 2013) *Bloody Foreigners: The story of immigration to Britain*, London: Little Brown

Winter K. (2006) 'Widening our knowledge concerning young looked after children: the case for research using sociological models of childhood', *Child & Family Social Work*, 11:1, pp 55–64

Winter K. (2008) 'Recent policy initiatives in early childhood and the challenges for the social challenges for the social work profession', *British Journal of Social Work*, 39, pp 1235–55

Wolanin T.R. (2005) *Higher Education Opportunities for Foster Youth: A Primer for policymakers*, Washington DC: The Institute for Higher Education Policy

Wolf A. (2011) *Review of Vocational Education: The Wolf Report*, London: Department for Education; http://media.education.gov.uk/assets/files/pdf/w/wolf%20review%20of%20vocational%20education%20%20%20government%20response.pdf

Wolfendale S. and Bryans T. (2004) *Evaluation of the Looking After Literacy Project in Kent for Children in Public Care*, London: University of East London

Woolfson R., Heffernan E., Marianne P. and Morven B. (2010) 'Young people's views of the child protection system in Scotland', *British Journal of Social Work*, 40, pp 2069–85

Zingraff M., Leiter J., Johnsen M. and Myers K. (1994) 'The mediating effect of good school performance on the maltreatment–delinquency relationship', *Journal of Research in Crime and Delinquency*, 31, pp 62–91

# About the contributors

**Sarah Ajayi** is Project Officer for Beat (National Eating Disorders Charity). Her main areas of interest are improving outcomes for marginalised groups – children, young people and adults – through research and practice. She is interested in exploring the transitions people make across the life course, in particular those in and leaving care as well as those within the mental health community.

**Julia Alfano** is an Educational Psychologist, Hampshire Educational Psychology Service.

**Dr Collette Isabel Bentley** currently works as a doctor in General Medicine at Addenbrooke's hospital, Cambridge. She is also a freelance health writer and journalist. Her main research interests are the health and education inequalities faced by looked after children and associated social policy.

**Kate Cairns** is an author, speaker and trainer with an international reputation for her work around attachment trauma and resilience. She has been a social worker for 40 years, a trainer for 20 years and, together with her husband Brian and their three birth children, provided a permanent family for 12 other children between 1975 and 1997. In 2004, Kate founded Akamas Ltd, which developed pioneering online qualifications for foster and the broader children's workforce before becoming part of the ALS group in 2009.

**Claire Cameron** is Reader in Education and Co-Deputy Director, Thomas Coram Research Unit, Institute of Education, University of London.

**Graham Connelly** is Strategic Research and Qualifying Courses Manager of CELCIS (Centre for Excellence for looked After Children in Scotland). He has researched and published widely on the education of looked after children, recently completing a two-year study of care leavers in further education for the Scottish Funding Council. Graham is a trustee of Who Cares? Scotland, a member of the Education Advisory Committee of Kibble Education and Care Centre and of the LACSIG learning "hub".

**Jenny Driscoll** is a Lecturer in Child Studies, Barrister and Programme Director, MA Child Studies/International Child Studies, King's College London. Before moving to King's College in 2005, she practised at the independent bar for over a decade, specialising in child protection. Her research interests include the protection and rights of vulnerable children, particularly looked after children, and ethical issues arising from research with children and young people.

**Robbie Gilligan** is Professor of Social Work and Social Policy, Trinity College, Dublin, Republic of Ireland.

**Mike Gorman** is Head of the Bath and North East Somerset Virtual School for children and young people in care and represents virtual schools on a number of national working groups. Prior to this he was a secondary school head teacher, with wide experience of schools in the South West.

**Rose Griffiths** is Director of Learning Initiatives in the University of Leicester's School of Education. Rose has taught in primary, secondary and special schools, and her publications include many books for children, parents and teachers. She is a former foster carer and her research interests include raising the achievement of looked after children, and the learning and teaching of mathematics.

**Kristin Hintze** is a Psychologist in the School and Social Services Administration, City of Helsingborg, Sweden.

**Anna Aldenius Isaksson** is a Special Education Teacher in the School and Social Services Administration, City of Helsingborg, Sweden.

**Caroline Leeson** is an Associate Professor of Early Childhood Studies at the University of Plymouth. She qualified as a social worker and currently works in the field of education. Her research interests mainly relate to education, communicating with younger children, safeguarding children during their early years and children in care.

**Peter McNamara** is Head Teacher of a virtual school of 360 children in the care of Salford City Council. His job is to look after the education of all the school-age children in the care of the authority as if they were on one school roll, despite the fact they are actually spread over as many as 120 "real" schools all over England. As one of the original 11 authorities piloting the virtual school scheme from 2007 to 2009, his school is now well established and he can point to real achievements: an improving set of primary school results, the best GCSE results they have ever had for looked after children and a halving of the number of children who have had 25 or more days off school in a year.

**Antony Mains** is *Way Ahead* Project Manager, Education and Children's Services, Children's Social Care and Safeguarding Looked After Service, Leicester City.

**Angela O'Sullivan** is a Principal Biology Lecturer at De Montfort University and the Faculty of Health & Life Sciences' Head of Widening Participation. Her original research focus was analytical science but her later experiences of teaching care leavers drew her towards the social sciences and inclusive practice. Her current research interest is the barriers to educational achievement for disadvantaged groups.

**Cara Osborne** is a Psychology Research Associate, based with Hampshire Educational Psychology's Research and Evaluation Unit. She carries out research on a range of areas, defined by the needs of educational psychology and children's services more widely. Recent projects have included work on the education of looked after children, support for foster carers, changes in pupils' attitudes to learning during transition and the role of emotional literacy support assistants in schools.

**Richard Parker** is Director of the Centre for Education Policy in Practice at Bath Spa University, having worked in youth services, schools and local government. A key focus of the Centre is to enable vulnerable groups, such as children and young people in care, to influence policy and practice in schools, and to improve outcomes and their overall experience of the education system.

**Maria Poyser** is currently employed as a Student Referral Centre Manager at an Academy in Nottingham, where she is also the Designated Teacher for Looked After Young People. More recently, she has also begun to manage and co-ordinate the implementation of Alternative Provisions for young people at the Academy. Her main areas of research and practice are the education of looked after young people, pupils with Emotional and Behavioural Difficulties and SEN as well as disaffected young people/non-attenders.

**Ala Sirriyeh** is Lecturer in Sociology at Keele University. Her research is centred in the field of migration and refugee studies, particularly with reference to children, young people, gender, identities and personal relationships. Her recent book, *Inhabiting Borders, Routes Home: Youth, gender, asylum* (Ashgate, 2013), explored young refugee women's narratives of home in the context of their migration to the UK and transitions to adulthood.

**Eva Tideman** is Senior Lecturer, Department of Psychology, University of Lund, Sweden.

**Bo Vinnerljung** is Professor of Social Work at the University of Stockholm, Sweden. His research work includes a long line of national cohort studies on the long-term development of children in public care or children growing up in adverse childhood circumstances, international/national adoption, but also intervention studies targeting young people in public care.

**Jim Wade** is a Senior Research Fellow in the Social Policy Research Unit, University of York. For more than 20 years he has published widely in the area of social work and related services for vulnerable groups of children and young people, including looked after children, care leavers, young runaways and asylum-seeking and refugee children

**Penelope Welbourne** is Associate Professor of Social Work at Plymouth University. Her background is as a child and family social worker. Her current research and teaching interests reflect a continuing interest in child protection and professional development in child and family social work, including children involved in legal proceedings and cross-cultural studies in child protection.

**Rob Westerman** is Assistant Leader, Raising the Attainment of Looked After Children team, Leicester City Council and Young People's Service.

**Tanya Winn** is Acting Lead Officer, Education of Children in Care Team, Hampshire Educational Psychology Service.

# Index

abuse
    child development and  33–4
    Collette's story  45–6
    entry to care  223
    trauma in  150
academic potential *see* educational potential
accommodation difficulties, in FE  216–17
adolescents
    anticipation of failure  38
    behavioural issues  31–3
    school inclusion or PRUs  129–34
    work experience  82–3
    *see also* care leavers
*Adoption & Fostering* journal  2
    on barriers to achievement  66–7
    foster care and HE  159–73
    self-reliance among care leavers  206–19
    support beyond Key Stage 4  220–33
    Swedish study  87–100
adult supervision, in spare-time activities
    79–83
adversity
    adaptations to  38
    child development and  33–4
    overcoming  1–4
Afghan young people  193–204
ages
    educational progress in care  36–7
    at entry to care  31–3
    refugees and asylum seekers  192–3, 198
Aim Higher partnership  67, 75, 137
anhedonia  154
ASDAN (Awards Scheme Accreditation
    Network)  137, 139, 140
aspirations  227–9
    Collette's story  45–52
    influences on  38–40, 50–2
    refugees and asylum seekers  195–6

Assessment and Action Records (AARs)
    17–18
assessments
    behavioural difficulties  91, 95
    educational potential  91, 92, 93–4, 96–7
    emotional difficulties  91, 94
    psychological  91, 93–4
    reading  56–9, 92, 96, 97, 120–6
    refugees and asylum seekers  200–1
asylum seekers (unaccompanied)
    education pathways  192–204
    educational aspirations  161
    educational outcomes  7
attachment
    in child welfare policy  12–13
    at entry to care  38, 150
    neglect and abuse and  34
    use of Letterbox Club materials  63–4
attachment awareness, training packages
    143
attachment difficulties
    training needs  108–9
    traumatic stress  151

Bath and North East Somerset (B&NES),
    In Care, In School project  135–45
Bath Spa University  137–43
Beck Young People Inventories  91, 94
behavioural difficulties  31–3
    assessment  91, 95
    barrier to HE  188
    fictional account  146–9
    school inclusion  129–34
*A Better Education for Children in Care*
    (SEU, 2003)  21–3, 25–6, 66
*see also* Social Exclusion Unit (SEU)
*Big Brother Big Sister* (US), mentoring
    scheme  84